THE FAMILY LIFE OF
GEORGE WASHINGTON

THE WASHINGTON FAMILY
Painted from life by Edward Savage

THE FAMILY LIFE OF
GEORGE WASHINGTON

BY

CHARLES MOORE

WITH AN INTRODUCTION BY

MRS. THEODORE ROOSEVELT

AND WITH ILLUSTRATIONS

BOSTON AND NEW YORK

HOUGHTON MIFFLIN COMPANY

The Riverside Press Cambridge

1926

The Riverside Press
CAMBRIDGE · MASSACHUSETTS
PRINTED IN THE U.S.A.

PREFACE

Two centuries ago, lacking six years, George Washington was born on the banks of the Potomac in Westmoreland, a Virginia county that produced three Signers of the Declaration of Independence, two Presidents of the United States, a Justice of the Supreme Court, and — Robert E. Lee. In 1932 the two hundredth anniversary of Washington's birth will be celebrated officially by the Nation, and with more or less ceremony throughout this land and in foreign countries as well. His fame, growing with the years, keeps him one of the foremost characters of the world.

Washington was very human. True, he became a personage before attaining his majority and during nearly half a century of public life maintained his supremacy; but there never was a time in camp or forum when he was out of touch with his farms, or when his deeply affectionate nature even temporarily lost concern for his wife and his relatives.

A radius of a hundred miles from the city that bears his name comprises the scene of his activities, save when he was called from home by public duties, or when he made a few journeys North or South or West. He dearly loved companionship; he did not like to be alone, and when condemned to pass the time with only himself for company he sets the fact down in his diaries almost with a note of complaint. His affections overflowed toward his own and his wife's relatives; toward the members of his military family in camp and the Mount Vernon household in times of peace.

Washington had weaknesses; but they were not of a kind to subtract from his character. None of the tales whispered about him has any foundation in fact; and the facts of his life are patent. From the days of the Revolution spurious letters purporting to have been written by him have been published; but the fraud has been exposed quickly. He has suffered from the implied reproach of having been thrifty in money matters. So he was, else he could not have given his services freely to the Nation. His friends and admirers never were called upon to extricate him from harassing debt. Yet no needy person was ever turned from his door either by himself or by his agents.

Years of familiarity with the places which knew Washington as boy and man, almost daily contact with the very papers on which his hand rested as he wrote the words that came from brain and heart, acquaintance with many persons among whom he is still looked up to as the head of the family — all of these things induced me to write these chapters at first as casual contributions to the *Magazine of the Daughters of the American Revolution*, and then, with the kind permission of the Daughters, to rearrange and enlarge them for publication in book form.

Perhaps an added impulse came from the circumstance that when I was a child a visitor from Virginia appeared at my home in the mid-West. Being fond of children, he took me on his knee, asking how old I was. 'When I was your age,' he said, 'I sat on George Washington's knee.' So all my life I have thought of Washington as one who took children on his knees. He has never been an abstraction. In finer way Mrs. Roosevelt has told how to her and hers Washington has ever been a familiar presence, one of the historic personages whom she would have been glad to know in the flesh.

It would be impossible to mention here all the persons to whom I am under obligations. That there are not more errors in the following pages (and I have never seen a book on Washington in which there were no mistakes) is due to the painstaking care of Miss Emily B. Mitchell, the helper of so many frequenters of the Division of Manuscripts in the Library of Congress. Mr. Levin C. Handy, the hereditary photographer of the City of Washington, has exercised his great skill in bringing into workable form faded and obscure manuscripts. Miss Natalie Sumner Lincoln, the editor of the *D.A.R. Magazine*, continuously extended to me the hospitality of its pages. The owners of various groups of family letters have permitted the use of their treasured manuscripts, as will be made known to the reader. The Frick Art Reference Library, which is doing real service in making adequate copies of historical portraits scattered in galleries and private homes throughout the country, has been laid under contribution.

Much time would have been spared if John C. Fitzpatrick's monumental *Diaries of George Washington* had been available in published form. Embodying his own extensive researches, together with those of Worthington C. Ford and that most indefatigable of collectors, the late Dr. J. M. Toner, they form the foundation for the study of the personal life of Washington. The recent publication of the *Diaries* represents one of the many great services rendered by the Ladies' Mount Vernon Association of the Union.

Readers will readily discover that in the opinion of the writer a very great deal remains for the American people still to do in order to realize the visions of Washington for the Capital City. Much also should be done to put his birthplace in order and to give proper sepulture to the bones of his ancestors. These pious duties should be made an integral part of the approaching Washington Bicentennial provided for on a large scale by Congress. Only so can George Washington be made a vital force for the generations to come. They will be our judges.

CHARLES MOORE

WASHINGTON, D.C.
 February, 1926

CONTENTS

ILLUSTRATIONS

ILLUSTRATIONS XV

ILLUSTRATIONS

INTRODUCTION

WASHINGTON's portrait hung beside his wife's on our nursery wall. He was a beloved and familiar friend, and I was taught to throw kisses to 'George and Martha.' The same lithographs in their round frames hang in the school-room of my children in this house; and partly on their account, perhaps, the childhood feeling of intimate friend-ship persists.

Once, while we were in the White House, we went on horseback to Mount Vernon, and came upon the house away from the river, under trees and up a quiet road, as Washington would have come. Almost his presence met us, not the leader who nursed the country 'thro' shifts and wants and pains,' but the man who loved his horses, his fields, and the same countless trivial pleasures and cares that fill our lives — the dear friend of my childhood days.

I don't know why some places have a curiously pene-trating atmosphere of sentiment — but in fact this seems true, and Wakefield, where Washington was born, is such a place. I have felt it in the spring, when the blue cloud of grape hyacinths almost hid the grass; and again in the late fall afternoon when I took my children on a pious pilgrimage. Even writing about it brings back some happy days of a happy life.

Edith Kermit Roosevelt

SAGAMORE HILL, OYSTER BAY
October 30, 1925

THE FAMILY LIFE OF
GEORGE WASHINGTON

.·.

CHAPTER I

THE LAND OF THE WASHINGTONS

FROM the monumental gateway of the City of Washington to Wakefield, the birthplace of George Washington, is a round hundred miles as the automobile speeds. With each changing figure on the cyclometer one passes some place or object associated with the Father of his Country.

Skimming across the semi-circular plaza of the Union Station, with its fountains like those in Rome, and its flagstaffs like those in Venice, one looks up at the United States Capitol, dazzlingly white in the morning sun. George Washington, in the regalia of the Grand Master Mason of Virginia, laid the corner-stone of the original building, on September 18, 1793.

Turning westward, the way leads through the Mall, which Washington and L'Enfant planned with taste and a knowledge of the world's best precedents in landscape architecture. Only now the Mall is beginning to be put into the order they intended — a park connection between the Congress House and the President's House.

Needlelike, the gleaming shaft of the Washington Monument towers in crystal air, seemingly a growth of nature rather than the creation of man's hands. When storms gather, there it stands stoutly amid the shifting billows of mist. To-day, under a bright sun, it seems to pierce bluest of skies. We shall carry the vision over miles of Virginia, so wide is its domination — an exemplification of the character it commemorates.

By 1889 the historic Long Bridge across the Potomac had become so decrepit that the stone dumped into the water to save its tottering piers created a dam; and when the spring rains descended and the floods came, Pennsylvania Avenue from White House to Capitol was turned into a navigable stream. To-day two strictly utilitarian bridges cross the river: one to accommodate railroad traffic into the South, while the other is crowded with trolley-cars, trucks, and pleasure vehicles, seeking either Washington's meager Coney Island or else the National Cemetery at Arlington. The way lies along one of the city dumps, smoking with the ill-smelling fires of Gehenna.

No approach to Washington, whether from Virginia or from Maryland, has any sort of distinction, and most of the approaches are squalid. Congress, however, has provided for a memorial bridge across the Potomac, a project mooted since the days of Andrew Jackson and Daniel Webster, who were its sponsors. This bridge, now under construction, will afford a connection between the Lincoln Memorial and the slopes of Arlington, where rest the Nation's dead. It will also link the parks on either side of the Potomac. From the Virginia end will radiate the boulevard to Mount Vernon and the highway to the valley of the Shenandoah. Ultimately the Potomac, from Great Falls to Alexandria, will flow through a continuous series of national parks.

THE CAPITOL, LIBRARY OF CONGRESS, SENATE AND HOUSE OF REPRESENTATIVES OFFICE BUILDINGS, UNION STATION, AND POST OFFICE, 1925

THE WASHINGTON MONUMENT IN WASHINGTON, D.C.

From the hill-road one obtains a view of the Washington panorama, with the dome of the Capitol, the Washington Monument, and the Lincoln Memorial on the great central axis, each a delight to the eye. These three structures, together with the White House at the head of the cross-axis, form the dominating features of a composition more extensive than any other ever devised for man's satisfaction. They also give the sense of unity, combined with great dignity and beauty.

Before ever the idea of this Nation and its Capital had entered into the mind of man, John Parke Custis, only son of Martha Washington, purchased some thousands of acres on the Potomac; and to the house, located opposite the mouth of the Eastern Branch, he brought his bride, the beautiful and spirited Eleanor Calvert, a descendant of Lord Baltimore. There three of their four children were born. To-day only an expert knows how to find the way to the dilapidated remnants of the once comfortable mansion. The present inmates are unfamiliar even with the history of Abingdon.

Before the Revolution, Jack Custis's lands marched with those of his stepfather, Hunting Creek being the common boundary. In the seventeen-fifties, young George Washington had surveyed for his elder brothers, and the Fairfaxes and the Alexanders, a town site which they first called 'Belhaven.' Shortly thereafter it came to be known as 'Alexandria.' The town grew slowly, as all Virginia towns did in those days of large estates. Christ Church represented the established religion; and the big house was owned by Major John Carlyle. For the accommodation

of himself and his wife, when business or pleasure held
them in town for the night, Washington built a small
house. They were fond of this little shelter, and in his
will he left it unreservedly to her; and it was occupied by
three generations of her family before modern improvements swept away all traces of it.

The Carlyle Mansion attained historic importance as
the headquarters of General Edward Braddock, while he
was preparing for his ill-starred expedition to the Monongahela in 1755. Christ Church, seated amid grave-
stones of the past, maintains its religious standing, while
at the same time it challenges the attention of students
among architects, as well as of curious visitors desiring to
sit, however briefly, in the seats of George Washington
and Robert E. Lee. The Lee family lived in Alexandria
during Robert's school-days.

On Shooters Hill, near the railroad station, the Masons
of America are building a Solomon's Temple to com-
memorate the fact that Alexandria Lodge was the scene of
Washington's fraternal activities. The grim lodge-room
in the town is a veritable treasure-house of Washington
and Fairfax relics.

Then, too, Alexandria has a Civil War record, brief but
tragic — the killing of Colonel Ellsworth when he removed
the Confederate flag floating over the Marshall House.
Ellsworth's Zouaves were one of the first three divisions
of Union troops to cross the Potomac in 1861; and, therefore, his death took on symbolic character. The Confederate monument, wrought by Buberl, after the figure
in Elder's painting of 'Appomattox,' at Richmond, is well
worth going one block out of the way to see. Of course,

pedestal and setting are bad; but the figure of the young Southerner, whipped but not defeated, is inspiring.

By devious but well-marked ways one emerges from Alexandria, and, after rattling over the long wooden bridge across Hunting Creek, is soon within the Washington precincts, howbeit it is still seven miles to the mansion house of Mount Vernon. Washington inherited twenty-five hundred acres; he increased his holdings of contiguous lands until he owned about nine thousand acres.

We are on the Richmond Pike, the main traveled road into the South; and pennants from every State in the Union are plastered on the passing motors. If we were visiting Mount Vernon on this trip, we should leave the pike at Gum Spring, noted in the wills of the Washingtons. As it is, we bear to the right, and soon come in sight of the mansion of Woodlawn, spreading its long lines complacently over the hill. Woodlawn recalls a long story of changing fortunes, and characters changing with the fortunes — a story which comes later in this narrative.

From his nine thousand acres Washington selected two thousand, including his mill and distillery, to give to Lawrence Lewis and his wife, Eleanor Parke Custis, known to the world as 'Nelly' Custis. Thornton, the architect of the Capitol, bestowed the design of the house on the happy couple, and both love and much money went into the building of the mansion; but for many reasons these well-laid plans came to naught. Woodlawn passed through many vicissitudes before it was restored to more than its pristine elegance by Miss Sharpe, of Wilkes-Barre, Pennsylvania. Now it has gone into the ownership of Senator Underwood, of Alabama, and will doubtless be maintained as the home of a statesman worthy of that title.

We are traversing country over which George Washington often and often 'rid after a fox,' in company with the four Fairfax men — Lord Fairfax, his brother from England, his cousin William, and his heir presumptive, George William Fairfax. The latter was the husband of the bewitching Sally Cary, who had so large a share in Washington's upbringing. When Lawrence Washington inherited Mount Vernon, he took to wife the eldest daughter of William Fairfax of Belvoir; and it was only natural that the intercourse between the two neighboring houses was quite unrestrained. Indeed, as Washington said, there were ties between the Fairfax and Washington families in both England and America; and so strong were these friendships that the Revolution could not break or even disturb them.

The Government asphalt ends at Fort Humphreys, and the State of Virginia has delayed building the continuation of it, even though this is the main southern highway. However, the rolling gravel is not so bad. We shall have to put up with it for almost all of the remainder of the eighty miles.

Next we speed past the ugly gates leading to Fort Humphreys, the permanent headquarters of the United States Corps of Engineers. Nothing in the appearance of the brutal electrical transformers suggests that here was once the stately entrance to the estate of Belvoir, owned by the Honorable William Fairfax, cousin and agent of Thomas, Lord Fairfax. His lordship divided his time between Belvoir and Greenway Court in the Shenandoah Valley; and his inheritance included some six or seven million acres, still known as the Northern Neck of Virginia, stretching between the Potomac and the Rappahannock, even into the mountains where the sources of those rivers are.

During the World War the Government took over about seven thousand acres, including the old Fairfax estate, and made it the scene of a bustling activity. To-day rotting bridges, blown-down trees, abandoned roads, and dilapidated buildings present a depressing spectacle of forlornness, scarcely mitigated by the attractiveness of the officers' quarters perched on the high wooded bluff overlooking the Potomac. Some day Fort Humphreys (as has happened to the Soldiers' Home, the War College, and Fort Myer) will be included in the outer park system of the District of Columbia.

Ten miles from Alexandria stands Pohick Church, into whose sandstone quoins and door-trims Federal and Confederate soldiers impartially carved their names. George Washington's father was a vestryman of Truro Parish: he attended two meetings, one to impose upon his fellows the selection of Charles Green as minister, and one to put Mr. Green securely into the place, in spite of apparent reluctance on the part of the other vestrymen. However, once seated, he drew his stipend of tobacco during the remainder of his life. Moreover, he frequently was called to render medical service at Mount Vernon during George Washington's incumbency. Lawrence Washington was never a member of the vestry, probably

because he objected to Mr. Green, as he had good reason
to.

For a quarter-century after the Civil War, Pohick
Church was in a forlorn state, although services were held
there. The interior finish had been torn out, even to the
window-frames and sash. The floor had been replaced with
cheap quality pine; a few wooden benches, with a rough
chancel-rail and desk, constituted the furniture. Such
were the unpromising conditions in 1894, when Mr.
Harrison H. Dodge, Superintendent of Mount Vernon,
accompanied by Mr. Glenn Brown, a Washington architect of taste, knowledge, and feeling, visited the place
in a buggy. Mr. Dodge secured promises of money to
begin the work of reconstruction: the Colonial Dames
undertook to supply a new pulpit; the descendants of the
original pew-holders contributed six box pews. Slowly
Mr. Dodge was raising funds, and Mr. Brown was working
out the plans, when Miss Amy Townsend, the New York
Regent of Mount Vernon, became so much interested
that she gave, or secured, the money necessary to complete the pews, wainscoting, walls and gateway, and to
plant the grounds. To-day the old church has a charm all
its own. The congregation is made up of descendants of
many of those who first worshiped within its walls;
numbers come by motor from Washington; and the
visiting that goes on after the Sunday morning service is a
reminder of Colonial days, when Fairfaxes, Washingtons,
and Masons foregathered there.[1]

[1] The present Pohick Church is the second of the name, the first, a frame
building, having been located two or three miles nearer the Potomac. Washington secured the change in site when the new brick church was erected, between 1769 and 1773, during the rectorship of the Reverend Lee Massey, who

If one should turn sharply to the left at Pohick Church, and make his way over six miles of such roads as were called good in Colonial times, he would come to Gunston Hall on the Potomac, built by the great statesman, George Mason, prior to 1758, about the time George Washington was putting Mount Vernon in order, to receive his bride. From the outside Gunston Hall appears small; but inside it is spacious. Here again Mr. Glenn Brown exercised his skill in restoration, and his original work has been supplemented by the owners, Mr. and Mrs. Louis Hertle, whose one thought has been to bring back house and gardens to the beauty and dignity that made them the fitting home of the author of the Virginia Constitution and of the Virginia Bill of Rights. Although George Mason helped to frame the Constitution of the United States, he would not vote for it, because it contained no bill of rights. His Virginia bill forms the first ten amendments to the Constitution.

In the eighteenth century George Mason's estate consisted of between five and six thousand acres of land, occupied by a community of some five hundred people, who manufactured or raised everything consumed on the premises, even to the brick for buildings. If there had been, in all Virginia, brick made in England, George

succeeded Charles Green (1737–65). There were thirty-four pews: Number 1, allotted to 'magistrates and strangers'; number 2, vestrymen and merchants; numbers 3 and 4, George Mason (now occupied by Mr. and Mrs. Hertle, of Gunston Hall); number 5, T. W. Coffer, sold to William Toeplet; numbers 6 to 10, 'most respectable inhabitants and housekeepers, men'; the pews on the opposite side of the church were reserved for wives of men of corresponding ranks. George Washington owned numbers 28 and 29 in the center, at the chancel end. His neighbors were George William Fairfax, A. Henderson, H. Manley, M. Cockburn, and D. McCarty. These facts are taken from Mr. Dodge's and Mr. Brown's notes, and from manuscripts in the Library of Congress.

Mason would have built Gunston Hall of them; but, in spite of assertions to the contrary, all brick in America was American made.

Chief among the glories of Gunston Hall are the two solid rows of box, twice the height of a tall man, between which one looks from the rear portico, to see at the vista's end the blue waters of the Potomac and the Maryland hills. What a procession has passed down that box alley since first it was planted! Washington came often to Gunston Hall, either in chariot or by his eight-oared barge; there were Rochambeau and Lafayette; Jefferson, Madison, and Patrick Henry; and Richard Henry Lee and Arthur Lee. In these later days foreign guests of the Nation like Arthur J. Balfour and M. Viviani, together with Presidents, Cabinet officers, Senators and Representatives, friends of the family, and curious visitors, all receive a welcome. Gunston Hall is still proverbial for hospitality.[1]

Too long, as usual, we have been lingering in a place where the present seems merged into the past. However, one finds no occasion to stop on the road over the hills of Occoquan, where the District of Columbia has spread a reformatory institution on a thousand acres; nor yet in Dumfries, in Washington's day a settlement of thrifty Scotch merchants. Two big, dilapidated mansions tell of former glories; but their once fine interiors now live only in books of historical architecture.[2] Quantico, on the Potomac, is the base of the Marine Corps of the Navy.

[1] From George Mason the estate passed to his eldest son, George Mason, of Lexington; thence to the third George Mason, all three of whom are buried in the quiet, tree-shaded graveyard, not far from the house. In 1867 the estate passed out of the Mason family. Mr. Hertle has owned it since 1912.

[2] Fiske Kimball: *Colonial and Early Republican Architecture.*

POHICK CHURCH

GUNSTON HALL ON THE POTOMAC
Built by Col. George Mason in 1755

BELMONT, AT FALMOUTH
The home of Mr. and Mrs. Gari Melchers

As we run through Stafford, we consider the new court-house, Colonial in its architecture, which contains the will of George Washington's father, for he was a resident of that county at the time of his death. Up hill and down dale, we drive to Falmouth Heights, and descend to the valley of the Rappahannock. The noise of the waters as they come over the falls sounds in our ears as it sounded to the boy Washington in his fishing and swimming days.

Perched on a hill commanding picturesque views up and down the Rappahannock is Belmont, the home of Mr. and Mrs. Gari Melchers, who have enriched the old seat of the Ficklins with treasures gathered during their years in Holland, and at Weimar, where the World War found them. With the Falmouth landscape for a back-ground, Mr. Melchers has painted 'Hunters Home from the Hill,' 'The Madonna of the Rappahannock,' and many another creation in which the life-history of real people is depicted with sureness, sincerity, and charm. Dividing his time between his New York and Falmouth studios, he changes his garb with his skies, but not his nature; and he takes reasonable pride in a spacious new combined studio and gallery, built from stone that has weathered since Revolutionary days.

On the left bank of the Rappahannock is the lordly estate of Chatham, one of many Fitzhugh places, once the home of William Fitzhugh, whose daughter married George Washington Parke Custis, of Arlington. According to a reasonable tradition, Colonel and Mrs. George Washington tarried here on their journey from White House, her home on the Pamunkey, to Mount Vernon;

and here, it is said, Lieutenant Robert E. Lee wooed and
won Mary Custis — but this is doubtful, because they
had known one another from childhood. We are on solid
historic ground in stating that at Chatham (then known
as the 'Lacy House') President Lincoln stayed when he
made his visit of encouragement to General Burnside's
army, awaiting the disastrous Battle of Fredericksburg.
In so far as I know, Chatham is the only roof that has
sheltered both Washington and Lincoln. The extensive
restoration just completed by the present owners, Colonel
and Mrs. Devore, has made Chatham one of the finest
country seats in all Virginia.

Fredericksburg fifteen years ago was a place to have
seen rather than a place to see; to-day it is a live, clean,
well-cared-for little city. The town is fairly steeped in the
Washington tradition. It was here that he threw a dollar
across the river — or could have done so, had there been
dollars in those days. Here, on the Ferry Farm, he cut
down the cherry-tree, and was on such friendly terms
with his father that he confessed the crime. Perhaps it
was because George was a sickly lad that Augustine
Washington gave up the Wakefield home and moved his
family to the Hunting Creek (Mount Vernon) property.
The second move, to Fredericksburg, was made in order
that he might be near his iron business.

The earliest home that George knew was Ferry Farm;
and all a precocious boy could acquire up to the age of
eleven years he here acquired, in company with his sister
and brothers and a large troop of cousins. There is no
place like a small town in which to gain a knowledge of
good and evil, together with some proficiency in practice,

and George was not unlike other boys. He even bore
teasing for romping with the big girls at school.

There is not left enough of the Ferry Farm buildings to
entice the relic-hunter; and the location of his school is so
uncertain that both Falmouth and Fredericksburg plausibly claim it. But here, open to inspection, is the Masonic
Lodge George Washington joined before reaching his
majority; the Sun Tavern where he and Rochambeau
danced with local maids and matrons after Yorktown.
Here, notably, is Kenmore, the mansion built in 1752 for
Washington's sister Betty, when she married Fielding
Lewis, one of the Warner Hall Lewises of Gloucester
County. A nation-wide movement, begun with addresses
by Vice-President Coolidge and Congressman R. Walton
Moore in 1922, has culminated in the purchase of Kenmore, and the beginning of its restoration as a typical
home of the Colonial period. 'Colonel Lewis,' said the
Vice-President, 'was a patriot who sacrificed a fortune in
supplying the Revolutionary forces with arms and ammunition. The mansion not only has these associations,
but is a good example of Colonial architecture, well fitted
to rank with the home of Jefferson, of Mason, of Lee, and
Mount Vernon itself. It ought to be preserved for its own
sake. It must be preserved for the sake of patriotic
America.'

During the Revolution, when British forces were overrunning Virginia, Washington and Fielding Lewis withdrew Mary Washington from Ferry Farm, and located
her in a home on the Kenmore estate, in the house still
preserved as a memorial of her. There George visited
her as often as his active duties permitted, taking his

last farewell before entering on the duties of the Presidency.

Standing on Meditation Rock, the afternoon resort of Mary Washington, one looks across the little town, through which the Union troops passed, fighting as they went, only to be hurled back by General Lee's forces concentrated on Marye's Heights, guarded by the Sunken Road. The Confederate cemetery in the town and the United States military cemetery on the hillside bear eloquent witness to the deadly combat of those days, and the later days when Grant fought the Battles of the Wilderness, only a few miles away. Colonial, Revolutionary, and Civil War memories cluster thick about this spot, making Fredericksburg one of the most historic of all American towns.

From Fredericksburg to Wakefield on the Potomac is a stretch of forty miles of good dirt road, with never a railroad in all that distance to make one 'stop, look, and listen.'

One would be sure of a cordial welcome from Mr. and Mrs. Carter Nicholas Grymes, at Marmion, reached by a left turn at Osso, and a drive through wood roads that have not changed character during the years. Marmion was first a Fitzhugh estate; after the Revolution it was the home of Captain George Lewis, a member of that small and devoted troop known as Washington's Life Guard. George Lewis was named for his uncle; he was the second son of Betty Washington Lewis; he lived at Marmion until his death in 1821, and Mrs. Grymes is his granddaughter. From Marmion came the dining-room interior

FREDERICKSBURG FROM FERRY FARM, THE BOYHOOD HOME
OF GEORGE WASHINGTON

STRATFORD, THE BIRTHPLACE OF GEN. ROBERT E. LEE

MARY WASHINGTON'S HOME IN FREDERICKSBURG

MEDITATION ROCK, FREDERICKSBURG
Mary Washington's favorite resting-place, near which is her burial-place

that forms one of the chief features in the Colonial building at the Metropolitan Museum in New York. When it
was painted, or by whom, neither history nor tradition
says. The favorite theory of Hessian prisoners as the
artists does not fit in this case.

On we go, through Oak Grove, until a granite stone
stops the way, and bids us turn into two miles of new,
broad, fine road, built by the Government and the State
of Virginia, leading from the highway straight to Wakefield, in Westmoreland County — the birthplace of
George Washington.

CHAPTER II

WASHINGTON FAMILY MIGRATIONS

'In the year 1657, or thereabouts, and during the usurpation of Oliver Cromwell, John and Lawrence Washington, brothers, immigrated from the north of England and settled at Bridges Creek on the Potomac River in the County of Westmoreland, but from whom they descended the subscriber is possessed of no document to ascertain.'

So, in 1791, President Washington wrote to Sir Isaac Heard, the Garter King-at-Arms in London. At that date the Washingtons had been Virginians for a hundred and thirty-three years, and George Washington had become 'a citizen of the United States,' as he described himself in his will.

Many persons, misled perhaps by James Russell Lowell's characterization of Abraham Lincoln [1] as 'the first American,' are apt to think and speak of Washington as an Englishman transplanted in America. As a matter of fact, his life, his fortunes, and his hopes were first Virginian and, after the Confederation was formed, they were national. He was English only in the sense that the spirit of liberty was in his blood.

Although the origin of his family was of only casual interest and of no importance to Washington, it is of moment to such as find in ancestry the controlling forces in the life of the individual. We smile at the title-page of

[1] *Commemoration Ode.*

Mr. Albert Welles's voluminous compilation entitled: 'The pedigree and history of the Washington family: derived from Odin, the founder of Scandinavia, B.C. 70, involving a period of eighteen centuries and including fifty-five generations, down to General George Washington, first President of the United States.' The chief value of Mr. Welles's record is in the portion subsequent to the date he set for his ending. After years of solemn absurdities printed by imaginative genealogists, it remained for Mr. Henry F. Waters to set forth clearly the genealogy of the Washingtons for seven generations in England, and to close the hiatus where the Atlantic Ocean comes in. In 1889, a century after Washington had confessed ignorance of his English ancestry, Mr. Waters proved that the father of the immigrants, John and Lawrence, was Lawrence Washington, M.A. (Oxford), a son of Lawrence Washington, of Sulgrave, a brother of Sir William Washington, of Packington, and of Sir John Washington, of Thrapton.

Lawrence was successively student, lector, and fellow of Brasenose and proctor of the University of Oxford. He left the university to become rector of Purleigh, a valuable living in Essex; and during 'the usurpation of Oliver Cromwell,' [1] he was deprived of his living by Parliament, ostensibly because he was a frequenter of ale-houses, a drunkard, and 'a malignant royalist.' As a matter of testimony, he appears to have been upright, pious, and exemplary in conduct. That he severely arraigned Parliament was sufficient excuse for taking from him a rich living. He died in 1652, at the age of fifty years; and after the Restoration,

---

[1] This was a phrase common in Virginia; it connoted no historical judgment, as may well be surmised from Washington's use of the term.

his widow enjoyed one fifth of the tithes and profits of Purleigh during the two years that she survived him.[1]

John Washington was about twenty-five years old when he came to America in 1658. The first ten years of his life had been spent amid the comforts of the Purleigh rectory, the home of a scholar of distinction. During the second decade he became acquainted with poverty and intolerance. His mother, Amphilis Rhoades, may have been the daughter of a tenant farmer; if so she must have possessed qualities of a high order, so that she easily rose to her new situation. Her eldest son, John, acted as the executor of her estate; and four years after her death he came to Virginia to make his home. His brother Lawrence and his sister Martha came later. Shortly after his arrival John married Ann, the daughter of Nathaniel Pope, a man of influence and property.

John Washington settled in Westmoreland County, then but recently set off from Northumberland, and extending nearly a hundred miles along the Potomac even to the Great Falls, whence the City of Washington now obtains its water supply. John located himself at Bridges Creek, and by this name the family estate was known until after George Washington's day. Wakefield, the present name, came later. The creek (now only a wide marsh) furnished power for a grist-mill; the level acres

[1] The Oxford records disclose that Christopher Washington, of Northhants, gentleman, matriculated at Oriel College, December 6, 1588, aged fifteen years; B.A., February 22, 1594–95 (son of Robert of Sulgrave). His brother William entered on the same date at the age of eleven years. Lawrence Washington, of Northhants, gentleman, matriculated at Brasenose College, November 2, 1621, aged nineteen years; B.A., May 16, 1623; fellow, 1624–33; M.A., February 1, 1625–26; proctor, 1631; rector of Purleigh, Essex, 1633 until ejected 1643 (son of Lawrence, of Sulgrave, Northhants). See also Walker's *Sufferings of the English Clergy*, vol. 2, p. 395, and Foster's *Index Eccl.*

PURLEIGH CHURCH, ESSEX, ENGLAND

Lawrence Washington, great-great-grandfather of George Washington, was rector from 1632 to 1642.
He was the father of the first Washingtons in America

THE GRAVEYARD AT BRIDGES CREEK
The first four generations of Washingtons in America are buried here

POPE'S CREEK TO-DAY, FROM THE SITE OF WASHINGTON'S
BIRTHPLACE

were virgin soil needed for tobacco; and the broad Potomac formed the highway to and from British markets.

The original house probably stood near Bridges Creek, on the tree-covered bluff overlooking the Potomac. Later a second and more commodious house was built near Pope's Creek. Like most Colonial houses, it had four rooms and a hall on the first floor, with chambers above. No picture of the house has come down to us, nor have any excavations been made to locate it. It seems certain, however, that it was a structure quite in keeping with the position of its owner, an active colonel in the joint war waged by Maryland and Virginia against the Indians, a member of the House of Burgesses, and the owner of fourteen thousand acres of land. Yet it did not belong in the same category with Stratford, the brick mansion of the Lees, seven miles lower down the river. Nor could it compare with Mount Airy, the seat of the Tayloes, or Sabine Hall, the Welford estate, both in the adjoining county of Richmond.

It was in this second dwelling that George Washington was born. Unfortunately the location has never been investigated; and there is reason to believe that the monument which ostensibly marks the site is built over the ruins of an outhouse, one chimney of which was standing within the memory of persons now living.

Ann Pope was the mother of the four children who survived infancy — Lawrence, John, Elizabeth, and Ann. On her death John took to wife the widow successively of his neighbor, Walter Broadhouse, and of Henry Brett. After her demise he married for a third time Frances, the widow of Captain John Appleton.

Land being the wealth of new communities, John Washington was assiduous in acquiring such possessions. In company with Nicholas Spencer, he secured a grant of five thousand acres on the Upper Potomac in consideration of bringing a shipload of immigrants to Virginia, a practice approved in those days, but now known to be a prolific and enduring source of ills to the Colony.[1] John Washington's moiety of this grant became the estate we know as Mount Vernon; and eventually George Washington acquired the entire five thousand acres.

In 1677, after nearly a score of busy and successful years [2] as a colonist, 'John Washington, of Washington Parish in the county of Westmoreland, gentleman,' was buried, by his own direction, on the plantation on which he lived, by the side of his first wife and their two children. In his will he remembered the church and its minister as well as his relatives. There was property in England, a diamond ring, and other articles implying possession of some of the luxuries of life.

John Washington's brother, Lawrence, had settled in Rappahannock County. Their wills were proved in January, 1677, within four days of one another.[3] John's eldest son, Lawrence, inherited the Bridges Creek property, and thither he brought his wife, Mildred Warner. She was the daughter of Colonel Augustine Warner, a member of the King's Council, whose seat was Warner Hall, a mansion of twenty-six rooms, in Gloucester County.[4] Lawrence died

[1] Fairfax Harrison: *Landmarks of Old Prince William*, p. 157 *et seq.*
[2] John Washington's personal estate was equal to about $2,000, and his lands to approximately $70,000, according to calculation in P. A. Bruce's *Economic History of Virginia*.
[3] Worthington C. Ford: *Wills of the Washingtons*.
[4] Fielding Lewis, who married Lawrence Washington's granddaughter, George's sister Betty, was born at Warner Hall.

in 1697, at the age of thirty-six years, leaving John, Augustine, and Mildred, the eldest child being five years old. The widow married George Gale, and together they went to England to settle the English portion of Lawrence Washington's estate, taking the three young Washington children with them. Within the year she died in England and was buried there. Just what became of the children during their minority is not certain. Eventually, John settled in Gloucester County, probably on the maternal acres; while Augustine occupied the old Washington home at Bridges Creek.

Augustine took after his grandfather, John Washington, being active, energetic, successful. The tract on the Upper Potomac having fallen to his sister Mildred, he bought it from her for £180. Also he acquired various other properties, including lands in King George's County, between Bridges Creek and Fredericksburg, which he sold, in 1725, to the Principo Company of Virginia and Maryland, to which enterprise he devoted the remainder of his short life.

This company, promoted by British capitalists, began the manufacture of pig-iron in Maryland in 1717, and the year following shipped three and a half tons to England, the first iron exported from America. Augustine Washington had a contract for getting out the ore, hauling it two miles to the furnace, and then transporting the pig-iron six miles to the Potomac landing. In 1751, the company controlled the foreign market, exporting three thousand tons, as compared with two hundred tons from Pennsylvania and sixty tons from the remainder of the country. At this time England's total production of iron was less than seventeen thousand tons. Augustine Washington's interest in the company probably amounted to one twelfth, besides the profits from his contract.[1]

On coming of age, Augustine married Jane Butler, the daughter of a Westmoreland neighbor. After thirteen years of married life his wife died, leaving two sons and a daughter. Three years later Augustine married Mary, the daughter of Colonel Joseph Ball, of Lancaster County, by whom he had six children — George, Elizabeth, Samuel, John Augustine, Charles, and Mildred.

Not much is known of Mary Ball's antecedents. There is small difficulty in providing for her a genealogy in England going back to William Ball, of Northamptonshire, who departed this life in 1480. It is certain enough that Colonel William Ball, son of William Ball, of Lincoln's Inn, came to Virginia about the time the Washington family arrived, and settled at the mouth of Corotoman Creek, in Lancaster County. Mary Ball's father, the second son of the original William, lived at Epping Forest, in the county of his birth. He married twice. Joseph, the son of his first wife, was alternately a London lawyer and a Virginia planter. His second wife, the Widow Johnson, so-called, was the mother of five daughters, all of whom married well. The youngest daughter, Mary, married Augustine Washington.[2] In her youth she was known as 'the Rose of Epping Forest'; but unfortunately no portrait of her, either as a young or an elderly woman, exists, and the

---

[1] *Pennsylvania Magazine of History and Biography*, vol. XI, 1887. The Virginia ore gave out in 1753; Lawrence Washington was then the resident officer of the company. In 1780, Maryland confiscated the property, which was sold for £90,000, George Washington's share being £7500. The manager had espoused the American cause and had manufactured iron for the Revolution. He thus saved his share, £10,000.

[2] March 6, 1730–31.

descriptions of her face in later years betoken strength of will rather than beauty.[1]

George Washington was born in the family home at Bridges Creek, in Westmoreland County, at ten o'clock on the morning of February 22, 1732, and on April 16th was baptized in due form, with Mrs. Beverly Whiting, Captain Christopher Brooks, and his aunt, Mrs. Mildred Gregory, as his sponsors. His father was thirty-eight and his mother was twenty-eight years old at the time of his birth. He was the fifth child of his father and the first child of his mother.

At the time of his birth the family included Lawrence, fourteen years old; Augustine, aged twelve (both probably at school at Appleby,[2] in Northumberland County, England); and Mildred, a girl of ten, who died when George was two years old. Besides these brothers and sister, there were two families of cousins. John Washington had eight children, the oldest of whom was seventeen years older than George, while the youngest was but two years his senior. His Aunt Mildred had three girls, the youngest of whom was twelve. Thus he had plenty of young companions.

Changes in production and transportation have left Westmoreland County stranded. The broad waterways of the Potomac and Rappahannock that once made it so accessible now act as a barrier to railroad-building. To-day the voice of the resorter is loudest in the land. In earlier days it was known, not without reason, as the 'Athens of

[1] G. W. Ball: *The Maternal Ancestry and Nearest of Kin of Washington.*

[2] The academy at Appleby was established by a friend of the Fairfaxes, whose children were educated there. This accounts for the presence of the Washington boys at that seemingly remote place.

America,' a title which has taken its way westward with the star of empire. In Westmoreland, Presidents Washington and Madison were born; here, too, is located the seat of Governor Thomas Lee, Stratford House, rebuilt after a fire with money contributed by the British Government, on the plea that the fire was set by convict immigrants to whom Governor Lee, as a magistrate, had meted out justice. Stratford was the birthplace of Francis Lightfoot Lee and Richard Henry Lee, Signers of the Declaration of Independence; and of Arthur Lee, representative of the Colonies in England and France; and Lighthorse Harry Lee, the friend and eulogist of Washington; and Robert Edward Lee, the general of the Confederate armies. Stratford House (which passed out of the Lee family shortly after Robert's birth) is falling into decay, and no more pious duty is laid on any community than that of preserving one of the most illustrious homes in all America.

It is plausibly said that Augustine Washington gave up living at Wakefield because either the house burned or the location was too malarial for the children. Inasmuch as the house was not burned, a better reason for removal is his desire to begin a home for his eldest son, on the Upper Potomac property, to which he first removed. That accomplished, he doubtless found that he could handle his iron business better from the town of Fredericksburg than from his farm at Wakefield.

In June, 1815, George Washington Parke Custis, the grandson of Martha Washington, set sail from his estate, Arlington, on his own vessel, the Lady of the Lake, a fine topsail schooner of ninety tons. He was bound for Wakefield, and he carried with him a slab of freestone bearing this inscription: 'Here on the 11th of February, 1732 (Old Style), George Washington was born.' Desiring to make as imposing a ceremony as circumstances permitted, as he tells:

The stone was enveloped in the 'Star-spangled banner' of our country, and was borne to its resting-place in the arms of descendants of four Revolutionary patriots and soldiers — Samuel Lewis, son of George Lewis, a captain in Baylor's regiment of horse, a nephew of Washington; William Grymes, the son of Benjamin Grymes, a gallant and distinguished officer of the life-guard; the captain of the vessel, the son of a brave soldier wounded at Guilford; and George W. P. Custis, son of John Parke Custis, aid-de-camp to the Commander-in-Chief at Cambridge and Yorktown.

We gathered together the bricks of an ancient chimney that once formed the hearth around which Washington in his infancy had played, and constructed a rude kind of pedestal, on which we reverently placed the First Stone, commending it to the respect and protection of the American people in general and the citizens of Westmoreland in particular. . . . We reëmbarked and hoisted our colors, and fired a salute, awakening the echoes that had slept for ages around the hallowed spot.

'The American people in general and the citizens of Westmoreland county in particular' seem to have been remiss in the care for 'the first stone' commemorating Washington. Lossing has a cut of it in his 'Field Book of the Revolution,' written in the forties, but when Bishop Meade visited Wakefield prior to 1857 the slab was in fragments, a brick chimney was all that remained of the 'Washington Mansion,' except broken bricks scattered over the spot where it was built. The then owner, John Gray, of Traveller's Rest, near Fredericksburg, 'either repaired one of the outhouses or built a small house for his overseer out of the materials.'

When President and Mrs. Coolidge visited Wakefield on a July Sunday in 1924, they were set ashore in a small boat from the Mayflower. Landing on the sandy beach near the ruined Government wharf at the mouth of Bridges Creek, they motored for a mile or more along an unimproved road reminiscent of Colonial days, their machine pushing aside the curious cattle pasturing in the lane. A hundred yards away on the right, in the center of a turnip-field, they might have seen a small enclosure framed by artificial stone. A sagging iron gate opens on a mass of weeds and brambles beneath which are the graves of four generations of Washingtons. At the lane's end the visitors came in sight of a funereal monument built by the Government in 1896, to mark the site of the birthplace of George Washington. An examination would probably show that the house in which Washington was born stood near the bank of Pope's Creek, several hundred feet from the monument.

The Government owns eleven acres of shore front and is spending a small amount of money on the lane road. The recently organized Wakefield Memorial Association has purchased seventy acres,[1] including the beautiful grove of cedars along the Potomac; also a right of way to, and fifty feet of land surrounding, the graveyard.

The tide being too far down to permit the Presidential party to reëmbark at Wakefield, they motored eight miles

[1] The title to Wakefield, Duck Hall, and Wakefield Barrens, containing 1099.5 acres, was confirmed to William C. and James Latané in December, 1923. The purpose of the Wakefield National Memorial Association is to purchase the entire thousand acres and to open the place to public uses.

THE ENTRANCE TO WAKEFIELD

THE GOVERNMENT MONUMENT AT WAKEFIELD, THE BIRTHPLACE
OF WASHINGTON

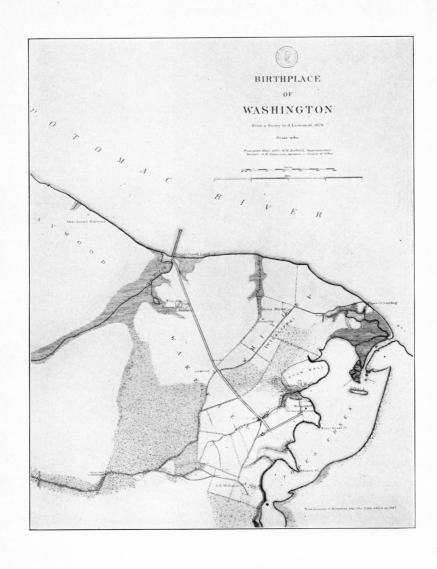

BIRTHPLACE

OF

WASHINGTON

From a Survey by A Lindenkohl. 1879

Scale 1/20000

Published May 1887, W.W. Duffield, Superintendent.
Revised by H. Telemann, Assistant in Charge of Office.

POTOMAC RIVER

AYWOOD

Abandoned Wharf

Bridge Creek Landing

Upper Cr Landing

New Mill Co

LAKE

WICKLIFFE

DUCK HALL

Hunter

Burnt House Pt

J.E. Wilson

Blake's Pt

Note Location of Monument and other Data added in 1887

to Colonial Beach, and there took ship. Congress has provided for the celebration of the two hundredth anniversary of Washington's birth, in 1932. The first detail of the celebration should be to put the home of the Washingtons in decent order.

CHAPTER III

THE EDUCATION OF GEORGE WASHINGTON

AUGUSTINE WASHINGTON died suddenly of gout of the stomach, at Ferry Farm, on April 12, 1743. Being imbued with the theories of his day in regard to the descent of property, he had already conveyed to his eldest son, Lawrence, the Hunting Creek property, which he had selected as the proper seat for the head of the family. Three months after his father's death, Lawrence married Anne, the eldest daughter of the Honorable William Fairfax, a member of the King's Council, and one of the first men in Virginia. Lawrence was the equal of his wife in social position. Born in 1718, he was educated in England; he had seen service as a Virginia officer in the Cartagena expedition under Admiral Vernon; and in 1742 he began a term of seven years in the House of Burgesses.

The second son, Augustine (called in the family Austin), was placed on the estate at Bridges Creek. Austin had returned from school at Appleby during the previous year, and had lost no time in marrying Anne Aylett, an heiress.

Mary Ball Washington and her children took what was left. She received ready money, a life-interest in Ferry Farm, and the management of the property left to the minor children. Mrs. Washington was quite capable of handling the Ferry Farm plantation, but family councils decided that she should relieve herself, or be relieved of, the task of bringing up her eldest son, George, then a precocious lad of eleven years. As a result, he returned to his birthplace and became a member of Augustine's family. During the five years before he was sixteen, George received all of the schooling he ever had. Either in Westmoreland County or at Fredericksburg, he learned more of mathematics than is required of college students to-day. In particular he became proficient in surveying, and thus was able to earn his living when the time came. Also he became familiar with the legal forms used in conveying land, making contracts and the like; he learned to calculate time and to determine the days which marked the divisions of the year according to the calendar then in use. He became an expert penman, training his hand to produce the handwriting that distinguished his letters throughout life, although later he generally eschewed those flourishes in which boyish exuberance found vent.

For copy in the art of writing he had set for him exercises containing one hundred and ten 'Rules of Civility,' adapted from a long popular translation by Hawkins of a French work on behavior. It has been assumed that the compilation was made by George himself; but this seems improbable. During twenty-five years the Hawkins translation ran through edition after edition in England; and copies of one edition or another have survived in the British Museum, in the Bodleian Library, Oxford, in Trinity College Library, Cambridge, and in the Library of Congress. The Rules, without exception, can be traced directly to Hawkins, but there is a gap of three quarters of a century between the latest known edition of Hawkins and the date when George Washington made his copy of them. When and by whom those copied by Washington were selected and condensed is as yet unexplained.

The fact that young Washington wrote out these Rules
.before he was sixteen years old, and that he practiced them
all his life, has caused them to be regarded as one of the
most important parts of his education. Undoubtedly they
were; they expressed in concrete form the ambition which
he always displayed, namely, by diligence to stand before
the best of the earth and not before mean men. Times
have changed what is simply accidental in the rules, but
the essence of them is as potent to-day as it was when they
were compiled by the Jesuit priests of centuries ago. The
boy of to-day who learns and practices them is fitted for
any society anywhere.[1]

Lawrence Washington as the head of the family, according to the ideas then prevailing, was concerned for his
half-brother's future. He urged strongly upon his stepmother that George should go to sea; and to this the latter
assented, not because of inclination, but on account of his
confidence in the disinterested friendship and experience of
Lawrence. But no amount of urging could persuade the
timid mother, who would be more influenced by one word
against the project than by ten words for it. In this stand
she was fortified by the pessimistic advice of her brother
Joseph, the London lawyer. Just what Lawrence had in
mind was contained in two letters, one to Mary Washington and also one to George, which he was cautioned not to
show to his mother. Lawrence had made many friends in
England during his school-days, and probably their influence was referred to in the 'strong recommendation' he

[1] The *Rules of Civility* and the mathematics notebook are in the Washington
Manuscript Collection in the Library of Congress; both are in the handwriting
of George Washington and are dated by him.

104th 6 belongs to ye Cheafest in Company 'to unfold his Napkin and fall
to Meat first, But he ought then to Begin in time & to Dispatch
wth Dexterity that ye Slowest may have time allowed him

p5th Be not Angry at Table whatever happens & if you have reason
to be So, Shew it not but on a Chearfull Countenance especially if
there be Strangers for Good Humour makes one Dish of Meat a Feast

156 Set not yourself at ye upper of ye Table but if it be your Due
or that ye Master of ye house will have it So, Contend not, least
you Should Trouble ye Company

107th If others talk at Table be attentive but talk not with
Meat in your Mouth

108 When you Speak of God or his Atributes, let it be Seriously &
wth Reverence Honour & Obey your Natural Parents although they be Poor

109th Let your Recreations be Manfull not Sinfull.

110. Labour to keep alive in your Breast that Little Spark of Celestial fire Called Conscience

Finis

LAST PAGE OF GEORGE WASHINGTON'S 110 RULES OF CIVILITY,
WRITTEN BEFORE HE WAS SIXTEEN YEARS OLD

LAWRENCE WASHINGTON

proposed to furnish to his younger brother.[1] There is no
basis for the oft-repeated statement that the youngster was
to become a midshipman in the Royal Navy.

At the age of sixteen, George went to live with his brother Lawrence at Mount Vernon, which was destined ever
afterward to be his home, or, better, his headquarters, for
he was rarely spared from public service. In England the
Washingtons were connected by many ties with the Fairfax
family, the head of which was Thomas, Lord Fairfax, who
had inherited through his mother the Culpeper grant, of
some six million acres between the Potomac and the
Rappahannock, known then and now as the Northern
Neck. The manager of this vast domain was the Honorable William Fairfax, a cousin of his lordship, whose seat
was Belvoir, immediately below Mount Vernon, on the
Potomac. Socially the two families were one; and so they
were in all material and political interests. It was in this
domestic environment that George Washington spent his
formative years from sixteen to twenty, both giving and
receiving.

William Fairfax became one of George Washington's
firmest friends, and merely from reading the frequent letters that passed between them one would not suspect the
disparity in their ages. Mr. Fairfax was born in Yorkshire,
the grandson of the fourth Lord Fairfax. He was educated
under the care of his uncle, Lord Lonsdale, and after entering the army he served in Spain and the Indies. He was
Chief Justice of the Bahamas when his health gave way,
and in 1725 he secured a transfer to the collectorship at

[1] William Fairfax to Lawrence Washington. Conway: *Barons of the Potomac
and Rappahanock*, p. 262.

Salem, Massachusetts. There his wife (Sarah Walker) died, leaving him with four children. Tradition has it that on her deathbed, in 1731, his wife selected as her successor Deborah, a daughter of Francis and Deborah (Gedney) Clarke, a choice which was confirmed later by the parties most interested.

About the time George came permanently to Mount Vernon, Deborah Clarke died, leaving three children. There are letters in which Mistress Deborah discusses frankly her position as wife and stepmother. She possessed a strong Puritan strain, relieved now and again by a tinge of humor. She had a good opinion of herself and was justified in it. Doubtless the partiality George Washington often and unmistakably showed for the New England character had its beginnings in his associations with this estimable Bay State woman.

The titular head of the household became Mrs. George William Fairfax (born Cary of Ceelys), then, at the age of eighteen, an experienced woman of the Virginian world. For beauty, liveliness, and social position Mistress Sally was without a superior in all Virginia. To George Washington, a tall, spare, unformed youth of sixteen, with big hands and feet, this demure matron, two years his senior, was quite the finest lady he had ever seen. On her part she evidently saw in the boy the promise which was so apparent to all men with whom he came in contact; and, within the limits of those conventions which she ever respected, she was ready to encourage his friendship. Then, too, she had a younger sister,[1] who added interest to the

[1] Mary Cary married the Reverend Bryan Fairfax, eldest son of William and Deborah Fairfax, who in 1800 entered into the enjoyment of the title of eighth Lord Fairfax. They are the direct ancestors of the present Lord Fairfax.

household, and there were several other young ladies who for a longer or shorter time touched the boyish affections of the susceptible youth. In short, George was like other boys of his age and circumstances; and no more serious attention is to be given to his protestations of love than belongs to those of boys in general.

The seat of the Fairfaxes was called Belvoir. A modest monument erected by Mr. Fairfax Harrison marks the burial-place of the original owners. The mansion was of brick, two stories in height; on the first floor were four rooms and a large hall; on the second floor, five rooms; and in the basement was a servants' hall and cellar. Convenient offices and stables adjoined; and the large garden was filled with valuable fruit-trees. Mount Vernon was in full view, only water separating the two estates.[1]

Another frequenter of Belvoir became a powerful influence on the future of George Washington. Lord Fairfax took a fancy to the youth and employed him to make surveys of his lands in the Shenandoah Valley. George seized the opportunity with avidity, because it meant activity, adventure, and financial independence. With him into the wilderness went George William Fairfax, and their friendship thus established never diminished.

Lord Fairfax lives in history and tradition as a graduate of Oxford, a man of fashion in London, and a member of the literary coterie who produced the 'Spectator.' He is believed to have fled to America because the lady with whom he was in love married a higher title. He was enough of a man to get on without this romantic English back-

---

[1] Edward D. Neill: *The Fairfaxes in England and America*, p. 153. Washington to Sir John Sinclair, December 11, 1796.

ground. As a matter of fact no member of his family ever matriculated at Oxford; he was quite too young to have belonged to the 'Spectator' set, and no paper therein has been identified as having come from his pen. There was ample reason for his presence at Greenway Court,[1] in the Shenandoah Valley; for the entire theory represented by him and his six million acres (granted by an English king to a favorite courtier) was disputed by the actual settlers, Germans and Scotch-Irish, who had come to this country to escape from such a system. With all his personal popularity and with many business and family alliances, he was ever playing a losing game. Democracy was in the air.

It has been assumed by Washington's biographers that, after a hard day's tramp in making surveys, or an even harder day's ride after the fox, Washington spent long evenings at Greenway Court, improving his mind by reading Mrs. Macaulay's histories, or Sir Walter Raleigh's works, or bound volumes of the English magazines. Of course, he never took from his lordship's shelves 'Tom Jones,' 'Joseph Andrews,' 'The Adventures of a Valet,' 'Amelia,' 'Peregrine Pickle,' 'Patty Landers,' 'Harriet Stuart,' or other books of like character, which made up more than half of that nobleman's not extensive library.[2]

Nevertheless, Lord Fairfax was one of the formative influences in the life of George Washington; he did belong to the great world to which the boy aspired; he dearly loved fox-hunting, followed by a good dinner and good stories;

[1] Greenway Court, then on the road from Ashby's Gap to Frederick Town, or Winchester; now in Clark County, near Berryville.

[2] Inventory of Lord Fairfax's estate, May, 1782. *The Virginia Magazine*, July, 1900. Most of the books mentioned in the inventory were published a little later than Washington's first visit to Greenway Court; but *Peregrine Pickle* was in his own library.

THOMAS, LORD FAIRFAX

WAKEFIELD, WESTMORELAND COUNTY
Conjectural design of the house in which George Washington was born
From a sketch by M. H. Lowell

GREENWAY COURT, THE VIRGINIA HOME OF THOMAS,
LORD FAIRFAX
The mansion disappeared a century ago, but the office used by George
Washington is substantially unchanged

and he was not niggardly about payment for services. From the old man the youth learned many things, but among them were neither political opinions nor yet morals. The friendship lasted for a third of a century, until the death of Lord Fairfax, at the ripe age of ninety-two years, after the surrender of Cornwallis.[1]

It was during the spring of 1748, when he was sixteen years old, that George Washington obtained his first experience of real life. His training in surveying had been excellent, and that accuracy which went with him through life was first made manifest in running the lines of Lord Fairfax's domains in the Shenandoah Valley. According to his own account, he was glad, after a long day's tramp, to roll himself in a blanket and lie down on 'a little hay or a bearskin with man, wife and children, like dogs and cats; and happy was he who got the berth nearest the fire.' Nor did he hesitate to supply to a band of Indians the liquor necessary to induce a war-dance — 'a comical sight,' he called it.

While these surveys were in progress, Lawrence and Augustine Washington, with others in Virginia and in England, organized the Ohio Company, and secured from the King a grant of half a million acres along the Ohio River. This territory, however, France claimed by right of discovery, and proceeded to occupy in force. The American affairs of the company fell into the hands of Lawrence Washington, who entered upon his task with energy. A company fort was built near the present site of Pittsburgh,

[1] Lord Fairfax was buried in the Episcopal Church he founded at Winchester. When the church gave way to business, his body was mingled with other bodies removed. In 1925 it was discovered and reinterred.

with a station at Piqua, north of the Ohio. Piqua was destroyed by the French, and plans were made to attack the forts at the forks of the Ohio. Such were the conditions when George Washington's boyhood was brought to a sudden end by the death, on July 26, 1752, of his brother Lawrence, at the age of thirty-four years.

CHAPTER IV

ARMS AND LADIES

LAWRENCE WASHINGTON'S death, neither sudden nor un-expected, placed upon his half-brother, George, then twenty years old, responsibilities that straightway changed the boy into a man. The Washingtons were not a long-lived family; and Lawrence had brought home from a British campaign against the Spanish in Cartagena the seeds of disease, which he vainly endeavored to eradicate by a trip to Barbados. For company he took his brother George, who then for the first and last time went beyond the bounds of his native country. An attack of smallpox left on the boy's face marks never wholly effaced. As soon as he was well enough to take ship, George returned to Mount Vernon to hasten the departure of Anne Fairfax Washington, who was to join her husband in Bermuda. Before she was ready to sail, Lawrence came back to Mount Vernon to die.

Augustine Washington had provided that in case of Lawrence's death without heirs, Mount Vernon should pass to George; and this provision Lawrence incorporated in his own will. To his widow he left a life-interest in the property, with the reversion to his infant daughter, Sarah, who, as it happened, survived her father only a few weeks. Thus there was only the widow's life-interest to be considered.

Anne Fairfax Washington, after enduring widowhood for the space of five months, married Colonel George Lee, of

Mount Pleasant, Westmoreland County, a member in the
fourth generation of the Stratford Lees. Probably she was
not loath to return to the scenes of her girlhood,[1] and an
amicable arrangement was made with her brother-in-law,
whereby he should enter immediately into possession of the
Mount Vernon estate, on an annual payment to her husband of fifteen thousand pounds of tobacco, equivalent to
£82. 10s., Virginia currency. This rental was paid punctu-
ally for nine years, until Mrs. Lee's death in 1761.[2]

In May, 1752, while yet he had no possessions and only
problematical prospects, George wrote to William Fauntleroy, Sr.:

I should have been down long before this, but my business in
Frederick [Winchester] detained me somewhat longer than I
expected, and immediately on my return from thence I was
taken with a violent plurise, which reduced me very low; but
purpose, as soon as I recover my strength, to wait on Miss Betsy
in hopes of a revocation of her former cruel sentence, and see if I
can meet with any alteration in my favor. I have inclosed a
letter to her, which I should be much obliged to you for the de-
livery of.[3]

Whether he ever pursued his intention to renew his suit is
doubtful.[4] Two months later he became a man of position
and property. Settling his brother's estate kept him busy;
and as the owner of Mount Vernon it behooved him to be
circumspect in the choice of a consort.

[1] Her father, William Fairfax, removed from Salem to Westmoreland County
before building Belvoir.
[2] George Lee survived his wife but a few months; of their three sons, the unmarried one lived to the age of eighty; the elder sons had daughters who were
absorbed in the Chipley, Sangster, and Cockrell families.
[3] Ford: *Writings of Washington*, vol. I, p. 9.
[4] Betsy Fauntleroy married an Adams, and became the mother of the Honorable Thomas Adams.

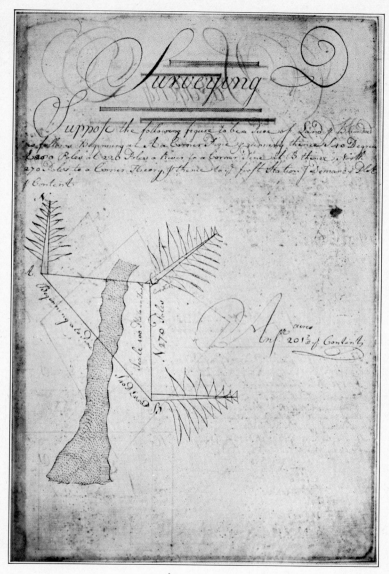

FROM GEORGE WASHINGTON'S COPY-BOOK, WRITTEN BEFORE HE
WAS SIXTEEN YEARS OLD

Sir

The General having been inform'd that you express'd
some desire to make the Campaigne. but that
you declin'd it upon some disagreeableness that
you thought might arise from the Regulation
of Command. has order'd me to acquaint you
that he will be very glad of your Company in
his Family by which all Inconveniencies
of that kind will be obviated

I shall think myself very happy to form an
acquaintance with a person so universally
esteem'd and will use every opportunity
of assuring you how much I am Sir
Your most obed't Servant
Rob Orme aid de Camp.

Williamsberg. Mh 2d 1755.

INVITATION TO COL. GEORGE WASHINGTON TO JOIN GENERAL
BRADDOCK'S MILITARY FAMILY

He joined the Masonic Lodge at Fredericksburg on November 4, 1752, before he became of age. Sincere in his practice of Masonry as in all his associations, he was a devoted member of that order. He held office in the Alexandria Lodge, which still possesses the furniture of his day. Later he encouraged Masonry in the Continental Army, because of the fraternal feelings it promoted among soldiers and officers, and also because it served to mitigate rancor in the case of captives.

In the autumn of 1753, Governor Dinwiddie started George Washington on his military career by sending him with a message to the French, demanding that they cease driving British traders from the Ohio country and breaking up their establishments. It was a winter journey of two months' duration, through a wilderness and over the mountains to Venango, on the Allegheny; it involved cajoling Indians, winning them to Virginia interests, and guarding them from the seductions of French officers. Not only did the French refuse to retire, but they also put forth a claim to the Ohio region by virtue of 'the discovery of one La-Salle, sixty years ago.'

To acknowledge these claims meant the ruin of the Ohio Company, and of all the hopes of fortune connected with that enterprise — a serious blow to Governor Dinwiddie, the Lees, and many other respectable men of the Colony. Virginia believed that her territory extended at least to the Mississippi. France claimed the entire valley of the Ohio. The Indians maintained that between English and French territories was a great hunting ground which of right belonged to the red men, and from which they proposed to exclude all settlements, although they were ever ready to welcome traders. The Indian policy favored the French, who wanted to trade, not to settle; whereas English strength in America was based on pioneer settlers taking possession of this country.

On the 11th of January, 1754, Washington reached Belvoir on his return to Williamsburg. Before the ink was dry on the report he submitted to Governor Dinwiddie, it went to the printer; and the next year it was published in London by the Lords of Trade, who thereupon directed the Colonial Governors to concert measures to drive the French from the territories of His Majesty.

The result was the Albany Convention of 1754, at which Benjamin Franklin vainly urged the Colonies to unite for the mutual protection of their frontiers. Another quarter-century was to elapse, however, before a common peril brought the Colonies to unite; and then not on behalf of the King, but against his policies.

Washington's report, lucid, straightforward, circumstantial, but not prolix, and withal modest, laid a firm foundation for the reputation he was building for himself not only in America, but also in both England and France. The Colonies began to see in him a leader in the field; the English regarded him as an enterprising youth who might be useful if properly curbed; and in him France recognized an enemy.

While the Albany Convention was in session, George Washington, at the head of a small force of Virginia militia and friendly Indians, fell upon a party of French and in an engagement of fifteen minutes' duration killed their commander and nine others and took twenty prisoners. On the 3d of July, however, he was surrounded by a superior force, and after nine hours' fighting was forced to capitulate.

In the postscript of a letter [1] to his brother John Augustine, whom he had left in charge of Mount Vernon, Washington says: 'I fortunately escaped without any wound, for the right wing, where I stood, was exposed to and received all the enemy's fire, and it was the part where the man was killed, and the rest wounded. I heard the bullets whistle, and, believe me, there is something charming in the sound.'

Horace Walpole reports that 'on hearing of this letter, the King said sensibly, "He would not say so if he had been used to hear many." However, this brave braggart learned to blush for his rodomontade, and, desiring to serve General Braddock as an aide-de-camp, acquitted himself nobly.' Walpole further characterizes this encounter as 'a trifling action indeed, but remarkable for giving a date to the war,' to which comment Walpole's editor, Lord Holland,[2] adds, 'and as remarkable for being the first action in which Washington was mentioned, who nearly thirty years afterwards became the principal figure in America.'

Such, indeed, was the beginning of the Seven Years' War, which ended in placing England in possession of Canada and India, and which proved for the Americans the training-ground for the Revolution. Such also was Washington's first appearance on the world's stage.

It so happened that, in signing the articles of capitulation prepared by the French, Washington unwittingly admitted the 'assassination' of French envoys, a mistake due

---

[1] Ford: *Writings of Washington*, vol. I, p. 90.

[2] Horace Walpole: *Memoirs of the Reign of King George the Second*, edited by the late Lord Holland; second edition, 1847, vol. I, p. 399.

to the fact that his interpreter, the old Dutch soldier Van Braam, had not enough French to furnish a correct translation of the articles. Not only was the error made much of in France, but it made trouble for Washington also in Maryland.

These misadventures were an essential part of a military education. Yet, when all had been said, the fact remained that a youth of twenty-two had been able to sustain an action all day with a superior force and had come off with the honors of war.

England now realized that, in order to retain her American possessions, she herself must fight for them; because the Colonies were too much concerned with individual quarrels between royal governors and popular assemblies to make common cause against the French. So it happened that in February, 1755, General Edward Braddock sailed up the Potomac with two regiments of British soldiers, sent to drive the French back to the St. Lawrence. From Governor Dinwiddie's palace at Williamsburg, General Braddock summoned the royal governors of five Colonies to meet him at Alexandria to prepare for the campaign.[1] The meeting took place in the home of Major John Carlyle, who had married a daughter of William Fairfax. To this day the Carlyle House, preserved as a monument of the occasion, is fragrant of the gayety incident to the headquarters of a commander distinguished not more for bravery in the field than for conviviality in the camp.

[1] The council was composed of General Braddock, Admiral Keppel, and Governors Shirley (Massachusetts), Dinwiddie (Virginia), De Lancey (New York), Sharpe (Maryland), and Morris (Pennsylvania). The minutes are in the MSS. of Sir William Johnson, *N.Y. Doc. Hist.*, vol. II.

George Washington at Mount Vernon longed for an opportunity to advance his military education by a campaign in company with trained soldiers; but he was precluded from doing so by the fact that, being only a provincial, he could hold no rank that would not subordinate him to the lowest officer who had purchased a royal commission. Having been told that the young man's knowledge of the country would prove useful, Braddock cut the knot by inviting him to become one of his own military family, an invitation accepted with alacrity. Between general and aide a feeling of mutual respect grew up quickly. The general took small offense at the spirit with which his aide defended his countrymen from aspersions; the aide learned the routine of army life as maintained by a soldier trained in the best traditions.

Best of all, Washington was brought into intimate companionship with Braddock's aides, Robert Orme, Roger Morris, and young William Shirley. Perhaps others of his contemporaries called Washington by his first name; but Orme is the only one whose pen naturally and easily writes the words 'dear George.' [1]

Washington's mother made the journey from Fredericksburg to Mount Vernon hoping to dissuade her son from undertaking another military expedition. But he was no longer a boy subject to parental control. He was a man of position and property, a youth with the world to conquer. He told his mother that she ought to want him to serve his country; but she was first of all a mother. She could not raise herself to such heights.

[1] Captain Orme and General Braddock were cronies, and before departing from London they spent a convivial evening at the house of an actress-friend of the General's.

After innumerable delays, exasperating to General Braddock, the army set forth in June to drive the French from the forks of the Ohio as a preliminary to the capture of Fort Niagara. Illness kept Washington from setting out with the expedition; but so soon as he could travel he pushed on, caught up with the advance, and although still weak took part in the battle near the banks of the Monongahela.

According to Washington's report to Governor Dinwiddie, Braddock's army, consisting of thirteen hundred well-armed men, chiefly regulars, had reached Frazier's within seven miles of Fort Duquesne, on July 9, 1755. There it was attacked unexpectedly by about three hundred French and Indians. The British were immediately struck with such deadly panic that nothing but confusion and disobedience of orders prevailed amongst them. The officers in general behaved with incomparable bravery, there being nearly sixty killed and wounded, a large proportion of the number engaged.

The Virginians behaved like men and died like soldiers; out of three companies scarce thirty were left alive. The dastardly behavior of the English soldiers exposed all those who were inclined to do their duty to almost certain death, and at length, in despite of every effort to the contrary, they broke and ran like sheep before the hounds, leaving the artillery, ammunition, and provisions and every individual thing they had with them a prey to the enemy. When the officers endeavored to rally them, it was with as much success as if they had attempted to stop the wild bears of the mountains.

General Braddock, fatally wounded, died three days

later. His two aides were wounded, but recovered. 'I luckily escaped without a wound,' are Washington's words, 'tho' I had four Bullets thro' my Coat and two Horses shot under me.' About three hundred dead were left on the field, and the same number brought off wounded. It was believed that two thirds of both numbers 'received their shot from our own cowardly dogs of soldiers, who gathered themselves into a body, contrary to orders, ten or twelve deep, and then levelled, fired, and shot down the men before them.'

Washington trembled at the consequences on the frontier inhabitants, who would be forced to leave their homes; and there was good reason for his concern. Although it was July, Colonel Dunbar, who assumed command, proposed to go into winter quarters in Philadelphia leaving the poor remains of the Virginian forces to guard the frontiers. Why Colonel Dunbar did not gather his troops and hold his ground is a puzzle. He knew he still had twice the force that attacked him. He might have known that the French officers were quite as timid as the English, and that Indians never fought unless they were safe in doing so. Their leadership, such as it was, came from a French trader, Charles de Langlade, from Lake Superior. A council of war never fights; and Colonel Dunbar's council was no exception to the rule. After suffering one ambush, the British army, that had danced and marched and bullied the Colonists, threw up their task, and retired.

From Fort Cumberland, Washington wrote to 'dear Jack,' as he called his brother John Augustine, that having heard a circumstantial account of his own death and

dying speech, he took that early opportunity of contradict-
ing the first and of assuring him that he had not as yet
composed the latter — a touch of ironic humor not uncommon in his letters.

Arriving at Mount Vernon on July 26th, Washington
was greeted by a note of heartfelt thankfulness from
William Fairfax, to which was appended a postscript in
the handwriting of Mrs. George William Fairfax. The
dainty little lady served notice of her displeasure that he
did not at once proceed to Belvoir, and she threatened a
descent upon Mount Vernon unless he should put in an
appearance early the next morning.

In August, Washington was commissioned colonel and
commander-in-chief of the Virginia Regiment, to be
composed of sixteen companies raised for the avowed
purpose of protecting the frontiers and driving out the
French, who had 'unjustly invaded His Majesty's lands
on the Ohio.' Governor Dinwiddie, in his instructions, desired the Colonel to 'inculcate morality and virtue among
his men, and to punish drunkenness and swearing.' When
on occasion Washington himself ripped out an oath,
history has decided that he expressed its opinion of the
transaction in question. When the Governor's letter
caused swearing at Fort Cumberland, the Colonel was in
no mood to stop it, although he was prompt to check
overt acts of mutiny.

To relieve the tedium of garrison life on the frontiers,
Washington urged Mrs. Carlyle [1] and Mrs. Fairfax to
write to him. The former, conscious of her own epistolary
deficiencies, warned him that 'he must not expect the

[1] Sarah Fairfax Carlyle. The two ladies were sisters-in-law.

113

to intend Marching, its supposed, to Philadephia or &c

Y'r affect.ᵗ W Fairfax

Dear Sir

After thanking Heaven for your safe return I must accuse you of great unkindness in refusing us the pleasure of seeing you this night I do assure you nothing but our being satisfied that our company would be disagreable should prevent us from trying if our Legs would not carry us to Mount Vernon this night, but if you will not come to us to morrow Morning very early we shall be at Mont Vernon

S Fairfax
Ann Spearing

Eliz^th Dent

NOTE FROM MRS. FAIRFAX

Postscript to a letter dated Belvoir, July 26, 1755, from William Fairfax to Washington, congratulating him upon his safe return from the disastrous Braddock expedition

MARY PHILIPSE
(Afterwards Mrs. Roger Morris)

SALLY CARY (MRS. GEORGE WILLIAM FAIRFAX OF
BELVOIR)
Born at Ceelys, 1730; died at Bath, England, 1811

corrispondence to be carried on on her side with such spirit as to enliven him, which would be her desire, if only she could.' She adds this sage advice:

Those pleasing reflections on the hours past ought to be banished out of your thoughts, you have now a nobler prospect — that of preserving your country from the insults of an enemy, and as God has blessed your first attempt, hope He may continer His blessing, and on your return who knows but fortune may have reserved you for some unknown She that may recompense you for all your trials.

Mrs. Fairfax discreetly stipulated that his letters should go to some third person, a suggestion at which he took quick offense, but he did not cease writing to her — nor did she cease writing to him.

A dispute arose over the pretensions of a Maryland captain to take rank over Washington by virtue of the fact that he once held a King's commission, and the Governors of Maryland and Virginia were unable or unwilling to compose the matter. Colonel Washington, therefore, sought a decision from Governor Shirley, the commander-in-chief. Leaving Alexandria on February 4, 1756, with his aide-de-camp, Captain Mercer, and two servants, he tarried in New York to visit his cousin, Beverly Robinson, at whose home he met for the first time Miss Mary Philipse, a beauty, a belle, and an heiress.

Riding through New London, Newport, and Providence, he proceeded to Boston, where he presented letters from Governor Dinwiddie to Governor Shirley, of whom he had conceived a high opinion when he met him at Alexandria. Governor Shirley promptly decided in his favor and for ten days entertained the two young Virginians, who listened to the legislative debates and 'accepted the hospitality of several prominent citizens.' On his travels Washington lost at cards, tipped men- and maid-servants, escorted ladies to exhibitions and dances, and patronized the 'tayler' and all his tribe. On his way back he tarried again in New York and again met Miss Philipse, with the result that their names have ever since been connected.

Much interest in the 'affair' was taken by Joseph Chew, who hoped to bring about a match between Washington and 'Miss Polly.' More than a year later Chew wrote:

As to the latter part of your letter, what shall I say? I often had the pleasure of breakfasting with the charming Polly. Roger Morris was there (don't be startled) but not always, you know him he is a lady's man, always something to say. The town talked of it as a sure and settled affair. I can't say I think so and that I much doubt it, but assure you had little acquaintance with Mr. Morris and only slightly hinted it to Miss Polly; but how can you be excused to continue so long at Phila. I think I should have made a kind of flying march of it if it had been only to have seen whether the Works were sufficient to withstand a vigorous attack, you a Soldier and a Lover. Mind, I have been arguing for my own interest now, for had you taken this method then I should have had the pleasure of seeing you. ... I intend to set out [from his home in New London] to-morrow for New York where I will not be wanting to let Miss Polly know the sincere regard a Friend of mine has for her, and I am sure if she had my eyes to see through she would prefer him to all others.[1]

The eager matchmaker's hopes were blasted, for not even his subsequent confidence that Miss Polly was suffering from pain in the face would spur on the reluctant George. Possibly it was tacitly if not openly realized that the life of a soldier's wife on a remote Virginia plantation,

[1] *Letters to Washington*, in five volumes; edited by S. M. Hamilton.

with its attendant domestic cares and duties, would not be productive of happiness to a young woman accustomed to New York social life.

Miss Philipse married in her own set. Twenty years later, when the Revolution came to sunder patriots and loyalists, she and her husband, Roger Morris, stayed with the De Lancey party in New York, as did also her brother-in-law, Beverly Robinson. Both men were active supporters of the King. Her property being needed by the Colonies, she was proclaimed a traitor and her possessions were confiscated. So ended a romance that scarcely had a beginning.

The tide of war swept northward, and left to Virginia only devastated frontiers. If George Washington had hoped, by reason of his visit to Governor Shirley, to obtain active employment with the northern troops, he was disappointed. He was attached to the expedition of General Forbes with Fort Duquesne as its objective, and he tried vainly to have that commander complete the Braddock Road to the Ohio. In spite of his arguments, Pennsylvania had sufficient influence to secure, instead, the building of the road from Philadelphia to the forks of the Ohio. The two routes are now traversed respectively by the Baltimore and Ohio and the Pennsylvania Railroads.

Here Washington's active military service ended for the time being. No Colonial soldier had equaled him in valor or capacity; his reputation was established, and he might well look forward to exchanging arduous garrison duty for the long-deferred joys of life as a Colonial gentleman at Mount Vernon, Virginia.

CHAPTER V

COURTSHIP AND MARRIAGE

ONE February day in 1758, Colonel George Washington, accompanied by his body-servant, Bishop, rode out of the gates of Mount Vernon on his way to Williamsburg on business connected with his duties as commander of the Virginia forces. Throughout the previous autumn he had been suffering from stomach trouble, which had become so acute during November that he could not walk, and so had been forced to repair to his home for recovery. He had gone back to Fort Louden in January, much to the apprehension of Dr. Craik, and of his superior officers and his friends, all of whom urged the plea that his prospective services to his country were too valuable to be risked by a premature return to duty — none of which things moved him. Indeed, his condition had been so precarious that the report of his death had again gone abroad.

Pursuing his way, Washington rode first past the estate of William Fairfax, Belvoir. Next he skirted the six thousand acres of George Mason, who was then completing Gunston Hall and who was in need of ready money to pay the workmen — if one may venture that explanation of the importunate request he had sent to Mount Vernon, almost demanding the payment to bearer of an account for military supplies.

Washington's way led through Dumfries, a settlement of Scotch traders, whose once fine mansions are now given over to transient tenants; then through the old town of

Good Cous?   Stratford 5.th of Sept.r 1755.

It is a sensible Pleasure to me to hear that
you have behaved your self with such a Martial
Spirit in all your Engagements with the French
nigh Ohio. Go on as you have begun; and God prosper
you.

We have heard of General Bradock's Defeat.
Every Body Blames his Rash Conduct
Every body Commends the Courage of the Virginian
and Carolina men: which is very Agreeable to me.

I desire you, as you may from time to time
have opportunity, to give me a Short Account how
you proceed. As I am your Mother's Brother, I
hope you won't deny my Request.

There is Little News here. One of our men
of war has taken in our Channell a French Ship
Ship of 16. Guns, 2. Brigs, and a Schooner,
for Martinico, and brought them in. And there
were 11. more in the Fleet; after after which another
Man of war is gone out in Chace.

What will be done with them 4. that are taken
I can't tell.

There is no war Declared yet either by the
French or us; though it is expected there Soon will.

The King is not Returned from Hanover yet; but
is lookt for very Soon; The yachts are gone for
him. I heartily wish you Good Success, and am
                              Yr. Loving Uncle
Please to dir.ct to me at Stratford   Jos. Ball
by Bow nigh London.

Since the writing the other above, I have Gotten G. more; so much so fast brought in. Though
                                        and to the best of our knowledge they are these   & now though.
                                                                    viz.t

MARTHA (DANDRIDGE) CUSTIS
(Afterwards Mrs. George Washington)

DANIEL PARKE CUSTIS
The first husband of Martha Washington

Falmouth, nestling on the hills of the Rappahannock near the falls. He may have passed the night at Ferry Farm, where his mother was then living; but probably he stayed at the house of Colonel and Mrs. Fielding Lewis, as usual.

Throughout the Northern Neck, as the country between the Potomac and Rappahannock is still called, the roads known to George Washington run their accustomed way through field and forest, over hills and down dales, much as they did in his day. Motor-bus and river-boat are the only regular connection with the industrial world; ferries are in use, with ferrymen just as leisurely and independent as they were a century and a half ago. The county court-house and the church in the woods remain social centers; but the great plantation, with its self-contained community life, was dissolved by the Civil War. Since the World War, new homes, new schools, and the omnipresent gas station, give an appearance of life to the country. In the towns, an occasional granite soldier of the Confederacy, rough-hewn at the quarries in Vermont, rises from a group of obsolete cannon and cannon-balls. On the wall of every house hangs a picture of General Robert E. Lee.

Enterprising youth, male and female, seek the opportunities afforded by the city. Occasionally men who have gained wealth in the big world have come to tidewater Virginia, to rejuvenate the old homes and to find refuge in a region where time is not the essence of life's contract. Many of the old estates, still in the possession of the original families, have never recovered from the ravages of the Civil War. Their glory has departed, and with difficulty one traces the outlines of formal gardens, or, in some God's-acre near the once stately mansion, scrapes the moss from the tombstone of a man whose name shines resplendent in American history. The most permanent thing among impermanent things is Virginia hospitality, exercised toward all whose credentials give claim to it.

It was the 25th day of February, 1758, when Colonel Washington came to a ferry on the Pamunkey, not far from the point where it changes its name to York River. In those days, a gentleman on his travels usually dined in the afternoon, or supped and passed the night, at the mansion of an acquaintance. The inns, or ordinaries, were for people of less consideration and for servants. Whether by accident or design, Washington dined that day with a Mr. Chamberlayne, who lived near the crossing. There he met, possibly for the first time, Mrs. Martha Dandridge Custis, the widow of Daniel Parke Custis.

If Washington was looking for a mistress for Mount Vernon, no marriage could have been more suitable than that of this man and this woman. Both were independent financially; they moved in the same social circles. Both were well-born and well-bred; they had the same ambitions and the same outlook on life. Mount Vernon needed a housekeeper; Mrs. Custis needed some one to guide and direct the education of her two children, and to care for their and her considerable property.

The story is that the young soldier was quickly smitten with the attractions of the beautiful widow; and that he lingered in her presence while the impatient Bishop led the horses around and around the drive, dispatches of the Royal Government being allowed to wait. It was not until the next morning that farewells were said, and then only for a brief interval before the returning officer should call at White House, the home of his inamorata, to plead his suit and win her consent.

There is not so much romance in Washington's life that one would willingly forego a whit of it; but as a matter of fact there were no dispatches. Washington had gone to Williamsburg on his own motion, perhaps for the very purpose of renewing an acquaintance with Mrs. Custis, possibly begun in Williamsburg some time before this meeting.

The real test of their romance, however, is found in a life-companionship of forty years, lived in home, in camp, and in official residence, and ever with admiration, helpfulness, and consideration on both sides.

Colonel Washington being the leader of the Virginia forces in a British war for the conquest of North America, both the interests of his country and his own honor required that he continue in his command to the end of the campaign for the recovery of the Ohio country. And inasmuch as this end was not then in sight, 'the happy hour when they made their pledges to each other' was to remain their secret, although, like most secrets of that kind, it gradually became known to the friends of both.

In April, Beverly Robinson, writing from New York, conveyed the compliments of Mr. and Mrs. Roger Morris. Thus the episode with Mary Philipse was closed. There remained the adjustment of the friendship with Mrs. George William Fairfax, whose proprietary interest in her protégé must of necessity cease with his marriage. Her fitful and uncertain letters had stopped during the spring, although probably he saw her at Belvoir on his way to and

54 THE FAMILY LIFE OF WASHINGTON

from Williamsburg in May, and possibly he then told her of the change in his fortunes. He wrote to her in September, expressing in his own vehement fashion his impatience at the delays in the campaign, due to mismanagement and, as he believed, to the politics played by the Pennsylvanians in the matter of cutting a new road to the Ohio instead of using the old Braddock Road.

The nimble-witted Mrs. Fairfax suggested that his impatience was due not so much to his devotion to public interests as to 'the animating prospects of possessing Mrs. Custis.' He admitted the imputation, and acknowledged himself 'a votary of love.' Then, after some enigmatical expressions referring to their friendship, he continues:

You have drawn me, dear Madam, or rather I have drawn myself, into an honest confession of a simple Fact. Misconstrue not my meaning; doubt it not, nor expose it. The world has no business to know the object of my love declared in this manner to you, when I want to conceal it. One thing above all things in this world I would wish to know and only one person of your acquaintance can solve me that, or guess my meaning. But adieu to this till happier times, if I shall ever see them. The hours at present are melancholy dull — Neither the rugged toils of war, nor the gentler conflict of A[ssembly] B[alls] is in my choice. I dare believe you are as happy as you say. I wish I was happy also. Mirth, good humor, ease of mind, and — what else? — cannot fail to render you so and consummate your wishes.[1]

Attempts, based largely on this letter and another written to Mrs. Fairfax when she was old, friendless, and alone at Bath, England, have been made to prove that she was 'the object of George Washington's early and passionate love.' [2] His obligations to her were great. She was the

[1] These letters are printed in Ford's *Writings of Washington*.
[2] Wilson Miles Cary: *Sally Cary* (privately printed).

JOHN PARKE CUSTIS AND MARTHA PARKE CUSTIS
Children of Mrs. Washington

MARTHA PARKE CUSTIS   JOHN PARKE CUSTIS

From Miniatures owned by Mrs. Wilfred P. Mustard

merriest, brightest, most sophisticated woman of his acquaintance. She rallied him on his seriousness, teased him about his affairs, played with his professions of interest, threw about their occasional letters a tantalizing air of mystery, and so for ten years contributed to his education. If she ever sacrificed either time or affection for his sake, that fact has not appeared.

Undoubtedly the training he received at her hands made him particular and discriminating in the choice of a wife. She, on her part, never swerved from her straight wifely path. There was never any diminution in the intercourse between the Fairfax and Washington families, save such as separation and death created.

In July, Mount Vernon was put into condition to receive its new mistress. The roof was raised; Triplett burned bricks for the underpinning, and under the competent direction of Mr. Patterson the repairs were made to the complete satisfaction of William Fairfax, whom Washington asked to have an eye to the job.[1]

On November 28, 1758, Washington wrote to Governor Fauquier that.

Fort du Quesne — or the ground rather on which it stood — was possessed by His Majesty's troops on the 25th instant. The enemy after letting us get within a day's march of the place burned the fort and ran away (by the light of it) at night. . . . The possession of this post has been a matter of great surprise to the whole army — and we cannot attribute it to more probable causes than those of weakness, want of provisions and desertion of their Indians who providentially fell into our hands at Loyal Hannon, at a time when we despaired of proceeding, and a council of war had determined that it was not advisable to advance beyond the place above mentioned this season.

[1] Fairfax letter of July 25, 1758.

On December 9th, Washington again wrote to the Governor that he was setting out (although much indisposed) for his own home; and that if he could get the better of his present disorder he 'should hope for the honor of kissing his hand about the 25th instant.'

On December 30th, he was in Williamsburg, and on Saturday, January 6, 1759, he was married to Mrs. Custis, probably at the bride's home, White House, on York River, New Kent County. The bride wore white brocaded silk interwoven with silver thread and an embroidered satin petticoat, from beneath which peeped the purple satin slippers trimmed with silver lace that are still preserved at the home of her descendants, Tudor Place, in Washington. Her ornaments were pearl necklace, earrings, and bracelets.

He appeared in citizen's dress of blue cloth, the waistcoat of embroidered white satin, shoe and knee buckles of gold, a dress sword, and powdered hair.

Among the guests were Speaker Robinson and several members of the House of Burgesses, who rode over from Williamsburg; but the wedding was a quiet one. The next day Colonel and Mrs. Washington attended Saint Peter's Church, the rector of which, the Reverend David Mossom, had performed the ceremony on the previous day. Probably the drive to and from church, and the greetings that followed the religious service, gave rise to the impression that there was a church wedding.

CHAPTER VI

THE DANDRIDGE, PARKE, AND CUSTIS FAMILIES

GEORGE WASHINGTON'S marriage to Mrs. Custis brought him into relationships that occupied a great portion of his private life. She herself embodied the traditions of the social system of Virginia. The care of her property and the education of her children and grandchildren became one of his absorbing occupations; for he gave to the task a punctilious consideration. The Washingtons in successive generations had made their own way in the world. Mrs. Washington's descendants inherited largely the traits of the Parkes and Custises, families that toiled not, neither did they spin. They were born Parke-Custises, and so they lived. Strive as he might, Washington never was able to overcome the forces of heredity, although he mitigated the effects. He won their affections and even their worship, but he could not transform their natures.

Martha Dandridge, the eldest child of Colonel John Dandridge and Frances Jones, was born June 21, 1731, which would make her eight months older than her husband, George Washington. Her father, the clerk of New Kent County, lived at the White House, on the right bank of the Pamunkey, while his brother William, a member of the King's Council, dwelt on the opposite shore. On her mother's side she was descended from the Reverend Roland Jones, a graduate of Merton College, Oxford, who was rector of Bruton Church, Williamsburg, for fourteen years, from 1674 to 1688. Such were her respectable, but in no way distinguished, antecedents.[1]

At the age of nineteen she married Daniel Parke Custis. Both the Parke and the Custis families were of consideration because of wealth, social standing, official position; and also because of a certain arrogance and lack of consideration for others which marked them as persons to be reckoned with.

John Custis, first of the name in America, came from Ireland, by way of Holland, leaving a son in Ireland, another in London, a third in Rotterdam, and bringing three boys with him, when he settled, about 1640, on the Eastern Shore of Virginia. His son John took an active part in suppressing Bacon's Rebellion in 1676. He married a daughter of Edmund Scarborough, thereby forming an alliance with a prominent family. He obtained from the Royal Governor, Lord Howard of Effingham, the lucrative post of collector of customs for the Eastern Shore, and died in the odor of sanctity, having given to the lower church of Hungar's Parish a silver communion service.

For sixty-four years a John Custis was a member of, first, the House of Burgesses and afterward of the King's Council of Virginia. The family estate on the Eastern Shore of Virginia, called Arlington, passed from the second John to his grandson, the fourth John Custis, who married Frances, the elder daughter of Daniel Parke. Her sister Lucy married William Byrd, of Westover, on the James River.

Daniel Parke, the immigrant, came from Sussex, Eng-

[1] A. H. Wharton: *Martha Washington.* 1897.

COL. DANIEL PARKE

FRANCES PARKE CUSTIS

MARLBOROUGH'S DISPATCH ANNOUNCING THE
VICTORY AT BLENHEIM

land; his name stands first on the first vestry of Bruton Church; he was a member of the House of Burgesses in 1692, and of the Council in 1696; and further he acquired the distinction of a tablet in the first church in Williamsburg. His son, the second Daniel Parke, may be considered the real founder of the family, by reason of his varied exploits and the manner of his life and particularly of his death. The tale is characteristic of the times.

The College of William and Mary had for its first president an able, argumentative and persistent Scotchman in the person of the Reverend James Blair, who encountered the opposition of the Governor, the notorious Sir Edmund Andros.[1] The latter, being no match for Mr. Commissary Blair in argument, opposed him by all the means his office and power could afford. There was

a handsome young man named Daniel Parke, who to all the other accomplishments that make a complete sparkish Gentleman added quick resentment of affronts or injuries. Having learned the art of fencing, he was as ready at giving a challenge as the greatest Hector in the Town. This Mr. Parke, being a proper tool for his designs, Sir Edmund Andros gained to his interest, advanced him into the Council, made him a Colonel and received him into particular favor. There was no way this gentleman had to merit a place of profit from Sir Edmund (which he then greatly wanted) so ready as to exercise his talent upon the Governor of Maryland to whom Sir Edmund owed a particular grudge and enmity.

In September, 1695, Colonel Parke,

having a sword about him much longer than what he commonly travelled withal (and which he afterwards bragged he had caused

[1] Andros was Governor of New York from 1674 to 1681; Governor of all of New England from 1686 until he was expelled by the Bostonians in 1689; Governor of Virginia from 1692 until his removal in 1698. His character is sufficiently indicated by the occurrences above adverted to.

to be ground sharp at the point that morning) came from Sir
Edmund's house to Mr. Blair's, where the Governor of Maryland then was.

Finding the company at breakfast, he waited until after
grace, and then said:

'Captain Nicholson, did you receive a letter I sent you from
New York?'

'Yes, I received it,' answered the Governor.

'And was it done like a gentleman to send that letter by the
hand of a common post to be read by everybody in Virginia — I
look upon it as an affront and demand satisfaction.'

'You must go to Pennsylvania then,' said the Governor of
Maryland; 'my hands are tied up in Virginia. But if you go
thither you shall have the satisfaction you desire.'

'Come out here,' said Parke, and so putting his hand upon his
sword, went towards the door.

'What, is this your way, Mr. Parke, of giving challenges before so much company? If you have anything to say you know
where to find me. I am often in these parts and you shall never
find that I fly the road for you.'

After some more talk, Colonel Parke said:

'You have affronted me and I have affronted you: now it lies
upon you to demand satisfaction.'

On the afternoon of the same day,

the Governor of Maryland being to wait on Sir Edmund Andros
at his house (as he never failed to do when he came to Virginia
about the business of the College) Sir Edmund took occasion to
quarrel with him, alleging that he reflected upon him in Maryland, and the Sheriff of James County being present, he ordered
the Governor of Maryland into custody. The Governor told Sir
Edmund that he knew that the design of the Governor of Virginia and Colonel Parke was to scare him from coming into Virginia to wait upon the business of the College, but that he would
still come and perform his duty on that trust.

Then Sir Edmund, fearing the effects of detaining a
King's governor, ordered Nicholson set at liberty.

After this Colonel Parke, 'being extremely caressed by Governor Andros,' was made collector of the lower district of the James River, although the place had been promised to Colonel Philip Lightfoot. Subsequently there was another altercation between the by now over-arrogant Colonel and the Governor, at which the lie was passed.

'A lie!' exclaimed Colonel Parke, running to the Governor, who was sitting bareheaded, and gave him a slash over the head with his horsewhip.

The Governor, having no weapon, flew at the Colonel with naked fists. The company parted the contestants. 'Governor Nicholson challenged Colonel Parke to meet him in Carolina, a day's journey from Jamestown; but for all his hectoring Colonel Parke would give the Governor no satisfaction.' [1]

Colonel Parke was not one to brook interference with his mode of free living. He even denied himself the privilege of attending church because of a sermon preached by Samuel Eburne, which discourse he construed as a reproof to himself for entertaining 'one Mistress Berry, whom he had conveyed away from her husband in London in the year 1692 and carried to Virginia along with him, calling her by the name of his cousin Brown.'

Colonel Parke, having conceived a great dislike for Mr. Commissary Blair, vented his spleen on Mrs. Blair,

---

[1] *Papers Relating to the Church in Virginia*, 1650–1776; edited by W. S. Perry; 1870. Dr. Blair's memorial, Fulham MSS. These statements, including the conversations, are taken from Dr. Blair's letters to the Bishop of London. There was a Conference at Lambeth, December 27, 1687, participated in by the Archbishop of Canterbury and the Lord Bishop of London, on which occasion Dr. Blair easily routed his opponents. William Byrd (then a young man), Mr. John Povey, Mr. Marshall, and Mr. Hanson were witnesses. The Parke matters came up at the Conference.

whom he found one Sunday seated in the pew of his father-in-law, Philip Ludwell. He rudely seized her by the arm and drew her out into the aisle, a breach of ecclesiastical decorum which reverberated through the courts of Lambeth Palace.[1]

If we may believe the Reverend Mr. Anderson's 'Colonial History,' quoted with approval by Bishop Meade,[2] the various offenses of Parke's early life compelled him to flee from Virginia to England, where he bought an estate in Hampshire and entered Parliament, only to be expelled for bribery.[3] After serving in Flanders with Lord Arron, he went as a volunteer under the Duke of Marlborough and became one of his aides-de-camp.[4]

In August, 1704, at the Battle of Blenheim, Marlborough broke the long spell of French victories, thereby shattering the pride of France and humbling Louis XIV. Both as a statesman and as a general, Marlborough was a character of the first order, and to-day, after two centuries of hot dispute, his abilities, devotion, and integrity emerge resplendent. That Colonel Parke was a member of the military family of a man renowned as a judge of character and worshiped by his officers is high testimony to the worth and valor of the Virginia soldier.

The Battle of Blenheim having ended in the rout of the French army, Marlborough dispatched two messengers:

[1] Mrs. Blair herself was something of a character. On her wedding-day she changed her mind and her bridegroom.

[2] *Old Churches and Families of Virginia*, vol. I, p. 181. Dr. Lyon G. Tyler says that Parke had the temerity to challenge Governor Francis Nicholson, of Maryland, a member of the Board of Visitors and Governors of William and Mary.

[3] Daniel Parke's name is not found in the Parliament lists.

[4] Parke to his daughter Frances, G. W. P. Custis: *Recollections*, p. 23.

MINIATURE OF QUEEN ANNE
Given by her to Col. Daniel Parke for bringing news of the victory of Blenheim

AN
ANSWER
TO A
Scurrilous Libel,
INTITLED

A Letter to Mr. G. French,
Occasion'd by his HISTORY of
Col. *PARKE*'s ADMINISTRATION, &c.

To which is added

The Character and Conduct, as well of
Walter Hamilton, Esq; the present Captain-
General of the *Leeward Islands*, as of the
principal Fomentors and Actors in the Re-
bellion and Murder mention'd in that
History.

By Mr. *GEORGE FRENCH.*

Thus Traytors glory in unpunish'd Guilt,
Slip thro' the Laws, and boast the Blood they spilt:
Bold ev'n to Impudence, the Miscreants dare
Contemn the very Mercy which they share!
For tho' the Sword is Pow'r's acknowledg'd Pledge,
It awes not Villains 'till they feel its Edge.

LONDON,

Printed for *J. Bettenham* at the *Crown* in *Pater-
noster Row.* 1719. Price stitch'd 3 s. 6 d. bound 4 s.

Where may be had the History of Colonel *Parke*'s Administration, Price 5 s.

one was a French prisoner pledged to make all haste to Versailles, where he arrived six days later to break the terrible suspense that formed the somber background of the rejoicings over the birth of a great-grandson of the Grand Monarch. The news was told to the King by Madame de Maintenon, who alone of all the court had the courage to do it.

On the same 21st of August, the second messenger, Colonel Parke, who had galloped from the Danube, arrived at Windsor without having uttered a word to give inkling of the momentous news he bore. London had passed an anxious summer, during which Marlborough was blamed for plunging recklessly into the heart of Germany, thereby taking the aggressive against a larger and better-disciplined force. England's nerves were on edge. The French were confident and boastful.

Colonel Parke, when he rode up Castle Hill at Windsor, found the Duchess of Marlborough (to whom his letter was addressed) in attendance on Queen Anne. No one detained the bearer of tidings from Marlborough. 'He was led straight into the little turreted chamber, high on the outer wall, which now forms part of the Royal Library, in which, in memory of that day, his portrait still hangs. It is still called Queen Anne's closet.' The two women, Mrs. Morley and Mrs. Freeman, as they then familiarly called one another, were seated at a tea-urn near the window that commands a view of Eton.

Colonel Parke was one of the most distinguished-looking officers in the British army — nearly as handsome as the great soldier who had sent him. Bowing low to the Queen, he handed the note to the Duchess. His wife, whom Marlborough worshiped throughout his life, was to be the first in all England to know of his victory. Imagine the feelings of the three persons in that little room of but ten feet square. To the Queen the message meant glory and honor beyond compare — a victory still ranked among the great victories of the world. To the Duchess it meant immortality for the man who was her slave in love; and for herself admiration, and consolation amid the troubles she brought on herself by her own arrogance and headstrong temper.

Colonel Parke, when assured by Queen Anne of the reward of five hundred guineas due to the bearer of news of victory, craved instead her own portrait. The next day he received the miniature set in diamonds and with it one thousand guineas.

The little note, hastily written by Marlborough on a leaf torn from his account book, is still preserved at Blenheim Castle.[1] The miniature, or, at least the diamonds surrounding it, remained with the English Parkes; but one copy in water-colors on cardboard came to this country and is now in the possession of Mrs. Mustard, of Baltimore, a descendant of Eliza Parke Custis (Mrs. Thomas Law); the silver plate also bestowed on him likewise found its way to America, and was once in the ownership of Mrs. Robert E. Lee, a daughter of George Washington Parke Custis. Now it is scattered among members of the Lee family. Colonel Parke's portrait with the miniature about his neck, painted by Sir Godfrey Kneller, is at Washington and Lee University, Lexington, Virginia.

[1] *Marlborough Despatches*, vol. I, p. 390. John and Sarah, Duke and Duchess of Marlborough, 1660–1744. Based on unpublished letters and documents at Blenheim Palace. By Stuart J. Reid (London, 1914), p. 208 *et seq*. G. W. P. Custis: *Recollections*, p. 23.

In further proof of Queen Anne's appreciation 'Colonel Parke, by Letters Patent, bearing Date the 25th Day of April, 1706, was appointed Captain-General and Governor in Chief of Nevis, St. Christopher, Antegoa, Mountserrat and other Leeward Caribbean Islands in America; and in June following arrived at Antegoa.' [1]

While Colonel Parke was still at the court of Queen Anne, John Custis, through his father, asked for the hand of the Colonel's elder daughter and received this favorable if brutal reply:

LONDON, *August 25, 1705*

SIR: I received yours relating to your son's desire of marrying my daughter, and your consent if I thought well of it. You may easily inform yourself that my daughter, Frances, will be heiress to all the land my father left, which is not a little, nor the worst. My personal estate is not very small in that country, and I have but two daughters, and there is no likelihood of my having more, as matters are, I being obliged to be on one side of the ocean, and my wife on the other. I do not know your young gentleman, nor have you or he thought fit to send me an account of his real and personal effects; however, if my daughter likes him, I will give her, upon her marriage with him, half as much as he can make appear he is worth.

I have no one else to give my estate to but my daughters. This is what I think convenient to write at present.

My service to you and all friends in Virginia.

From your humble servant

DANIEL PARKE

Whether John Custis really loved Frances Parke, or whether his ardent protestations of affection were (like the plans of the Colonial houses of the day) taken from some English books, [2] may well be doubted. She is reputed to

---

[1] *The History of Colonel Parke's Administration, etc.* London, 1717.

[2] Custis: *Recollections*, p. 16. He prays that angels may guard his dearest

have had a violent temper and a sharp tongue. For weeks at a time she and her husband communicated with one another only through the servants, after this fashion: 'Pompey, ask your master if he will have coffee or tea, and sugar and cream?' To which Mr. Custis would reply: 'Tell your mistress I will have coffee as usual, with no cream.'

On one occasion he surprised his wife by inviting her to go for a drive; and she surprised him by accepting. He headed the horse into Chesapeake Bay. 'Where are you going, Mr. Custis?' asked the wife. 'To hell, Madam,' he answered. 'Drive on,' she said, 'any place is better than Arlington.' When the lady's feet were drawn up on the seat and the horse was forced to swim, he headed for the shore, saying, 'I believe you would as lief meet the Devil himself, if I should drive to hell.' 'Quite true, Sir,' she retorted; 'I know you so well I would not be afraid to go anywhere you would go.' After this the two signed an agreement to keep the peace.[1] The poor woman lived but a few years longer, and then smallpox carried her off. She left a son, Daniel Parke Custis; and when her husband came to die he left all his considerable property to this son, with the proviso that, under pain of disinheritance, there be set up over his grave an English marble stone bearing this inscription, at once so unchivalrous and so vindictive as to give it place among the annals of Virginia as a crime against good manners and good taste:[2]

'Fidelia,' and deliver her safe to his arms, which 'won't refuse their protection to a creature so pure and charming that it would be easy for angels to mistake her for one of themselves.'

[1] Jennings Cropper Wise: *Ye Kingdome of Accawmacke; or the Eastern Shore of Virginia in the Seventeenth Century*, p. 333.

[2] He was born in 1678; was married in 1706; and died in 1749.

BENEATH THIS MARBLE TOMB LIES YE BODY
OF THE *HON. JOHN CUSTIS, ESQ.,*
OF THE CITY OF WILLIAMSBURG,
AND PARISH OF BRUTON.
FORMERLY OF HUNGAR'S PARISH,
ON THE EASTERN SHORE OF VIRGINIA,
AND COUNTY OF NORTHAMPTON,
THE PLACE OF HIS NATIVITY,
AGED 71 YEARS, AND YET LIVED BUT SEVEN YEARS,
WHICH WAS THE SPACE OF TIME HE KEPT
A BACHELOR'S HOME AT ARLINGTON
ON THE EASTERN SHORE OF VIRGINIA

The gay Colonel Parke, refusing all the importunities of his wife to come home to look after the welfare of his attractive daughters, sailed for the Leeward Islands, where he ruled with a strong arm for four years, during which period his wave-washed domain increased in population and in trade. He had a devoted band of followers to whom his arbitrary assertion of prerogative (both Her Majesty's and her Governor's) seemed the duty owed to government. But the people, an independent and lawless set, would brook no such assertion of authority. The members of the Assembly stood on their rights and gave encouragement to a mob that trapped the Governor in his house, and, at the cost of the lives of their leaders, killed his guards, wounded Colonel Parke, seized him by the leg and pulled him down his own stone steps, stripped him naked, broke his back, left him in the broiling sun, drove off those who would give him water, and abandoned him to die, as die he did a few hours afterward in a friendly home. It was a sorry ending of a headstrong career shot through with ambition and personal bravery.

When, at the instance of his sister in England (Mrs.

Parke Pepper), his murderers were brought to trial, Queen
Anne was dead, the Marlborough party was no longer in
power, the Leeward Islands were a long way off, and so no
punishment was meted out to the slayers; nor was any
recompense made for the five thousand pounds' worth of
personal property looted by the mob. When his estate
came to be settled, it was found that the entail on the lands
given to Mrs. Custis must be broken by the Assembly in
order to pay a portion of his Virginia debts. Her sister,
Mrs. Byrd, received by will but a petty one thousand
pounds, all of which sum, together with much of her husband's property, went to settle Colonel Parke's English
debts. Colonel Byrd seems to have acted, in this case as in
other cases, the part of a chivalrous gentleman, ready to
maintain his honor at any personal sacrifice.[1] He bought
from his brother-in-law, Custis, Virginia and English
lands and property sufficient, as was thought, to pay
Colonel Parke's debts; but was forced to pay one thousand
pounds more than the schedule showed.

The humiliating thing to the Virginia relatives was the
fact that Colonel Parke left by far the largest portion of his
property (that in the Leeward Islands) to Lucy, ostensibly
the daughter of Edward Chester, but, as was generally
believed, his own child by Catherine Chester, whose husband had turned her out of his house on Colonel Parke's
account.[2]

The irascible John Custis of tombstone notoriety desired an alliance for his son with the beautiful Evelyn

[1] *Writings of Colonel William Byrd*, edited by J. S. Bassett, p. 398.
[2] *An Answer to a Scurrilous Libel*, by Mr. George French (London, 1719), p.
214.

Byrd; but Colonel Byrd definitely refused the overtures, perhaps because he did not favor the marriage of cousins, or perhaps because he feared the Custis-Parke inheritance. His daughter had already determined that, since a difference in religion kept her from marrying the Earl of Peterborough, whom she loved, she would not marry another. She remained single to the end of the thirty years of her allotted span, thereby furnishing one of the most romantic stories of Colonial days.[1]

Disappointed in his first hopes, Daniel Parke Custis, at the age of thirty-nine years, sought the hand of Martha Dandridge, an alliance at first displeasing to the paternal Custis. Such, however, was the beauty of her person and the tactfulness of her speech that the parent unbent, and before he could change his mind the marriage took place, in June, 1749. It is euphemistically said that this girl of sixteen was the belle of the Williamsburg balls. Be that as it may, it is evident that she took her position easily and naturally as the wife of Daniel Custis, a man of large property, of high social standing, and with a disposition much more pacific than his turbulent ancestry would lead one to anticipate.

Children came — two who died in infancy, then a boy

[1] The name, following the English fashion, is always pronounced in Virginia *E*-velyn. She was born July 16, 1707, died November 13, 1737, and is buried at Westover; but her ghost is still abroad. Evidently she had a touch of her grandfather, both in her beauty and also in her determination. Her brother, a son of the second William Byrd, of Westover, married Elizabeth Carter, of Shirley. He was under twenty and she was not seventeen years old at the time of their marriage. Six months after her demise, he married Miss Mary Willing, of Philadelphia. He became a member of the Council; and at Braddock's defeat he was in command of the Second Virginia Regiment, Washington being his senior officer. During the Revolution his sympathies were with the British. His passion for gaming played havoc with the Byrd estate, and on New Year's Day, 1777, he died by his own hand, leaving a widow and eight children.

and girl, who inherited from their father delicate consti-
tutions. After eight years of married life, Daniel Parke
Custis slept with the Custises; and at twenty-five she was
left a widow, with large possessions, with a charm that had
in it more of the matron than of the girl, and with capacity
and strong will.

Within two years she married Colonel Washington. In
all her relations with him there was manifested a shade of
motherliness; while on his part, to the very last day of his
life, he was solicitous for her happiness and comfort, both
in mind and in body. It was the union of two fine, strong
natures that took the responsibilities of life seriously and
as a matter of course. Genuinely fond of one another,
neither of them ever shirked a duty, no matter how danger-
ous, or at what personal sacrifice.

CHAPTER VII

IN THE HOUSE OF BURGESSES

COLONEL WASHINGTON had prepared the way for retirement from military life by securing an election to the House of Burgesses, a position to which every Virginia gentleman aspired, and which both his half-brothers had held. Fairfax County being represented by George Mason and George Johnston, he decided to take the poll for Frederick County at Winchester, where he could count on the influence of Lord Fairfax.

'I fear,' wrote his lordship, 'that Coll. Washington will be very hard pushed,' a prognostication quite justified by the fact. The election cost him £39.6s., spent on a hogshead and a barrel of punch, thirty-five gallons of wine, forty-three gallons of strong beer, cider, and a dinner for his workers.[1] His colleague was Thomas Bryan Martin, nephew and agent of Lord Fairfax.

On his twenty-seventh birthday George Washington began his legislative career. The journal entry records:

A new Member, having taken the Oaths appointed to be taken by Act of Parliament, instead of the Oaths of Allegiance and Supremacy, and taken and subscribed the Oath of Abjuration, and also subscribed to the Test, was admitted to his Place in the House.

On the day following he was appointed a member of the Committee of Propositions and Grievances, Richard Bland being the chairman and George Wythe, Henry

[1] Neill: *Fairfaxes of England and America*, p. 98.

Peyton, Randolph Dandridge, Lewis Burwell, Archibald Cary, Benjamin Harrison, and Francis Lightfoot Lee being among the members.

The Journal for February 26, 1759,[1] states that

Upon a Motion made, Resolved, *Nemine contradicente*, That the Thanks of this House be given to George Washington, Esq.; a Member of this House, late Colonel of the First Virginia Regiment, for his faithful services to his Majesty, and this Colony, and for his brave and steady Behaviour, from the first Encroachments and Hostilities of the French and their Indians, to his Resignation, after the happy Reduction of Fort De Quesne. And accordingly Mr. Speaker, from the Chair, returned him (he standing in his Place) the Thanks of the House.

As the story goes, Speaker Robinson,

following the impulse of his own generous and grateful heart, discharged the duty with great dignity, but with such warmth of coloring, and strength of expression as entirely to confound the young hero. He rose to express his acknowledgments for the honor; but such was his trepidation and confusion, that he could not give distinct utterance to a syllable. He blushed, stammered, and trembled, for a second; when the Speaker relieved him, by a stroke of address, that would have done honor to Louis the Fourteenth, in his proudest and happiest moment. 'Sit down, Mr. Washington,' said he, with a conciliating smile, 'your modesty is equal to your valor, and that surpasses the power of any language I possess.'[2]

No introduction could have been more flattering to a young member of a legislative body made up of men who were soon to lay the firm foundations of a new nation.

Colonel Washington, having entered on his legislative career, took pains to learn his new duties. He did not make the common mistake of flattering himself that,

[1] *Journals of the House of Burgesses of Virginia*, 1758–61, p. 65.
[2] Wirt: *Life of Patrick Henry.*

because he was proficient in the military calling, he had
no need to apply himself to learning the business of a
legislator and the methods of procedure in the Assembly.
After the first session he took an active part in the pro-
ceedings. Particularly did he concern himself with the
claims of officers whose services were rendered under his
personal command.

The first law with which his name is associated origi-
nated on April 4, 1761, when 'leave was given to bring in
a bill to preserve the Water for the Use of the Inhabitants
of the Town of Winchester, and the limits thereof, by
preventing Hogs from running at large therein, and it is
referred to Mr. Pendleton and Mr. Washington to prepare
and bring in the same.' The bill having been passed, it
was 'Ordered that Mr. Washington do carry up said
bill to the Council for their concurrence.'

Mrs. Washington owned in Williamsburg the House of
Six Chimneys, and there the newly married couple made
their home during sessions of the Assembly.

Williamsburg was laid out on a generous scale for those
days. The main features of its design were used in 1792
for the location of the Congress House and the President's
House in the Federal City, when Washington was charged
with planning the National Capital. A broad avenue still
known as Duke of Gloucester Street, begins at Capitol
Square and extends to the grounds of the College of
William and Mary, next to Harvard the oldest college in
America. This main axis of the town had a broad cross-
axis terminating at the gardens of the Governor's Palace.
Capitol and Palace, together with Mrs. Washington's

house, have disappeared. George Wythe's stone mansion on Palace Green is now a college club; and Tazewell Hall (the home of Edmund Randolph) and the Coleman, Blair, Tucker, and Cary houses remain to tell of departed glory; while the Powder Horn, built by Governor Spotswood in 1714, carries one back over two centuries. The great Sir Christopher Wren (whose office turned out the plans of a hundred London churches built after the Great Fire of 1666) is credited with the design also of the modest little court-house, but the records do not so show.

Near the entrance to the college grounds stands a marble statue of Lord Botetourt. Designed by Haward, a London sculptor, this refined and delicate work has withstood not only the vicissitudes of the War of the Revolution and the Civil War, but also the thoughtless indignities practiced by generations of college students and the well-meant but ill-considered efforts of would-be restorers. Marred and discolored, it stands to-day one of the art treasures of America.

The older buildings of the college, notably the president's house, are substantially as they were in Colonial times. After the long and scholarly career of President Lyon Gardiner Tyler, a son of the President of the United States, the rapid expansion of the ancient seat of learning is being directed physically as well as scholastically by President J. A. C. Chandler, a man of feeling for fine architectural traditions, and himself a graduate of William and Mary.

The crowning feature, however, of Williamsburg, is Old Bruton Parish Church (1714), whose white tower rises above an ancient graveyard, the whole mellowed with age and half cov-

OLD CAPITOL AT WILLIAMSBURG, VIRGINIA

BRUTON CHURCH, WILLIAMSBURG, VIRGINIA

STATUE OF LORD BOTETOURT AT WILLIAM AND MARY COLLEGE
The oldest of the College buildings is in the background

ered with vine. It is a building of supreme beauty, the color of
its brick walls laid up in a Flemish bond with glazed headers, the
white blinds and fat muntins, the rare colored vines clambering
up the walls and along the perfect cornice, giving an effect in
Colonial unsurpassed.[1]

In the well-executed restoration of 1907, King Edward
VII contributed the Bible, and President Roosevelt gave
the lectern. Hangings similar to those of Governor
Spotswood's day were placed above the pew once occupied
by the royal governors.

On May 1, 1761, Washington wrote from Mount Vernon
to Robert Cary & Co., merchants, London, enclosing the
minister's certificate of his marriage with Mrs. Martha
Custis, and requesting that 'for the future they address to
him all letters which relate to the affairs of the late Daniel
Parke Custis, Esqr., as by marriage he was entitled to a
third part of that estate, and was invested likewise with
the care of the other two-thirds by a decree of the General
Court, which he obtained in order to strengthen the power
he had by reason of the fact that his wife had the administration of the estate.' He promised to continue to deal
with the firm so long as they satisfied him of due attention
to his business; and at the same time he ordered a considerable quantity of furniture and apparel, seeds and agricul-
tural books.

In September he sent another large order: for Mrs.
Washington 'a salmon-colored Tabby of the enclosed
pattern, with satin flowers, to be made in a sack and coat,'
and 'a Cap, Handkerchief, Tucker and Ruffles to be made

[1] *Brick Architecture of the Colonial Period in Maryland and Virginia.*

of Brussels lace, or point, proper to wear with the above negligee, to cost £20,' together with satin shoes, both black and white, 'of the smallest 5s'; for the house three pounds of Scotch snuff, an hogshead of best porter, three gallons of 'Rhenish in bottles,' and busts of Alexander the Great, Julius Cæsar, Charles XII of Sweden, Prince Eugene, the Duke of Marlborough, and 'two Wild Beasts, not to exceed twelve inches in height nor eighteen in length.'

John Augustine Washington had occupied and managed Mount Vernon during his elder brother's military service; and when the former married Hannah, daughter of Colonel John Bushrod, the bride and groom passed their honeymoon there. After the Colonel's marriage, John Augustine Washington repaired to his wife's ancestral home, Bushfield, in Westmoreland County. The substantial brick house, set in the midst of spacious gardens, still looks out on the broad Potomac, where the river is joined by Nomini Creek.[1]

From the time he left Fredericksburg at the age of eleven years, George Washington had been used to the amenities of life. Ease of living, the luxuries of the table, the sports of the hunting-field, association with governors and soldiers from the courts and camps of Europe, acquaintance with society in New York, Boston, and Philadelphia, the intimate friendship of Lord Fairfax and his family connections male and female, all these opportunities for education were earnestly embraced by a man who from early youth had aspired to be a gentleman.

---

[1] The estate is now owned by Mr. and Mrs. Willing, of Chicago, and is profitably managed by Mrs. Willing's brother, Mr. McFadon.

At the same time, he acquired a thorough understanding of human nature. Essentially a man of action rather than a student, his mind was so trained that in matters where he had no first-hand knowledge, his unerring instinct led him to seek out the advice of those best acquainted with the particular subject. He was patient in listening to all sides; and his judgments were sure. In all Virginia there was no man better fitted for leadership, and, on the other hand, none to whom life could bring more real satisfactions. Therefore it was with profound conviction that he could write to his cousin in London: 'I am now I believe fixed at this seat [Mount Vernon] with an agreeable Consort for Life. And hope to find more happiness in retirement than I ever experienced amidst a wide and bustling world.'

Thanks to the friendly supervision exercised by the Honorable William Fairfax, the mansion house at Mount Vernon was in good order for the advent of Colonel and Mrs. Washington. The great problem of the garret stairs was successfully solved after repeated letters, and rooms were finished in the attic for the entertainment of guests too numerous to find accommodations on the second floor. The house then was about half the size of the one we know; for the dining-room and the library ends were not built until after the Revolution.

The overseer, also, had got the plantations in fairly good shape, and, weather permitting, there would be a good crop of tobacco to pay for the goods ordered from England.

What Colonel Washington wrote about retiring from a busy world must be taken with a grain of salt; for he had too many irons in the fire and withal was too ambitious to settle down to the self-contained life of a plantation. Moreover, his services in the French and Indian War would entitle him to large grants of land in the Ohio country, so soon as the King could be induced to act.

Also schemes were afoot to set up proprietary colonies in the western country. Benjamin Franklin and his son, Sir William Franklin, Governor of New Jersey, together with Sir William Johnson, were urging the Walpole grant, with Johnson as the prospective governor; and Washington himself drew up articles of association for the Mississippi Company, in which he was to be associated with his brother John Augustine, Francis Lightfoot Lee and Richard Henry Lee, Henry Fitzhugh and Thomas Bullitt, the latter one of the earliest settlers of Kentucky.

Mrs. Washington, for her part, had a numerous household to administer. In addition to her two children, there were many servants to be trained and kept busy, and a constant stream of visitors to be entertained and cared for, since the established reputation of Mount Vernon for hospitality must be restored after the vacant years. Altogether Colonel and Mrs. Washington had a large task cut out for them.

Moreover, although Quebec and Montreal had fallen to the British, and the French had surrendered Detroit, with the control of the western country, Indian troubles were by no means ended, and at any time Washington might be compelled again to take the field in defense of the frontiers of Virginia.

CHAPTER VIII

FAMILY LIFE AT MOUNT VERNON

NEW YEAR'S DAY, 1760, at Mount Vernon was spent by Washington in visiting his plantations. On his return he found Mrs. Washington 'broke out with the Meazles,' and the next day he took the occasion of her indisposition to post his books and put them in good order. On the fifth day of her illness, Mr. Green came from Pohick Rectory and 'prescribed the needful,' and at dinnertime Dr. James Laurie (the family physician on an annual stipend of fifteen pounds) appeared. Mrs. George William Fairfax spent the day with Mrs. Washington, and, the evening being cold and windy, was sent home to Belvoir in the chariot, which did not return in time to take the family to church next day.[1]

Relieved by the improvement of his wife's health, Washington was plagued by the disorderly conduct of an oysterman, who interfered with hauling the seine for fish; and there was further trouble over 'Mr. French's great love of money,' which led the latter to break his contract, because pork had risen from 20s. to 22s. 6d.

Mrs. Washington's sister Anna, Mrs. Burwell Bassett of Eltham, on York River, came for a visit. She and Colonel Washington spent a day at Belvoir, and on a

---

[1] Moncure D. Conway's gossip that 'Martha Washington was always rather cool to this beautiful Mrs. G. W. Fairfax of Belvoir,' has no better basis than the presumption that a wife must of necessity be jealous of her husband's prenuptial female friends. The abundant correspondence between the families gives no substance for even a shadow.

Saturday the two set out for Port Royal, where Washington was to meet her husband, Colonel Bassett, on matters of estate business. The morning was clear and fine, but remarkable white frosts presaged falling weather. The travelers 'past Occoquan witht. any great difficulty notwithstanding the wind was something high and lodgd at Mr. McCrae's in Dumfries.' Here Washington was told 'that Colonel Cocke was disgusted at my House and left it because he see an old negro there resembling his own Image,' a not uncommon but always disagreeable reminder.[1]

Monday afternoon they were met by Colonel Bassett, who ferried them across the Rappahannock to Port Royal. Business concluded, Colonel Washington again set out on Tuesday morning. He dined at Colonel Carter's where the host had assembled a goodly company; but Colonel Champe, with whom he supped and passed the night, had been less provident, and the result was 'a very lonesome evening, not anybody favoring us with their company but himself.' Slipping out of the Champe house before the family was stirring, Washington writes in his diary: 'abt 10 reachd my mothr. where I breakfasted and then went to Fredericksburg with my brother Sam who I found there; . . . was disappointed of seeing my Sister [Betty] Lewis & getting a few goods which I wanted out of the [Fielding Lewis] Stores, returned in ye Evening to Mother's all alone with her.' The next noon, the snow and rain having turned to mist, he set out in time to reach Dumfries at dusk, and on Friday he returned to Mount Vernon, to find there Dr. Craik, who was attending Mrs. Washington.

[1] When this chapter was written *The Diaries of George Washington*, edited by John C. Fitzpatrick, had not appeared. The wealth of genealogical notes in those four volumes makes them a treasure-house of historical lore.

Went to a Ball at
Alexandria - where Mu-
sick and Dancing was
the chief Entertainment
however in a convenient
Room detached for the
purpose abounded great
plenty of Bread and
Butter, some Biscuets
with Tea, & Coffee which
the Drinkers of coud
not distinguish from
Hot water sweetned —
  Be it remembered that
Pocket handkercheifs
servd the purposes of
Table Cloths & Napkins
and that no Apologies
were made for either
  The Proprietors of
this Ball were Messrs.
Carlyle Laurie & Robt.
Wilson. but the Doctr.
not getting it conducted
agreeable to his own taste
woud claim no share of

the Merit of it.
* I shall therefore
distinguish this Ball
by the stile & title of the
Bread & Butter Ball
  We lodgd at Colo.
Carlyles.
Saturday Feb 7. 16
  Returnd home — re-
ceiving an Invitation
to Wm. Henies Ball on Mon-
day night next, first —
  The Morning lowerd,
and dript as yesterday
but abt. 10 Oclock the Wind
Sotly, blew fresh, and cleerd
  Sunday Feb 7. 17th
  The Wind blew cold - &
fresh from the No West.
  Went to Church & Dined at
Belvoir -
  Sent 4 Yews & Lambs
to the Mill to be fatted

THE BREAD-AND-BUTTER BALL AT ALEXANDRIA
Pages from Washington's Diary

CARLYLE HOUSE, ALEXANDRIA

FAMILY LIFE AT MOUNT VERNON 81

On the evening of February 15, the Washingtons

went to a Ball at Alexandria, where Musick and Dancing was the
chief Entertainment; however, in a convenient room detached
for the purpose abounded great plenty of bread and butter, some
biscuits, with tea and coffee, which the drinkers could not distinguish from hot water sweet'ned. Be it remembered that
pocket handkerchiefs served as Table cloths & Napkins and that
no apologies were made for either. I shall therefore distinguish
this ball by the stile and title of the Bread & Butter Ball. The
Proprietors of the ball were Messrs. Carlyle, Laurie and Robert
Wilson; but the Doctr. [Laurie] not getting it conducted agreeable to his own taste would claim no share of the merit of it. We
lodged at Colo. Carlyles.[1]

To Colonel Washington it must have been a humiliation
to take his wife, used as she was to the formality and state
of the Williamsburg entertainments, to so meager and ill-
arranged an affair; and that night, before they climbed
the winding stairs of the 'Braddock House,' the Washingtons doubtless joked with Colonel and Mrs. Carlyle over
the 'Bread & Butter Ball.' On the Colonel's part the
chagrin shown in his diary probably found vent in his
speech, for he was a plain-spoken man, even to his friends.

Ten days later the Washingtons gave a dinner for Lord
Fairfax, who was visiting at Belvoir. Colonel George
William Fairfax and his lady; Colonel Martin, nephew
and companion of the chief guest; Bryan Fairfax, who was
destined to succeed to the title as the eighth Lord Fairfax;
Mr. Green, the minister at Pohick, and the lady who came
to be accepted as his wife, were of the party. The day had
been particularly fine, and Washington had spent the
morning 'laying the worm' and fencing the peach orchard,

[1] Washington's *Diary.*

and disposing of Jolly, one of his best wagon-horses, that had a right foreleg smashed by a falling tree. He was 'unprovided for a demand of £90, his note of hand to Sampson Darrell; but promised the payment and interest at the April Court next.'

So the days passed at Mount Vernon. Dr. Laurie was drunk when he came for a professional visit; Nation's horse, distrained for rent, was sold for five pounds: a bad compass prevented accurate surveying; '91 dozn. Cyder' was bottled. Mr. Clifton bargained with Thomson (brother of George) Mason to sell eighteen hundred acres of Northern Neck lands for fifty pounds more than he had agreed to sell to Washington, thereby convicting himself of being 'nothing less than a thorough pac'd rascall disregardful of any engagements of words or oaths not bound by penalties.' However, Washington did not think himself 're-strained by any rules of honor conscience or &c' from raising Thomson Mason's offer by fifty pounds, and finally he bought the land at a court sale for twelve hundred and ten pounds, thereby saving forty pounds. Meantime, he had been in Winchester to care for his negroes, who had come down with smallpox; and had made a trip to Williamsburg, visiting his brother at Bushfield on the way.

After 1759, Washington kept a diary of his daily doings, usually confining himself closely to facts, with occasional brief comments on things that annoyed or distressed him. Also he kept records of the weather and statements of crops, using for the purpose blank pages of the Virginia Almanac, printed and sold at Williamsburg. The calendar for the month was headed by a bit of verse; and at the back of the little book were recipes for various concoctions, and pages of jokes. Several of the verses and witticisms are so Elizabethan in character that they could not now be printed; but evidently in those days the publication circulated freely and no one took offense thereat.[1]

George Washington never had any boyhood. He was only eleven years old when his father died and he left Fredericksburg to live with his brother Augustine in Westmoreland County. For five years he must have worked incessantly at school in order to learn surveying; for learn he did, as his neat, exact, and well-ordered copy-books abundantly prove. During the years from sixteen to twenty-two, instead of going to England for his education as his elder brothers had done, he was working for his living. Before he was twenty-one he had responsibilities that might well have taxed the judgment of a mature man. Nothing illustrates his wisdom better than the tone of letters addressed to him by men twice his years, who sought his advice and were satisfied with his decision.[2]

Having himself been deprived of that pleasurable period in the life of a Virginia boy of good family with comfortable means, the prospect of acting as stepfather to a boy and a girl of distinguished and proud ancestry and of wealth may well have seemed to Washington a duty preëminent among his many large responsibilities, especially as it was one for which he had no training. However, he undertook the task with the same conscientiousness that he bestowed upon all his duties.

From the time of his marriage to the day of his death

[1] For a complete statement as to the *Diaries*, their number, dates, survivals, see *The Diaries of George Washington*, vol. i, p. vii *et seq.*
[2] *Letters to Washington*, in five volumes, edited by S. M. Hamilton.

there were young people depending upon him for guidance and direction. Naturally affectionate to the point of indulgence, and dearly loving children, he was keenly disappointed at not having offspring; and he made up for this lack by fatherly care of his wife's children and grandchildren and his own nephews and nieces. It is this particular phase of Washington's development which hereafter will receive especial attention.

In September, 1759, Washington had directed Robert Cary & Co., of London, who had been the agents of Daniel Custis, to raise three accounts, one for him, one for the Custis estate and one for Miss Martha Parke Custis, or, if more eligible, to make him debtor for both John Parke and Miss Patty Custis. Their part of the estate would be assigned to them in the fall; the whole would remain in his management, and he 'would take particular care to distinguish always from whom tobaccos were shipped and for whose use the goods were purchased.' He insisted on particular care, so that settlements might be made from time to time in the General Court. In all financial matters he was punctilious to the last degree.

For Master Custis, six years old, he ordered, among other things, six pocket-handkerchiefs small and fine; six pairs of gloves and two laced hats; six pairs of fine thread stockings, four pairs of pumps; one piece of black hair-ribbon; one pair of handsome silver shoe and knee buckles; ten shillings' worth of toys; six little books for children beginning to read; and one light duffel cloak with silver frogs. For Miss Custis, four years old, the order included eight pairs of kid mits, four pairs of gloves, two pairs of silk shoes, four pairs of Calamanco shoes, four pairs of leather

pumps, besides caps, tuckers, bibs, and aprons (if fashionable), two fans, two masks, two bonnets, a stiffened coat
of fashionable silk made to pack thread stays, silver sleeve-
buttons with stones, a fashionably dressed baby (ten shillings), and other toys (ten shillings).

The portraits of the Custis children at about this age
show the little manikins arrayed in all the finery worn by
their elders, after the fashion of the day. It is to be presumed that at this stage of his career the Colonel had to
rely on lists furnished by his wife, but the items are set
down in his own faultless chirography, and if mistakes
were made in carrying out the orders the fault lay with
Cary & Co., and not with the guardian. It is to be observed that the requirements of fashion were consonant
with his own ideas. The price, when mentioned, was
rather a guide than a limit; for in his dealings with his
agents there was no question of expense; everything must
be the best the market afforded. English goods represented the fine arts of life; and in all that pertained to
living Washington was an artist.

On June 1, 1760, Mrs. Washington wrote to her sister,
Mrs. Bassett, this one of the few of her letters extant.[1]

DEAR SISTER: I have had the pleasure of receiving your very
welcome and affecte Letters of the 10th of may intended to come
by Jack and the 23d by Mr. Bassett who I must acknowledge
myself greatly obliged to for the favour of his last visit. I should
not have suffered him to go without a letter to you had I not
known of the opportunity that now offers and here I must do
myself the pleasure of congratulating you very sincerely on your
happy deliverance of, I wish I could say boy, as I know how
much one of that sex was desired by you all. I am very sorry to

[1] *Harper's Magazine*, April, 1889, p. 739.

hear my mamma's [1] complaints of ill health and I feel the same uneasiness on that account that you doe but I hope Mr. S[co]tt's prescriptions will have the desired effect — the children are now very well and I think myself in a better state of helth than I have been in for a long time and don't dout but I shall present you a fine healthy girl again when I come down in the Fall which is as soon as Mr. W—ns business will suffer him to leave home. I am very much pleased to hear Betsey continues to grow a fine hearty child. . . .

Mr. Bassett will inform you of the mirth and gaietys that he has seen so I hope I have no occasion to enlarge upon that head in order to induce you to Try Fairfax in a pleasanter season than you did last time. I shall now conclude but not till I have desired you to present my Best good wishes to Mrs. Dawson and Judy in which Mr. Washington desires to join. we also beg you will give our Blessing to the dear little children and to Each of them half a dozen Kisses and hope you will not imagin that yourself and Mr. Bassett is forgot by my dear nancy your sincere and Loveing sister.

MARTHA WASHINGTON

The hope of offspring having come to naught, George Washington's pent-up affections turned themselves first to Mrs. Washington's children; and when they too passed out of his life through death, to her grandchildren, whom, 'since his expectation of having issue had ceased,' he came 'to consider in the same light as he did his own relations and to act the friendly part by them.' [2]

[1] Mrs. Washington's father had died two years before her marriage. His widow was Mrs. W.'s stepmother.
[2] Washington's Will.

CHAPTER IX

JOHN PARKE CUSTIS AND MARTHA PARKE CUSTIS

GEORGE WASHINGTON, on marrying Martha Dandridge Custis, quite deliberately took upon himself the duties of a husband and a stepfather. These duties he performed to the day of his death with his heart as well as his head. His admonitions to the younger generations, as almost invariably happens to parental admonitions, were unheeded; but his character and his affection were a potent influence for good in the lives of more than a score of young men and maidens who were directly the beneficiaries of his care and of his purse as well.

Moreover, he was very tolerant with youth. He suffered in mind and feelings from the idleness, the inattention, and the perverted tastes of those to whom he furnished opportunities; he formed (and often expressed) a shrewd estimate of their characters; but he was never harsh, intolerant, or vindictive. Indeed, few fathers could equal this stepfather in all those qualities that go to make up an ideal parent.

His apprenticeship began even before his marriage. When Bryan Fairfax, disappointed in love, enlisted as a private and was found by his family in a Baltimore jail, his father, William Fairfax, sent him to Colonel Washington to bring him back to the ways of soberness. The friendship thus began never wavered, in spite of the fact that throughout the Revolution, Bryan Fairfax was a pacifist and a loyalist.[1]

---

[1] *Letters to Washington*, vol. II.

Martha Custis, Mrs. Washington's eleven-years-old daughter, was 'seized with fits' in January, 1768, and the very sensitive mother was driven nearly distracted. Every remedy that Dr. Rumney could think of was tried; and in February, 1769, one Joshua Evans 'put an iron ring on Patsy' — as a talisman against the dread disease of epilepsy. In August the family took her to the Berkeley Warm Springs, hoping much from the famed efficacy of those waters; but she derived little benefit therefrom.[1]

The journey, made by wagon, consumed six days; and the stay was enlivened by all the social gayety of a Colonial watering-place. There were dinners, tea-drinkings, and mountain-climbings. Lord Fairfax rode over from Greenway Court, accompanied by his brother Robert from London, and his nephew George William Fairfax from Belvoir; and there were the Barclays and the Cadwalladers from Philadelphia. Several times Colonel and Mrs. Washington, Patsy Custis, and the three Fairfaxes rode to Cacapehon (Capon) Mountain to enjoy 'the wide and beautiful prospect'; and once Washington crossed the narrow neck of Maryland and penetrated into Pennsylvania in the direction of the present town of Gettysburg.

The family returned about the middle of September, for the election of Burgesses for Fairfax County. Washington was chosen by acclamation, without the formality of a poll.[2]

---

[1] Washington's *Diary*.

[2] At this time Washington was building a house at the southwest corner of Pitt and Cameron Streets in Alexandria, a story-and-a-half frame building, where he and Mrs. Washington often stayed when business kept him too late in the day to return to Mount Vernon. This little house ranked next to Mount Vernon in their affections. Washington left the property to his wife, who in turn bequeathed it to her nephew, Bartholomew Dandridge. It remained, perched upon an eminence, looking down on graded streets and other improvements, until after a century of usefulness it was torn down by Mr. Waters, a lumber dealer.

During the last two months of 1769, the entire family made headquarters at Williamsburg, where Colonel Washington attended the session of the Assembly called by Lord Botetourt (Bot-i-tot). It was a busy time, no fewer than eighty-nine laws being enacted. Among them were acts laying a duty on liquors, to suppress private lotteries, to prevent private innoculations for smallpox, to care for idiots, and, last and most ominous, to pay the Burgesses who attended the session of the convention held at the Raleigh Tavern after Governor Botetourt had dissolved the Assembly, on May 17, 1769.

The diary entries for the two months give evidence of a season of gayety:

Dec. 1. Dined at Mrs. Campbell's with the Speaker, Treasurer and other Company. Mrs. Washington & Children Dined at the Attorney's. Myself and J. P. Custis supped at Mrs. Campbell's.

Dec. 2. Mrs. Washington & Children, Myself, Colo. Bassett, Mrs. Bassett & Betsy Basett all Eat oysters at Mrs. Campbell's at abt. One o'clock and afterwards went up to Eltham.

Dec. 13. Dined at Mrs. Campbells and went to the Ball at the Capitol.

Dec. 14. Dined at Mrs. Campbells & spent part of the Evening in drawing Colo. Moore's Lottery.

Dec. 15. Dined at the Attorney's and went to Southalls in the evening to draw Colo. Moore's Lottery.

Dec. 16. Dined at Mrs. Campbells and drawg. Colo. Moore's Lottery till 10 o'clock & then compleated it.

Dec. 17. Dined at the Palace and then went up to Colo. Bassetts.

Dec. 19. Dined at Mrs. Campbell's an hour after Candle light and spent the Eveng. in my own Room.[1]

---

[1] Mrs. Campbell's boarding-place was as select then as Miss Cora Smith's is to-day.

Late dinners were noted on several occasions, an innovation which did not then obtain outside the capital city of Williamsburg.

Mrs. Washington improved the opportunity to visit her relatives on the York River, and particularly her sister Mrs. Bassett at Eltham, within easy riding distance from Williamsburg. The House adjourned December 21st, and Washington joined the family at Eltham, setting out for Mount Vernon the next day. He tarried three days at Fredericksburg, dining with the Lewises at Kenmore and going across the river to lodge with his mother at Ferry Farm. At Dumfries, John Parke Custis overtook him, and they finished the journey in company. Mrs. Washington and Patsy probably lingered with relatives on the Pamunkey.

On September 4, 1772, Colonel Washington 'set out with Mrs. Washington and Miss Custis, attended by Mr. Custis, on a visit to Mr. Boucher,' the tutor of young Custis, who lived near Annapolis. The horses and carriage were got across the Potomac the day before, and the family breakfasted at Warburton Manor, the home of William Digges, on the present site of Fort Washington. They reached Mr. Boucher's in time for dinner. Invited to meet them were Governor Eden and Mr. Benedict Calvert and his two daughters.

The Calverts returned to Mount Airy the next day, but Governor Eden remained and on Sunday drove Colonel Washington to church in his phaëton. On Monday the Washingtons and Governor Eden drove back to Mount Airy, where they met at dinner the Ignatius Digges family. There they stayed until Wednesday, when Washington and the Calverts dined and lodged at Ignatius Digges's, crossing to Mount Vernon on Saturday after dinner with William Digges.

Such was a typical round of visits in Colonial days. To-day the Washingtonian lunches at Mount Airy (falsely called Dower House), dines at Carvel Hall in Annapolis, and motors home in time for a good night's sleep.

The following April Mr. Calvert and lady and the two daughters returned the visit of the Washingtons, spending four days at Mount Vernon, where they met Lord Fairfax and his nephew. On the 27th, Mrs. Calvert accompanied Mrs. Washington to Gunston Hall to attend the funeral of the first Mrs. George Mason, she whose tomb, ordered from England, has withstood the storms of a century and a half in the family burying-ground near the Hall. Even the Sir Philip Sidney-esque epitaph, composed by her husband, is still legible. The other side of the monument evidently was reserved for George Mason himself, but is still unoccupied. No one knows the month or day in 1725 of George Mason's birth. Some day, perhaps, a suitable inscription may take the place of the curiously inappropriate modern monument erected to his memory by his descendants.

While these social functions of the elders were in progress, the young people had been not entirely idle. 'Jack' Custis was one of the finest young fellows in all Virginia. He had been brought up to enjoy the best of everything. His pumps and doe breeches, his hat laced with silver, his sleeve-buttons and handsome gold seal with the Custis arms engraved on the stone, his garters, his fowling piece, the accouterments of his horses and his servants, no less than his Greek Grammar, 'Roman Antiquities' and 'Method of Bookkeeping,' all came from London. He had a prodigious amount of fashionable equipment which he carried with ease and grace; for Washington had taught him to ride hard after the fox, and had taken the boy with him to entertainments official and social at Williamsburg and Annapolis. To the social side of life the boy took with avidity. But much to Washington's disappointment, 'all Cicero in a very neat edition of twelve volumes by Forbes of Glasgow,' not to speak of Livy and Martial's 'Epigrams,' were as much neglected as the 'Essay on Crimes and Punishments,' the poems of Milton and Thomson and the histories of Hume and Macaulay. He may have dipped into the 'History of England in Letters from a Nobleman to his Son,' but probably the leaves of the 'five religious books' ordered for the twelve-years-old boy remained uncut.

In vain the Reverend Mr. Boucher, himself no ascetic,[1] endeavored to instill the learning of the ancients and the precepts of the moderns into a mind filled with dogs, horses, and guns. Moreover, Mrs. Washington was an overfond mother; also she was a timid woman — so timid that when Jack was to be innoculated against smallpox at Baltimore in 1770, the clergyman was bade to write in a disguised hand to Lund Washington, so that the matter might be concealed from the mother until the boy should be safely through the ordeal.

Added to perils ordinarily encountered in the upbringing of a youth of taste and fortune, the boy fell in love with Eleanor Calvert, as merry, smart, and winsome a beauty

[1] For letters from Washington to Boucher and an account of the latter worthy see *Frederick Locker-Lampson*, by Augustine Birrell.

ELEANOR CALVERT
(Mrs. John Parke Custis)

MOUNT AIRY (NOW KNOWN AS DOWER HOUSE) NEAR
UPPER MARLBOROUGH, MARYLAND

ABINGDON, OPPOSITE THE CITY OF WASHINGTON

as ever led lover a brisk chase over the hunting field. The painter has fixed on canvas her slight figure in riding costume, with open jacket and boy's hat.

Naturally Washington was 'embarassed' on being informed that his stepson and ward had 'paid his addresses' to Mr. Calvert's second daughter, and, having made some progress in her affections, had solicited her in marriage. 'How far a union of this sort may be agreeable to you, you best can tell,' writes Washington to Mr. Calvert, 'but I should think myself wanting in candor, were I not to confess that Nelly's amiable qualities are acknowledged on all hands, and that an alliance with your family will be pleasing to his.'

An 'alliance' between the Calvert and Custis families was almost a union between Maryland and Virginia. Putting aside for the moment any Victorian ideas in our minds, let us remember that Jack Custis's maternal grandfather, in spite of erratic morals, had his portrait in Windsor Castle for services rendered, and that his silver plate as well as his name were the proud heritage of his descendants.

On the other side, Benedict Calvert was the favorite son of Charles Calvert, the fifth Lord Baltimore. He was born about 1724, several years before his father's marriage to Mary Jannsen. While Lord Baltimore acknowledged the paternity of his natural son and was devoted to him, the name of the mother has never been revealed. Whether or not she was a daughter of George II, as was surmised, certainly she was a woman of rank and station. Young Benedict (first known as Benedict Swingate) was sent to Maryland with Captain Vernon, and was brought up by Dr. George Stewart, of Annapolis. Lord Baltimore bestowed upon him lands in Prince George's County, made him Collector at Patuxent and a member of the Council. On his wide acres Benedict Calvert built, about 1751, Mount Airy where he lived until his death in 1788. .

It was to be expected that a young man of Calvert's antecedents would follow his own inclinations in matters of love. Benedict's affections were set on his cousin Elizabeth, the daughter of the Honorable Charles Carroll, who had been Governor of Maryland from 1720 to 1727, but who in England had been known as Captain Charles Calvert Lazenby, of His Majesty's Footguards.

When Benedict cautiously intimated to his father in England his desire and intention to marry, his lordship promptly informed him that the only person suitable was his cousin Elizabeth. So this course of true love ran true to form.

While Washington welcomed the prospect of such an alliance in the future, he opposed it at that time. Jack's 'youth [he was eighteen], inexperience and unripened education' were 'insuperable obstacles.' The cautious stepfather, mindful of his own numerous youthful admirations, and also an incipient affair of the boy's in Annapolis, did not conceive that Jack 'was capable of bestowing that attention to the important consequences of the married state which is necessary to be given by those about to enter into it.'

He sagely observes that 'if, unfortunately, as they are both young, there should be an abatement of affection on either side, or both, it had better precede than follow marriage.'

Although the young man 'did not vouchsafe to consult

either his mother or me on the occasion,' Washington was willing that Jack 'should consider himself as much engaged to your daughter as if the indissoluble knot were tied, and, as the surest means of effecting this, to apply himself closely to his studies, . . . by which he will, in a great measure, avoid those little flirtations with other young ladies that may, by dividing the attentions, contribute not a little to divide the affection.'

Not without a natural touch of pride, and also with an eye to settlements, Washington states that Mr. Custis's

estate consists of about fifteen thousand acres of land, a good part of it adjoining the city of Williamsburg, and none of it forty miles from that place; several lots in the said city; between two and three hundred negroes; and about eight or ten thousand pounds upon bond or in the hands of his merchants. This estate he now holds independent of his mother's dower, which will be an addition to it at her death; and upon the whole such an estate as you will readily acknowledge, ought to entitle him to a handsome portion with a wife. But as I should never require a child of my own to make a sacrifice of himself to interest, so neither do I think it incumbent on me to recommend it as a guardian.

Washington concludes this characteristic letter with a cordial invitation from Mrs. Washington, Miss Custis, and himself to Mr. and Mrs. Calvert or the young ladies to favor them with a visit.

Family councils prevailed. Later in April the Calverts spent four days at Mount Vernon, and on the 8th of May, Jack Custis 'set off for Mr. Calvert's on his way to New York,' where he was to enter King's (Columbia) College. Two days later, Washington joined him at Mount Airy, and they proceeded to New York, by way of Philadelphia, where for several days they enjoyed the abundant hospitality of that city.

The shadow of Patsy Custis's death had long been hanging over the family. On June 19, 1773, she died, at the age of sixteen. She was devotedly attached to Washington, who was the only father she had known and who had bestowed upon her all the affection of his large nature.

In his diary for February 3, 1774, Washington wrote: 'Set out after an early dinner (with Lund Washington) for Mr. Calvert's, to Mr. Custis's wedding, who was this evening married to Miss Nelly Calvert.' On the 4th he was 'at Mr. Calvert's all day with much other company,' and on the 5th he 'returned home.' The bridegroom was nineteen and the bride sixteen. In spite of, or perhaps because of, the youth of the contracting parties, the marriage turned out to be both successful and happy. The new home, called 'Abingdon,' was built on the Virginia side of the Potomac, opposite the mouth of the Eastern Branch. The house, a commodious structure, is yet standing. Located near the river's bank, the site still commands a fine view, and a few old trees remain from the days of departed glory; but never since this house was built has it been so isolated and remote as it now is. Even to find the entrance from the lower road to Alexandria is a matter of experiment. But, like all Colonial and Revolutionary homes in Virginia, it is well worth a visit.[1]

There, two and a half years after the marriage, the first child was born and named Elizabeth after her maternal

[1] The estate, purchased by Custis from the Alexanders, reverted to them owing to peculiarities in the agreement. At the outbreak of the Civil War it was owned by Bushrod Washington Hunter, who joined the Confederate Navy. It was confiscated and sold for taxes. A suit on behalf of the heirs was prosecuted by Jeremiah Black and James A. Garfield, who received part of the land as fees. Only recently the Garfield estate sold their remaining acres.

PORTIONS OF A LETTER FROM MRS. GEORGE WASHINGTON WRITTEN
FROM THE HEADQUARTERS AT CAMBRIDGE, MASSACHUSETTS

(also over)

please to give my love and good wishes to your
mamma & grand-mamma, Mr Ramsay and family,
my complements to all enquiring friends, the good
gentlemen that came with me up to Baltimore,
and Mrs Herbert — in which the general and Mr &
Mrs Custis join. please to remember me to
Mr — Clerk and family

    I am Dear miss your most
      affectionate friend

      Martha Washington

grandmother; the next year came Martha, called after Mrs. Washington; then Eleanor, for the mother. The favored name of Parke also was borne by each of the children. The first boy and the last child of this marriage was born in 1781 at Mount Airy, while the father was in the Revolution, and the mother was lodged at the paternal home. He was named George Washington Parke Custis.[1]

When Washington was called upon by the unanimous voice of the Colonies to take command of the Continental Army,[2] two apprehensions oppressed him. The first was a conviction of his own inexperience; but that one he dismissed with the consciousness that he had not sought the place. His great concern was leaving his wife 'under the uneasiness which he feared that affair would throw her into.' Upon Jack Custis he placed the duty of 'keeping up her spirits' and promoting her quiet. He enjoined both Jack and Nelly to abide at Mount Vernon, as 'absolutely necessary for the peace and satisfaction of your mother.' Thereafter Jack must manage his own estate, as he was abundantly able to do, 'as you have never discovered a disposition to put it to bad use.'

In August, 1776, Custis writes from Mount Airy to Washington about the appearance of British men-of-war in the 'Potowmack, as far as Mr. Brent's, whose house they burnt.' 'A Captain James with sixty militia were stationed there who all got drunk and kept challenging the men-of-war to come ashore, and upbraiding them with

[1] Elizabeth, b. August 21, 1776, m. Thomas Law, March 20, 1796. Martha, b. December 31, 1777, m. Thomas Peter, January 6, 1795. Eleanor, b. March 21, 1779, m. Lawrence Lewis, February 22, 1799. George Washington Parke Custis, b. April 30, 1781, m. Mary Lee Fitzhugh, 1802.
[2] Letter to J. P. Custis, June 19, 1775.

cowardice.' When the British accepted the challenge, the militia were asleep after their drunken frolic. 'Captain James desired his men to shift for themselves and ran off without firing a gun.' So Mr. Brent lost house and grain, before Colonel Grayson with thirty militia drove off the British, who dropped down the river.

On February 1, 1778, Washington wrote from Valley Forge congratulating Custis on the birth of his second daughter Martha, and on Nelly's good health, adding, 'I heartily wish the last may continue and the other be a blessing to you.' Mrs. Washington was hourly expected at camp. 'We are in a dreary kind of place, and uncomfortably provided.'

Mrs. Washington arrived at Valley Forge in due season, and wrote so cheerfully of her situation as to occasion the surmise that the worst was kept from her.

On March 19th, from Middlebrook she addressed to her 'dear children' one of those spunky letters which parents not infrequently find occasion to indite. In it she says:

I hear so very seldom from you, that I don't know where you are, or whether you intend to come to Alexandria to live this spring or not. The last letter from Nelly she says both the children have been very ill; they were, she hoped, getting better. If you do not write to me I will not write again, or till I get letters from you. Let me know how all the friends below are; they have forgot to write to me I believe. Remember me to all inquiring friends. Give the dear little girls a kiss from me, and tell Bett I have got a pretty new doll for her, but don't know how to send it to her. The General joins in love to you both and begs to be remembered to all our friends that inquire after us. I am, with sincere love

Your truly affectionate Mother
MARTHA WASHINGTON

Jack Custis proved a good correspondent so far as local matters were concerned: he was elected to the Assembly; he and General Washington had shares in a privateer which was never completed; crops were good, but prices of necessities soared; profiteers were overrunning the country and wages were high; neither soldiers nor officers could be had for the army, the ardor of the people had dwindled, paper money was an affliction, and there came from the Virginia members of the Congress (purposely exaggerated) stories of the defection of the Eastern troops, which even Washington's denials, as given out by Custis, could not counteract. Washington on his part wrote long letters in relation to home affairs, and particularly in regard to the effects of a depreciation of the paper currency on rents, values of land and commodities, a matter on which Custis had the usual hazy ideas, while Washington's exposition was clear and logical. He was what we call 'a sound money man.'

Jack Custis was serving as an extra aide to Washington at Yorktown during the October of 1781. The weather was Indian summer and the headquarters were of canvas. Within the town itself smallpox and camp-fever were doing deadly work among British troops and negro refugees. The still air was filled with pestilence, which was increased by a habit the British had of driving their useless horses into the river and shooting them, leaving their bodies to go up with the tide. Custis caught the camp-fever. Family tradition has it that he saw the ceremonial of the surrender before Dr. Craik hurried him to Eltham, the home of his mother's sister.

In the midst of rejoicings that marked the end of long-drawn-out war, Washington slipped away and rode hard to the bedside of the dying boy whom he loved, who loved him, and in whom the hopes and ambitions of Martha Washington were fixed. The end came quickly. Then and there Washington announced that he would adopt the two younger children, who were already domiciled at Mount Vernon.

CHAPTER X

ELIZA PARKE CUSTIS AND THOMAS LAW, HER SOMETIME HUSBAND

AFTER the death of her husband, John Parke Custis, in October, 1781, Eleanor (Calvert) Custis returned to Abingdon with her two elder children. Eliza was six and Martha was five years old.

It was no sudden burst of unpremeditated generosity that caused General Washington to adopt the two younger children at the deathbed of their father. Mrs. Washington was devoted to children. When she lost her own children (one in infancy, one at seventeen, and one at thirty-six), she transferred her affections to her grandchildren. Indeed, when Nelly Custis, the third grandchild, was born, the mother was so ill that she was forced to send her baby to Mount Vernon to be nursed by Mrs. Anderson (the wife of the English steward), under the direction of Mrs. Lund Washington,[1] and there Nelly made her home until her marriage in 1799. So, also, with George Washington Parke Custis. Born at Mount Airy, the home of his maternal grandfather, six months before his father's death, he, too, received the ministrations of 'Mammy' Anderson at Mount Vernon, where his home was until Mrs. Washington's death placed that estate in the hands of Bushrod Washington.

Eleanor Custis inherited from her husband a handsome

[1] For twenty-five years Lund Washington, a distant cousin of the General, was the capable and successful manager of the Mount Vernon estate.

property, but the depreciation of the currency and some unlucky speculations (which called forth from Washington a whole treatise on the nature of money and the theory of value) [1] had impaired that portion which was in the form of notes and bonds.

Abingdon was some three miles up the Potomac from Alexandria, and the tobacco ships bound for Bladensburg and Georgetown gave to the estate much more interest than it has to-day, hemmed in as it now is between railroad terminals on the west and a few dilapidated tenements on the east, and reached by a mile or so of winding dirt road used only by the occupants of the house.

After two years of widowhood, Mrs. Custis bestowed her hand on Dr. David Stuart, then thirty years old, a grandson of the Reverend David Stuart, who had come to America from Scotland after Culloden. The first David died in 1749 as the rector of Saint Paul's Church, King George County, and was succeeded by his son, the Reverend William S. Stuart, who had graduated at William and Mary College, and had been ordained by the Bishop of London. The seat of the Stuarts was Cedar Grove, King George County, an estate which came by the marriage of the first David to a daughter of Richard Foote.

Mrs. Custis, on the prospect of her second marriage, observed the proprieties neglected on the first occasion — she wrote to Washington to ask his advice. But the canny General dryly remarked that undoubtedly she had made up her mind to take the step, and therefore he should not waste words with advice which was quite unnecessary. She is credited generally with seven children by her second

[1] Custis MSS., in the Library of Congress.

marriage; but in a letter from Nelly Custis to Mrs. Charles Cotesworth Pinckney, dated January 3, 1802, we read:

My Dear Mother has just recovered from her confinement with her twentieth child, it is a fine Girl, large and healthy. Mama has suffered extremely and is still weak. I passed a fortnight with her & my two eldest single sisters have been here [Mount Vernon] with us since Christmas.

After the marriage the Stuart family removed to Hope Park, about twenty miles from Alexandria and five miles northwest of Fairfax Court-House. The estate came to comprise some two thousand acres, mostly in timber, with five or six hundred acres under cultivation; there was a commodious dwelling, a grist-mill located on a never-failing stream, peach and apple orchards, a fruit garden,[1] and numerous barns and outbuildings, all in good order. Besides this farm, Dr. Stuart owned, at the time of his death in 1815, some thirty-four hundred acres in other portions of Virginia.

Washington often consulted Dr. Stuart in regard to the education of the children, and he had so much confidence in his judgment that he appointed him the Virginia member of the Commission to lay out the Federal City. It is often carelessly charged that Washington gave the place to one of his own relations, but the second husband of a stepson's widow could hardly be termed a relative.

It is the fortunes of the eldest daughter, Eliza Parke Custis, that we are now about to follow. She was a beautiful and a lively girl, and quite susceptible to the attentions of men. At one time her sisters feared that an attachment would be formed between her and Joseph Alston who mar-

[1] *National Intelligencer*, May 11, 1815; advertisement of sale of Hope Park.

ried Aaron Burr's daughter Theodosia. But fate had quite
other designs upon Eliza.

On January 16, 1796, President Washington wrote from
Philadelphia to Nelly Custis:

This day, according to our information, gives a husband to
your elder sister and consummates, it is to be presumed, her
fondest desires. The dawn with us is bright, and propitious, I
hope, of her future happiness, for a full measure of which she and
Mr. Law have my earnest wishes. Compliments and congratu-
lations on this occasion, and best regards are presented to your
Mamma, Dr. Stuart and family; and every blessing, among
which a good husband when you want and deserve one, is bestowed on you and yours by yours, affectionately. . . .

In spite of his good words, Washington had his apprehensions as to this marriage of March and September. The
bride was a fitful miss of nineteen and the groom a tem-
pestuous individual of thirty-nine, who already had had a
career and three sons. Presumably there was once a wife,
although by searching I have never been able to find her.
Mr. Law had met Miss Custis at the President's House in
Philadelphia in 1795 and they were married at the home
of Dr. and Mrs. Stuart, at Hope Park, on March 20 (not
January 16, as Washington had it), 1796. For fourteen
months her younger sister Martha had been the wife of
Thomas Peter, a prosperous Georgetown merchant.

Thomas Law was born in Cambridge, England, on October 23, 1756, the fifth child of a family of nine children.
His grandfather and his father were clergymen, and when
he was twelve years old his father became Lord Bishop of
Carlisle. At the age of seventeen he entered the service of
the East India Company as a 'writer' — the lowest round
of a ladder that reached into the clouds. In ten years he

ELIZA PARKE CUSTIS
Sometime wife of Thomas Law

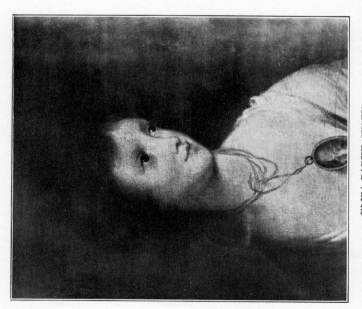

ELIZA PARKE CUSTIS
Showing the miniature of President Washington painted for
her in Philadelphia

ELIZA LAW
(Mrs. Lloyd Nicholas Rogers)

THOMAS LAW

was Collector of Bahar, where he reformed the tax system and incidentally gathered a fortune of fifty thousand pounds. At the age of thirty-five, with health impaired and one fifth of his property sequestered, he returned to England, accompanied by three sons born in India.

The family fortunes had not suffered during his absence. To be sure, the body of his father had been reposing in Carlisle Cathedral for four years; but the actual presence of the quiet, mild-mannered bishop was more than compensated for by a biography written by Dr. William Paley and three portraits by Romney. Meantime, Thomas Law's brother John had become Bishop of Elphin; his sister was the wealthy widow of Sir Thomas Rumbold, former Governor of Madras; his brother Evan had married the daughter of the Archbishop of York and was in Parliament.

Better even than all this, the trial of Warren Hastings was about to begin, and Law's older brother Edward was to prepare the defense, a task which he performed against such odds and with such astuteness that he became successively the Attorney-General, the Lord Chief Justice, and Baron Ellenborough.

In 1794, after spending four uneventful years in England, Thomas Law and his three sons — George, John, and Edmund — arrived in New York, where they occupied a house on Broadway near the Battery. Congress being in session in Philadelphia, Mr. Law lost no time in paying his respects to President Washington, whose name and fame had drawn him to America, his avowed purpose being to have a part in the upbuilding of the Federal City of the new nation.

Mr. and Mrs. Law made their first Washington home at Greenleaf Point (Square 502); but soon they built a house on New Jersey Avenue where the Potomac Hotel now stands. On January 19, 1797, their only child was born and named Eliza.

Thomas Law invested his fortune of forty thousand pounds in the District of Columbia, and when, in 1799, his suit against the East India Company was settled in his favor, another ten thousand pounds also went into Washington improvements. His father-in-law, Dr. Stuart, was one of the Commissioners of the new city; Mr. and Mrs. Peter were living on K Street near Rock Creek, and President Washington himself was building on North Capitol Street two houses for members of Congress. Also the latter had bought the square west of the Naval Hospital, on which to build a home for his last years.

The house of the Laws was a center of hospitality. Distinguished strangers, interested in the novel experiment of creating a capital city on farm lands, came in great numbers, and invariably were entertained by the Laws — Louis Philippe, Twining, and Volney among others. Then, in 1797, Law's eldest son was married and another social center was formed.

There comes a time in the life of a busy man when he should stop writing what seems to him poetry, and what indulgent friends term 'occasional verse.' That Thomas Law never for a day ceased rhyming is an index to his character. In 1800 he wrote the prologue for the first play presented in Washington, and four years later he was one of the promoters of the first theater in the capital, at the corner of C and Eleventh Streets; in fact, there was nothing in the way of Washington improvements that he did not promote, usually to his cost.

In May, 1803, Thomas Law went to England to raise eighty thousand dollars to build the canal that was to make Georgetown and Alexandria commercial centers. Unhappily, he was so inconsiderate as to leave his wife in this country. What good times the bright and handsome Eliza, accustomed all her life to the best America afforded, would have had among her husband's relatives — the Speaker of the House of Lords; John, Bishop of Elphin; Lady Rumbold, and Evan Law, M.P. for Westbury, Wilts, and the Isle of Wight, whose wife was an archbishop's daughter! Eliza was a tactful lady, and, when once the barriers were overcome, Mrs. Washington's granddaughter would have made firm friends in England. But Mr. Law, being a self-centered individual, left his young wife in America to follow her own devices.

After a year's absence, Thomas Law returned to America. In April, 1804, a break came between husband and wife; and on August 9th they agreed to separate. The daughter, seven years old, remained with the father, and Eliza was to receive an annuity of fifteen hundred dollars, which was paid with the unpunctuality characteristic of all Mr. Law's business affairs. She elected to call herself Mrs. Custis. From this time on until her death, twenty-eight years later, she was a restless, wandering spirit, coming to and going from Washington, often ill for long periods of time, but always noted for her wit, vivacity, charm, and devotion to the memory of George Washington.

In an age of scandal the breath of suspicion could not be expected to spare her alone. Reading many of her letters, and many letters about her, I have come to the conclusion that while, like most women of her environment, she liked to be made love to, she had her own high standards and kept to them.

Of the few jests perpetrated by Washington that have come down to us, one was at the expense of Eliza Custis. With characteristic impulsiveness she had written to the President that the dearest wish of her heart was to have his portrait; to which he rejoined that her request should be gratified, although he could not think that the fondest desire of a young girl's heart was to possess the portrait of an old man! However, the miniature was painted. The back of the case is of blue enamel, and in an opening bordered with pearls is a lock of the first President's hair.

Although Washington was apprehensive as to the outcome of a marriage in which there was such discrepancy in ages, yet he came to entrust to Mr. Law matters of business; and the very fact that a wealthy, experienced, and highly connected Englishman was ready to hazard his considerable fortune in the upbuilding of the Federal City was enough to make even Washington blind to his faults of vanity, egotism, and bad judgment. And, indeed, it was not until after the President's death that these faults became besetting sins.

In 1810, after the separation had endured for six years, Law established a residence in Westminster, Vermont, and a year later he obtained a divorce in that State. By way of celebrating his freedom, he distributed among his new-made friends the china he had brought from England as a present for himself and his wife. 'Law china' is still counted among the 'antiques' prized in the Connecticut Valley.

The fact seems to be that there was no real companionship on either side. Eliza, a gay, impulsive girl, fell in love with the wealth, position, and ambitions of her mature suitor. But she was intelligent, sensible, and capable of great devotion. Mr. Law's hero-worship of Washington, combined perhaps with a bit of that shrewdness which enabled him to amass a quick fortune in India, led him to seek an alliance with the President's family. Rage for popularity, pride, and vanity were his chief qualities, and when the neglected young wife outraged these elements of his character, he turned on her with a malignancy which increased with the years of separation and was carried by him beyond his unknown grave.

To Mr. Law's credit let it be said that of the estrangement he wrote:

That, although a separation did unhappily ensue, originating in a disagreement in disposition, yet I have always paid tribute correctly due to Mrs. Law's purity of conduct, which I never did impeach.

She, on her part, showed the spirit of her Calvert mother. Remaining in Washington, as Mrs. Custis, she enjoyed the friendship and consideration of men and women of distinction. Among these friends of hers was Dr. David Bailie Warden, a Scotchman of some thirty years, who had been permitted to come to America as a means of keeping him out of Irish political troubles. He studied medicine in New York, whence he was lured to Washington by the fascination of building a new capital. Then he became the first American Consul in Paris, where he enjoyed the society of every person worth knowing in the world of art and letters and even was elected a corresponding member of the Institute. He published a multitude of articles and books on America, and was for foreigners the chief authority on the geography and resources of the United States and the attractions of the City of Washington.

Mrs. Custis's letters to Dr. Warden, covering a period of twenty years, abound in Washington gossip. She gives one the impression of always acting on the spur of the moment and finding a spur in every moment. Shortly after the divorce she wrote:

If I can find a Being who will love me & who can obtain my affections, I will once more enter the Marriage state — then, Warden, I will be the best of wives — go with the object of my love to the world's end if, [torn] wills it & devote my whole life to love — if this be not my fate I shall remain as I am now — not happy — but determined to employ all my power to promote the good of others & deserve heaven's blessing.

Be careful of all my letters & notes. I go to pass this evening with the [Joel] Barlow party. I regret their going away; they are sensible agreeable people & I have passed many pleasant hours in their company.

May all good angels guard my much valued Warden is the prayer of his Sister, his unalterable friend

E. P. CUSTIS

Monday, 4 o'clock. With this you will receive a coarse cotton gown to have my Riding dress made by, an addition to the list I gave you — let all you get be plain, neat, & not extravagant.

The latter touch is truly Washingtonian.

Several times Mrs. Custis professed herself violently in love, during which periods she was ready to follow her to-be husband to France or even to 'Siberian wilds.' She was desperately lonely and wanted some one to take care of.

ELIZA PARKE CUSTIS

111

The one great interest in Mrs. Custis's life was devotion to her daughter. From Philadelphia she writes to Warden, in 1814:

I came from Washington to see my beloved Child — She has finished her school studies, but is to live with Madame Greland & a friend of Mr. L's alternately. She is now as tall as I am & stouter than I thought she would be — well improved. All I wish her to be — My fervent prayers are that she may meet with some good amiable man worthy of such a cherub & find in him a friend and protector for life. She is past 17 years. You saw the misery I endured when she was taken from me. I fear'd then it was separation forever. Mr. L. never intended to restore her & I have suffered more than I can express from his enmity, to gratify which he has prevented my staying near her — poor man, may God forgive him. Separated from my child, with a numerous family of relations all of whom have families, who are all prosperous, who want nothing from me, I stand alone in the world & let no one blame me if I venture once more upon that state where my peace was wrecked before, the most lonely and desolate of mortals.

Meantime Mr. Law was pursuing his career in Washington. When the Capitol, the White House, and other public buildings were burned by the British in 1814, a formidable agitation was started to remove the seat of government to a more central interior location. Thereupon Thomas Law and Daniel Carroll, with some assistance, built at the corner of First Street East and Maryland Avenue a temporary capitol, which was occupied until the original structure should be rebuilt. During the Civil War this building became the famous Old Capitol Prison, and in its yard Wirtz, of Andersonville notoriety, was hanged. Then Mr. Justice Field converted it into three dwellings, one of which he occupied. Now it is the headquarters of the Woman's Party.

In 1815, Law's second son, John, a graduate of Harvard College in the class of 1804, and a brilliant Washington lawyer, married Frances Ann, a daughter of George Carter.[1] In 1816, Thomas Law and Edward Cutbush founded the Columbian Institution, from which the National Museum developed.

The only daughter of Thomas and Eliza (Custis) Law, Eliza, was married on April 5, 1817, to Lloyd Nicholas Rogers, of Druid Hill, Baltimore. They had three children — Edmund, Eliza, and Eleanor. After only five years of married life she died on August 10, 1822, and was buried on the Rogers estate. Thirty-eight years later her husband's body was placed beside hers, in what is now Druid Hill Park, his gift to his native city.

In 1819, Law sold his New Jersey Avenue house to Dr. Frederick May, and retired to 'The Retreat,' a manor he had built two miles below the mouth of the Eastern Branch, on the Maryland side of the Potomac. There in May, 1820, he gave a 'splash' to one hundred farmers of Prince George's County, for whose singing President Monroe beat time.

Law's fortunes, owing to large holdings of land and high taxes, had been so reduced that when his son-in-law, Rogers, reproached him for not paying Mrs. Custis's annuity, he made plea that whereas he once had an income of thirty thousand dollars he was now reduced to from three hundred to five hundred dollars. In 1824, he went to London, saw Stephenson's railroad, and returned to advocate railroads for America.

---

[1] John Law died in 1822; his son, Edward Ellinborough Law, Harvard, 1819, died in 1889, a member of the American Philosophical Society.

Early in 1831, Mrs. Law wrote her last letter to Dr. Warden:

I recd. your letter of the 26th of Decr. — which was sent me by Mr. Levernier some days after his arrival — I have not been well enough to write before since I recd. it & do so now, with an aching head tied up — I have ever regarded you with a Sister's kindness, I felt much for the injustice done to you by removal from the consulate of Paris — where your talents & time were devoted to the service of Americans but I soon saw there was little chance of your being replaced in your old post — & after doing all I could to serve you — I gave you true information — I have no power of serving any one now — I formerly knew all our public people — but most now in Congress, or the offices, are strangers to me — when my child married I devoted all my cares to her & her family, & gave up general society — since I lost her, I came here & devoted all my time to her beloved children — when they were removed by their savage father, the sorrow I felt has de-stroy'd my health — except one journey I took to gratify my friends, who thought it would improve my health, I have been confined to my room, & most of the time to my bed, for the last four years — seeing none but my own relations & most particular friends — I do not wish ever to do so again. I have neither health nor spirits to make it desirable. . . .

Dear Warden, I have been the last [torn] months at the house of my old & dear friend Mrs. Jones, I wrote you a long letter from here by Gen Bernard — I then expected to go soon to My Sister Lewis in Alexa— but my health was so bad all the winter I was unable to remove, nor can I yet. I did not intend to stay more than a few days, but am so infirm — I can never be sure of executing any plan. . . .

I have heard within a few days that my darling children are well — I have not seen them for a year & nearly eleven months — how much longer, Oh God must thy poor servant suffer! Ever yr sincere & aff friend

E. P. Custis

Washington *April 5* — 1831

The enclosed letter was written sometime since — I was so ill since, that I could not till now write others, which were to go

with it — I grieve my dear valued friend, for the contents of this
letter — but I cannot with limited means I possess in a sick-
room, hear of any plan of change in the consulate or Legation
at Paris — I have ask'd Gen Lafayette if he hears of such a
change, to recommend you to this Govt — & his recommendation
would be a host in your favor —

You will greatly oblige me, if you can ascertain what *Mr. Law
has been doing in Paris* — breathe not to any mortal my name —
but write me what you hear — he has mismanaged his affairs for
years — owes large sums to me, & I am told to others — he has a
great deal of property, but may involve the whole in some wild
speculation. He never gave his angel daughter any fortune, nor
her children since. Give your letter to Gen. Bernard if he has
not left France. If he has Gen Lafayette will enclose it to me —
Ever yr sincere & devoted fd.

E. P. CUSTIS

To David B. Warden Esqr
   Care of Gen Lafayette
     Paris

On New Year's Day, 1832, Eliza Parke Custis died
while on a visit to Mrs. J. A. Chevallie at Richmond, and
her body is buried at Mount Vernon. Thomas Law died
July 31, 1834, and was buried in Saint John's Cemetery.
Later his remains were removed to Rock Creek Cemetery
and are with 'the unknown.' He left one thousand dollars
to the son of his colored housekeeper and the remainder
to William Blane, of London, 'the only one who suffered
through him.' When his estate was finally settled in 1850,
it amounted to $175,000. His wife, his daughter, and the
three sons who had come with him to America, all died
before him.[1]

---

[1] *Greenleaf and Law in the Federal City,* by Allen C. Clark, contains the most
information in regard to the career of Thomas Law. In the *Columbia Historical
Society Collections,* vol. IV, is a characteristic sketch of him by George Alfred
Townsend. The David Bailie Warden Papers and copies of Mrs. Custis's letters
to him are in the Library of Congress. Thomas Law's 'reply to certain insinua-

So ends the tragic story of the Law family in America, in so far as one may piece it together from the fragments that remain.

Mrs. Custis was one of the residuary legatees of General Washington, from whose estate she received one twenty-third part of the remainder, amounting with interest to $6456.14.[1] From her grandmother she inherited many family relics. One of her descendants [2] has shown me a moth-eaten military cape once worn by the General, a satin gown of Mrs. Washington, an original sketch in oil, by Trumbull, of General Washington, a contemporary copy of the miniature of Queen Anne given by her to Colonel Parke, and many another portrait, all comprising one of the richest of the private collections of Custis-Washington material.

tions' is in the *Washington Quarterly Review* for 1824. See also Howard's *Reports*, U.S. Supreme Court, vol. XVII, 1855, p. 417, and Vesey, *Junior High Court of Chancery Reports* (London, 1788–99), p. 824.

[1] Bushrod Washington's accounts; Library of Congress.
[2] Mrs. Wilfred P. Mustard, of Baltimore.

CHAPTER XI

MARTHA PARKE (CUSTIS) PETER, OF TUDOR PLACE

MARTHA PARKE CUSTIS, the second of Martha Washington's grandchildren, is the one least in the public eye. Apparently she was as happy as the country that has no history.

Mrs. Washington, writing from winter headquarters at Valley Forge to the wife of General Warren in Boston, tells of the birth of a second daughter (Martha) to Mr. and Mrs. John Parke Custis, whom Mrs. Warren had met two years before, when they accompanied Mrs. Washington to Cambridge, during the earliest days of the Revolution.[1]

Martha was born at Abingdon on the last day of 1777. The first six or eight years of her life were spent on what is now known as Hunter's Point, directly opposite the mouth of the Anacostia. To-day the white dome of the Capitol and the needle-like Washington Monument form the chief elements in the picture seen from Abingdon. Martha lived to see the beginnings of both structures. Indeed, the new City of Washington was a stage on which was enacted the play she watched from her seat of Tudor Place.

Martha was three years old when her father died; when she was five her mother married Dr. David Stuart, and some time later the family gave up Abingdon and went to

[1] Mrs. Washington to Mrs. [General] Warren, Valley Forge, March 7, 1778; and Mrs. Washington to Miss Ramsay, of Alexandria; Cambridge, November 5, 1775. Photostat copies in Library of Congress, from originals in the Pierpont Morgan Library and the Massachusetts Historical Society.

live at Dr. Stuart's home, Hope Park. There, at the age of seventeen, she was married to Thomas Peter, of Georgetown — the first wedding in the family. Her older sister, Eliza, had been on the brink of matrimony more than once, but it was not until fourteen months later that she became Mrs. Thomas Law.

The alliance between the Custis and Peter families was eminently suitable. Among the earliest merchants of Georgetown was Robert Peter, born in Scotland in 1726. In his upward progress he became the agent for John Glassford & Company, who had secured a monopoly of the Potomac River tobacco trade. If not an ardent patriot, at least he had a decent respect for the opinions of his neighbors; and when Maryland joined other Colonies in refusing to take British tea, Mr. Peter willingly agreed to turn over to a special committee the chests consigned to him, and he 'pawned his honor for the faithful observance of his engagement.' [1] For thirty-two years he was a member of the board of commissioners that managed the affairs of Georgetown, and on the incorporation of the city, in 1789, he became its first mayor.

Four years previous to the marriage of Thomas Peter and Martha Parke Custis, Congress had placed upon the already burdened shoulders of George Washington the task of selecting, on the banks of the Potomac, the exact location of a district not exceeding ten miles square, which, by cession of particular States and the acceptance of Congress, might become the seat of government of the United States. With characteristic tact, Washington called to Mount Vernon Thomas Jefferson and James Madison;

[1] Columbia Historical Society, vol. ii.

and, after discussing the subject, he asked them to call on George Mason at Gunston Hall to get his opinions.[1]

The result of these conferences was the choice of an area so bounded as to include the Virginia town of Alexandria and the Maryland city of Georgetown. Between the two, on the Maryland bank of the Potomac, the Federal City was to be laid out. For the particular work of planning the National Capital the President accepted the application of a young French engineer, Pierre Charles L'Enfant, who had served with distinction in the Revolution. L'Enfant had spent his youth at Versailles, a royal city designed by Le Nôtre and the French architects of Louis XIV. Jefferson furnished him maps of the great capitals of Europe, gathered during his foreign service. By nature an artist and by training an engineer, L'Enfant made his designs under the immediate supervision of Washington. Together they climbed the steeps to survey the prospect, and to locate the two focal points from which the great thoroughfares were to radiate — the Congress House and the President's House.

The plan Washington and L'Enfant worked out resembled that of Williamsburg in respect of the locations of capitol and mansion; Annapolis had its principal streets radiating from the State House. Hence the basic ideas were familiar to Washington, and his military experience had trained him to see things in the large. L'Enfant's

[1] Jefferson had given the dinner at which Alexander Hamilton made the bargain that the capital should be located in the South, in return for the agreement of that section to the assumption by the Federal Government of the Revolutionary debts of the States. Madison had secured the insertion in the Constitution of the provision creating a Federal District. George Mason was a large landowner on the Virginia bank of the Potomac, including Mason's (now Analostan) Island.

genius led him to seize upon the physical features of the
landscape and adapt them to the elements of his design.
He planned a city embodying every necessity of a great
capital, every convenience then known to man, every
adornment devised by the master of landscape as connected with public buildings — Le Nôtre.

In a letter to Washington L'Enfant set forth clearly and
distinctly the fundamental principle of all adequate city
planning:

Although the means now within the power of the country is
not such as to pursue the design to any great extent, it will be
obvious that the plan should be drawn on such a scale as to leave
room for that aggrandizement and embellishment which the increase of the wealth of the nation will permit it to pursue at any
period however remote.

If Washington had been a timid man, if his mind had
dealt only with the present, if he had not been endowed
with a vision that penetrated into a boundless future, and a
faith that was the evidence of things not seen, he never
would have appreciated L'Enfant's plan and adopted it for
the Nation, nor would he have striven with all his tact and
energy and influence to realize it. The proof of this is at
hand.

A century after Washington's death, when the people
gathered to celebrate the one hundredth anniversary of the
removal of the seat of government from Philadelphia to
the District of Columbia, there was a profound sense that
the stability, power, and wealth of the Nation demanded
that the National Capital should be set in order. A commission was created to study the subject and report a
plan. That commission, made up of artists trained in

planning, found the L'Enfant plan better intrinsically, and more comprehensive, than any other plan ever devised for a capital city. Therefore they extended that plan to meet the new conditions a century had created; and in so doing they expressed appreciation of Washington's vision and prevision in this as in other matters of high importance.

Plans, however, do not execute themselves. It devolved upon Washington personally to deal with the seventeen owners of the lands included in the Federal City; and probably there never was a group of seventeen men who exhibited more varieties of narrow-mindedness. Added to this, L'Enfant himself expected to achieve fortune as well as fame; and his arbitrariness, lack of accommodation, and vanity exceeded even the patience of Washington.

The President understood the artistic temperament and was ready to accommodate himself to its vagaries and vanities. Seeing clearly the intrinsic merits in the L'Enfant plan, he strove by every means in his power to create harmony among the artist, the commissioners, and the public; but the task was hopeless. L'Enfant would not work in his place. Reluctantly, and sorely against his will, Washington was obliged to separate him from the task of carrying out his design. But the plan itself Washington secured, and by his approval of it, and the confirmation by Congress, it became and has since remained the official plan of the Federal City.

Among the original proprietors of the lands between Rock Creek and the Anacostia River (the exact site selected for the city), Robert Peter was one of the largest. Probably by reason of his high standing in the community, he was also influential in the stormy councils that took place in the little building still shown in Georgetown as the place where the National Capital was planned. Dr. David Stuart was appointed one of three commissioners charged with the responsibility of having the new city ready for the executive and legislative branches of the Government by the year 1800. None of the commissioners lived near the city, nor could Washington persuade them to cast their lots therein when the town began to take form. He might serve his country for love; but they could not afford to. The result was that all disputes came to the President and all decisions were made by him. Sometimes he became impatient; often he grieved over lack of public spirit; but always he persevered.

Washington did not attend the wedding of Martha Custis to Thomas Peter at Hope Park, as we know from a letter dated at Philadelphia on the next day (January 7, 1795), in which he expresses his dissatisfaction with the action of the commissioners in making a second sale of a large number of lots in the Federal City to a syndicate made up of James Greenleaf, Robert Morris (the financier of the Revolution), and John Nicholson, who were the first of an endless line of speculators in Washington real estate.

Already Thomas Law (who was destined to marry Eliza Parke Custis a year later) had appeared on Washington's horizon with fifty thousand pounds to buy five hundred Federal City lots. 'Will it not be asked,' Washington pointedly writes to Commissioner Carroll, 'why are speculators to pocket so much money? Are not the Commissioners as competent to make bargains?' Alas, they were not. Mr. Law bought from the syndicate and not from the commissioners.

' Washington, being concerned about the building-up of the city, was pleased to lodge alternately with Mr. and Mrs. Peter, at what is now 2618–20 K Street, and with Mr. and Mrs. Law, who lived on Capitol Hill. He was familiar with Mr. Law's eccentricities, and he could joke about them, as when he asks Dr. William Thornton to forgive him for writing in haste — 'Mr. Law is waiting — & you know he does not wait patiently for anything not even for dinner.'

In 1793, Washington bought four lots on the Eastern Branch, and 'being unwilling it should be believed he had a greater predilection for the southern part of the city than to the northern,' he proposed to buy a like number of lots near Rock Creek; but no attention was paid to his suggestion. However, during the two years following he did buy all of Square 21, directly west of the present Naval Hospital grounds, between Twenty-Fifth, Twenty-Sixth, D and E Streets, a site now occupied by a storage warehouse and a disused brewery. His first purchase was accidental, he says; his second was deliberate, for the purpose of building a home for his later years. Had he lived for another decade, as might reasonably have been expected, he would have built on that eminence a house suited to his position, dignity, and wealth. There were to be extensive gardens sloping to the south; and although the development of the site would be expensive, he expected to finance it from the proceeds of the sale of western lands. Had he lived to carry out his intentions, the Nation's shrine would have been in the City of Washington rather than at Mount Vernon. His faith in the future of the city was unbounded. 'A century hence,' he writes to his boyhood friend, Mrs.

George William Fairfax (then an exile in England), 'if this country keeps united, will produce a city, not as large as London, yet of a magnitude inferior to few others in Europe ... a situation not excelled for commanding prospect, good water, salubrious air and safe harbor, by any in the world.'

One other real estate venture Washington made in the Federal City. Fearful lest members of Congress should have no roofs over their heads when they assembled at the permanent seat of government in 1800, he built on North Capitol Street a double house for their accommodation. By his example he hoped to stimulate other building. This building passed through many tribulations. At last it was the scene of a mysterious murder. It developed that a frenzied woman climbed the fire escape and shot the lover who had tired of her. Shortly thereafter the structure was torn down.

Denied the satisfaction of children of his body, Washington put into the Federal City, child of his brain and heart, his hopes and ambitions for the future of his country. Who shall say that he has not builded even more wisely than he knew?

Savage's well-known picture of the Mount Vernon family shows the President and Mrs. Washington seated at a table on which is spread L'Enfant's plan of the National Capital. Its broad avenues and focal points were designed while yet London was a labyrinth of narrow, twisting streets and the present Thames Embankment existed only on the discarded plans of Sir Christopher Wren. The Paris of that day had no quays along the Seine, no Arch of Triumph; the Gardens of the Tuileries were a stone quarry;

the boulevards were slums. It was the First Napoleon who aimed to make Paris the capital of the world's taste; it was the Third Napoleon who gave to the city beauty with convenience and ordered grandeur. These facts show how boldly Washington sailed uncharted seas.

Washington died a year before the removal of the Government from Philadelphia to the Federal City; but he lived long enough to see the L'Enfant plan adopted by the Congress, the walls of the Capitol and the President's House rising, and such private activity as assured the success of the undertaking.

Next to Washington, the one person who entered most wisely and whole-heartedly into the plans for the Federal City was William Thornton. Born of English Quaker parents in the West Indies, in 1761, he was educated as a physician in Edinburgh and Paris. In 1786, he came to the United States, and lived successively in New York, Wilmington, and Philadelphia, until the acceptance of his design for the Capitol brought him to the City of Washington. He was a student of architecture, but was not trained as an architect. As a designer he combined a sense of proportion with fertility of invention and rare good taste. His plans commended themselves to the President by their undeniable quality of elegant simplicity. Moreover, Thornton was a man of education and intelligence; and he quickly established himself, not only with the Peter and Law families, but also with the Mount Vernon household.

Hoban, the successful competitor for the President's House, was an architect trained in Dublin. He followed closely precedents well established in England and Ireland. Later, Latrobe, another trained architect, added attractive features to the mansion; and, after it was burned in 1814, Hoban rebuilt it according to the original style. In 1903, during the Presidency of Theodore Roosevelt, the White House was shorn of excrescences accumulated with the years; the exterior was brought back to its pristine dignity by Charles McKim, who gave to the interior a simple dignity, elegance, and appropriateness for its purposes, which it had never before possessed.

Of Mrs. Washington's four grandchildren, Mrs. Thomas Peter was most like the Dandridges. She was part and parcel of the social life of Georgetown, and also she had dealings with the more stable of the new people, like the Thorntons,[1] whom the building of the new capital brought thither; but she and her husband kept themselves aloof from the political set. He followed in the footsteps of his father, and his increasing prosperity was steady and solid. Speculation in Washington real estate dragged down his brother-in-law, Thomas Law, and sent Robert Morris, the financier of the Revolution, to a debtor's prison; but it never came nigh Thomas Peter.

Soon he forsook the K Street house which his father had built, and on the heights of Georgetown erected a mansion designed by his friend Thornton, the architect of the Capitol, of The Octagon, and of that other Tayloe home, the House on the Square, now the southern portion of the Cosmos Club.

First the Peters built and occupied the two wings of

[1] William Thornton for a time was a Commissioner of the District of Columbia, and afterward was appointed the first Commissioner of Patents by President Jefferson, to whom he furnished a plan for the University of Virginia. In 1790, he married Anna Maria Brodeau, of Philadelphia. He died March 28, 1828; she lived until August 16, 1865. Her diaries, covering a period of sixty-three years, from Washington to Lincoln, are in the Library of Congress.

their house; and when Mrs. Peter received from the Washington residuary estate her one twenty-third, she expended it on the central portion of the house. They called the new home 'Tudor Place.' Located beyond the platted portion of Georgetown, it was not subject to being cut into by streets; it stretched from the present Q Street to R Street, and from Thirty-First to Thirty-Third.

From its tree-clad eminence one looked over the busy wharves lined with bold-water ships, and off down the broad Potomac toward Mount Vernon. On the north the Peters planted a garden, after the fashion of their ancestors, with a hedge-encircled driveway, and mazes of odoriferous box, for the pleasure of themselves, their children, and their intimate friends.

Near by, on the east, was 'Peter's Grove,' built by Thomas Peter's brother David; and to the north was an estate later known as 'The Oaks,' where dwelt a niece of Thomas Peter.[1] She had married into the Beverly and Tayloe families, whose seats were on the Rappahannock. George Washington Peter, a son of Thomas and Martha, married a sister of Captain Boyce, of 'Montrose,' now Montrose Park — so closely were all these Georgetown families allied by marriage. It is interesting also to note how the Carrolls, the Tayloes, the Diggeses, the Beverlys, the Masons, and other Virginia and Maryland families established themselves within the District of Columbia.

Tudor Place was finished in 1815, the same year that saw the overthrow of Napoleon and the birth of that one of the Peter children who was called upon to bear witness

[1] Now the home of the Honorable and Mrs. Robert Woods Bliss, who have restored house and gardens to more than their original stately beauty.

North Front

South Front

TUDOR PLACE, GEORGETOWN
Designed by Dr. William Thornton

MARTHA PARKE CUSTIS
(Mrs. Thomas Peter)

to the feelings of the parents by supporting the name of Britannia Wellington. One of her sisters rejoiced in the name America. Britannia was ten years old when Lafayette came to Tudor Place straight from his call on the President, to do homage to Mrs. Peter, whom he had known when she was a girl at Mount Vernon. He sent back, as a memorial of his visit, a workstand which still occupies a place in the room where it has been used for a century.

When Britannia was twenty-seven years old, she became the wife of Commodore Beverly Kennon, U.S.N. On February 28, 1844, after less than two years of married life, Commodore Kennon, together with Secretary of State Upshur and Secretary of the Navy Thomas W. Gilmer, was killed by the accidental explosion of a gun on the U.S.S. Princeton.

For ninety-six years, lacking one day, Mrs. Kennon lived at Tudor Place, and for sixty-seven years of that period she was a widow. The estate had been held by George Washington Parke Custis in trust for his sister, Martha Peter. Upon his death in 1857, it was vested in Mrs. Kennon by a deed from Robert E. Lee and Mary Custis Lee, the latter the only child of Mr. Custis, of Arlington.

The Kennons had one daughter, who married her cousin, Dr. Armistead Peter, and their son and grandson, both bearing the name of Armistead, now make Tudor Place their home.

I was so fortunate as to know Mrs. Kennon during the last decade of her life. Very tall, very slender, with the figure and grace of a young woman, she ever retained her interest in life and especially in the continued development of the Capital.

It has been said that Tudor Place was to the District of Columbia what Windsor Castle is to England: the seat of royalty. Mrs. Peter, in her own person, in her spacious mansion, and in her not ungracious aloofness, represented the Federalist dynasty. When that dynasty was rudely overturned by the election of Thomas Jefferson instead of General Charles Cotesworth Pinckney, the Washington family almost despaired for the life of the Republic.

When Mrs. Kennon came to rule at Tudor Place, she carried on the old traditions. Whether or not she feared lest, during the Civil War, Tudor Place might go the way of Arlington, at least she averted such a calamity by renting the mansion to Union Army officers. The war over, she resumed her throne and occupied it during the remainder of her life.

Mrs. Washington in her will gave to her granddaughter, Martha Peter, 'my writing table and seat to it standing in my chamber.' This little mahogany table was found to contain the only two letters extant written by Washington to his wife after their marriage. All the others she had burned. One of these letters, still preserved at Tudor Place, reads thus:

PHILADELPHIA, *April 23*, 1775

MY DEAREST:

As I am within a few minutes of leaving this city, I could not think of departing from it without dropping you a line, especially as I do not know whether it may be in my power to write again till I get to the camp at Boston. I go fully trusting in that Providence, which has been more bountiful to me than I deserve, and in full confidence of a happy meeting with you some time in the fall.

I have not time to add more as I am surrounded with company to take leave of me. I retain an unalterable affection for you, which neither time nor distance can change. My best love to Jack and Nelly, and regards to the rest of the Family, . . . with the utmost truth and sincerity.

Yr entire

G. WASHINGTON

To her inherited share of Washington relics, Mrs. Kennon added others rescued from Arlington in 1861, when that estate was seized by the Federal troops. These, together with her own possessions, glorified her home. I recall, besides the Lafayette workstand, the miniature by Robertson that President Washington had painted for Martha Custis at the time of her marriage; also two miniatures of Mrs. Washington — one as the young widow, Mrs. Custis, in lavender gown and a drapery of lace caught at the breast with a butterfly; and the other by Field, painted after her husband's death, in the cap of the period. Accompanying the first miniature are the actual slippers in which the bride stood. The lavender satin is faded and the silver lace is tarnished and torn; but what a sense of personality clings to them and to the filmy stockings and fans and card-plates and the hundred other intimate belongings of this consort and companion.

Then there are portraits of the Thorntons, and of Mrs. Alexander Hamilton, who died in one of Mrs. Kennon's houses in Georgetown, while she was urging her claim against the Government.

The living at Tudor Place might be, and was, plain, but the thinking was high in courage, and in love and veneration for George Washington. In Mrs. Kennon's august presence, listening to her bright and witty talk of family and affairs, one felt not far removed from the actual presence of the personage who was the father of his country, indeed, but also who stood in vital relations with a numerous company of flesh-and-blood boys and girls and men and women.

In beautiful Oak Hill, amid the forest trees under which she played as a girl, Britannia W. Kennon and Commodore Beverly Kennon rest side by side, with nothing more than their names on the low marble headstones to give clue to the identity of the peaceful sleepers.

CHAPTER XII

NELLY CUSTIS

CUSTIS she was born. Eleanor Parke she was named by her sponsors in baptism. Mrs. Lawrence Lewis she became by marriage. But as Nelly Custis she grew up in the hearts of the American people — the bright particular star in that numerous galaxy of youths revolving about Washington as sun and center of their universe. And as Nelly Custis she will ever live in the history of the Washington era.

The third daughter of John Parke Custis and Eleanor Calvert, his wife, she was born at Abingdon, on the Potomac, opposite the present City of Washington, during the March of 1779, when General and Mrs. Washington were with the army at Middlebrook, New Jersey. Because of the serious illness of her mother, the baby was taken to Mount Vernon to be nursed by 'Mammy' Anderson, the English wife of the steward. Mrs. Lund Washington, wife of the overseer at Mount Vernon, had the general oversight of the child, and gave to that task the conscientious care she bestowed on all other duties; but she had never reared children of her own, and because of an overplus of conventional religion she never quite fitted into the Mount Vernon family, where true religion was a matter of everyday practice.

Nelly Custis was two and a half years old before her eyes first saw her foster-father. General Washington returned to Mount Vernon in September, 1781, for a visit of but three days, the first since he had taken command of the

Continental Army six years previously. It was a happy
stay, for the end of the war was in sight; a month later
Cornwallis surrendered.[1]

In the midst of the rejoicings at Yorktown, John Parke
Custis, Nelly's father, was stricken by camp-fever, and
died on November 5, 1781, at Eltham, the home of his
maternal uncle. She was too young to remember him, and
thus it happened that when she and her six-months-old
brother were adopted by General and Mrs. Washington
there was no break in her young life. During the Revolution she remained at Abingdon; but Mount Vernon was the
only home she really knew so long as her foster-parents
lived. Her mother, engrossed by the care of Nelly's two
older sisters, and afterward by the steadily recurring
children by her second husband, was well persuaded to
spare the two younger Custis children to be the interest
and comfort of the otherwise lonely Mount Vernon family.[2]

On the Christmas Eve of 1783, when Nelly Custis was
nearly four years old, General Washington returned from
duties connected with disbanding the army, and family
life at Mount Vernon was resumed.

Things had changed during the war. The Virginia
planter who had ridden away from friends and neighbors
eight years before now returned as the first public character of the world. Wherever in Europe or America liberty
was invoked, Washington was hailed as its incarnation.
His home, of which he spoke as 'little better than a well

[1] October 19, 1781.
[2] The letters of Lund Washington indicate that both of the younger children
were with their mother at Abingdon when Mrs. Washington was with the
General in camp. Certainly there was no lack of affection on the part of parent
or children. Copies of these letters, and also Mrs. Lund Washington's diary, are
in the Library of Congress.

resorted tavern,' became, in fact, the gathering-place of
every traveler of note, of statesmen consulting for the
future of the country, of soldiers ardent in living over the
days of camp and battle, and of a horde of painters and
sculptors seeking their own immortality by representations
of an immortal.[1] To live up to these demands the house at
Mount Vernon was nearly doubled in size and took on the
character of the mansion we know.

Two family matters seriously disturbed General Washington's equanimity while he was at Newburgh in the
January of 1783. 'In God's name,' he writes to John Augustine Washington, 'how did my brother Samuel contrive
to get himself so enormously in debt? Was it by making
purchases? By misfortunes? or sheer indolence and inattention to business? From whatever cause it proceeded
the matter is now the same, and curiosity only prompts me
to the enquiry, as it does to know what will be saved and
how it is disposed of.'[2]

The other matter was more serious. His mother's overseer was eating up the whole profit of the Little Falls
quarter, the annual rental of which (between eighty and a
hundred pounds) George Washington was paying at a
time when public business caused him to neglect all matters of private concern so that he was 'hardly able to keep
his own estate from sale.' The thing that gave him 'much

[1] Gilbert Stuart told J. D. Herbert, in Dublin, that when he could net a
sum sufficient to take him to America, he should be off for his native soil,
where he expected to make a fortune by Washington alone. He calculated to
make a plurality of his portraits — whole lengths — and he did. See *Irish
Varieties*, London, 1836, p. 248.

[2] Samuel Washington died at Harewood, Berkeley County, in 1781, at the age
of forty-seven years. He had five wives, by two of whom he had children who
survived. He owed his brother George for certain lands, the title to which the
latter cleared in his will.

pain' was information which came to him from Benjamin Harrison that a proposition to grant a pension to his mother was to be made to the Virginia Assembly. This he instantly and decisively stopped, for he 'was sure she had not a child that would not be hurt at the idea of her becoming a pensioner — or in other words, receiving *charity* from the public.' In her old age she had complained 'upon all occasions and in all companies' of the hardness of the times, of her wants and difficulties. He asks his brother John Augustine to reason with her. 'That she can have no *real* wants that may not easily be supplied I am sure of. *Imaginary* wants are indefinite; and oftentimes insatiable; because they sometimes are boundless, and always changing. . . . If the rent is insufficient [to make her comfortable] while I have anything I will part with it to make her so; and wish you to take measures in my behalf accordingly.' [1]

Four years later, in 1787, he sent his mother fifteen guineas, all the money he had, and strongly advised her to give up the management of the plantation, rent the land and also her house, and go to live with one of her children, where 'her income would be sufficient for all her wants and make ample amends to the child she lived with.' This solution of her problems had been agreed upon between George and John Augustine, but the death of the latter (in February, 1787) made it impossible for her to go to Bushfield as they had planned; and at Mount Vernon she would not be happy because of the requirements of a house that

may be compared to a well resorted tavern, as scarcely any strangers who are going from north to south or from south to north do not spend a day or two at it. This would, were you an

[1] Ford: *Writings of Washington*, vol. x, p. 136. Letter of January 16, 1783.

NELLY CUSTIS

inhabitant of it [Mount Vernon], oblige you to do one of 3 things: 1st, to be always dressing to appear in company; 2d, to come into [the room] in a dishabille; or 3d, to be as it were a prisoner in your own chamber. The first you'ld not like; indeed for a person at your time of life it would be too fatiguing. The 2d, I should not like, because those who resort here are, as I observed before, strangers and people of the first distinction. And the 3d more than probably, would not be pleasing to either of us. Nor indeed could you be retired in any room in my house; for what with the sitting up of company, the noise and bustle of servants, and many other things, you would not be able to enjoy that calmness and serenity of mind, which in my opinion you ought now to prefer to every other consideration in life. . . .

A man, a maid, the phaeton and two horses, are all you would want. To lay in a sufficiency for the support of these would not require ¼ of your income, the rest would purchase every necessity you could possibly want, and place it in your power to be serviceable to those with whom you may live, which no doubt would be agreeable to all parties. . . . By the mode I have pointed out you may reduce your income to a certainty, be eased of all trouble, and if you are so disposed, may be perfectly happy; for happiness depends more upon the internal frame of a person's own mind than on the externals of the world.

Like many another mother, Mary Washington never could be persuaded that an end had come to maternal control over her children. Her dominant will continued to the very end of her life, making it necessary that she should maintain her own establishment, however small; for she would not have been happy in any house which she did not rule. Her early life was a succession of troubles. Her father died before she was five years old; her mother married three times and was thrice a widow. On her mother's death, Mary came under the 'tutelage and government' of Captain George Eskridge, a Westmoreland lawyer, in whose family she lived for nine years, until her marriage with Augustine Washington. It was George Eskridge for whom her first child was named George. After eleven years of married life she herself became a widow, with narrow means, and a large family dependent on her management for their upbringing. So she early developed self-reliance.

In spite of the troubles with which her life was filled, she gained the affection of her various relatives, as is abundantly shown by their wills, in which she is remembered by gifts of lands, negroes, saddle-horses, and household equipment.[1]

On the Kenmore lands, near her favorite resting-place, known as 'Meditation Rock,' the mother of Washington was buried. A monument to her, begun during the administration of President Andrew Jackson, was never completed. In 1889, at the time of the inauguration of President Benjamin Harrison, the lands containing Mary Washington's grave were offered for sale at auction. So shocked were the American people at the predicament brought about by their own neglect that a fund was raised for a new monument that was dedicated during the second administration of President Cleveland.

Washington has been accounted the richest of our Presidents; and his estate turned out to be a large one for its day; but the only times when he was not in want of cash were just after he had borrowed to meet the demands that his public duties imposed upon him; and to pay these debts he sacrificed lands won by military service.

Gideon Snow, of Boston, was Nelly's first teacher, and

[1] *The Virginia Magazine of History and Biography;* January, 1901.

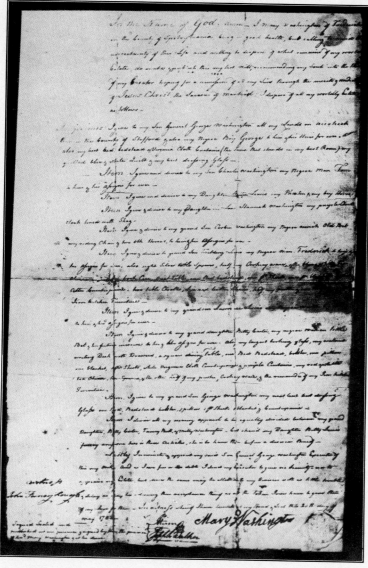

WILL OF MARY WASHINGTON, MOTHER OF GEORGE WASHINGTON

ELEANOR PARKE CUSTIS (MRS. LAWRENCE LEWIS)
From a drawing by James Sharpless

the acquaintance then formed was continued through life. In 1824, when she was in Boston with her own daughter, Gideon Snow called on her; and twenty-six years later, in 1850, he was corresponding with Washington Custis [1] about Mount Vernon days. When Nelly was seven years old, Tobias Lear, another New-Englander, a graduate of Harvard, appeared at Mount Vernon, and began an association with the family which lasted until Colonel Lear's death by his own despondent hand in 1816. First as tutor, then as secretary to the President, and finally as Washington's man of business in the new capital, Tobias Lear grew into the trust and affections of the entire household. [2]

Nelly Custis early learned to write a hand that must have satisfied even the particular Washington; and (what was then uncommon for a girl) she could, and usually did, spell the same word in the same way and as printed in the dictionary rather than as it sounded to the ear. But her real education she received directly from her foster-mother, who took her through all the grades in the school of the housewife and mistress of a plantation — certainly the most exacting, perplexing, and complicated task ever put upon woman. It had to do not only with providing for an elastic table and the sleeping arrangements for unexpected guests, but there was also the problem of the slaves of the house and the field, which called for the exercise of the utmost patience.

A Virginia girl brought up on a plantation was ac-

[1] In the family, George Washington Parke Custis was known as 'Washington.'
[2] In his will General Washington gave to Tobias Lear the life use of the Wellington House (built by William Clifton prior to 1760). After Colonel Lear's death the house was occupied by two generations of the Washington family until 1859.

quainted with problems and facts carefully ignored in the upbringing of town girls. Happily for Nelly Custis, the Mount Vernon plantation was conducted with consideration and propriety. There she came to know and admire chivalry and gallant conduct, and she heard discussed by the actors themselves the gravest and the most inspiring ideas of free government and the upbuilding of a new nation.

All these things Nelly Custis and her sisters experienced, and each one of them showed in after life the results of their early training. They were ardent Federalists; they believed firmly in the rule of the fittest; and when the rising tide of democracy swept their friends from power and exploited itself with the detraction of brave and true men, the girls nailed the Federalist flag to the mast — and were overwhelmed in the Jeffersonian flood.

Nelly's parental instruction was by no means confined to domestic duties. Mrs. Washington taught her to play the harpsichord; and since music was scarce and hard to obtain, the good lady copied with her own deft hand pieces by Mozart, Scotch songs, marches, and dance music, enough to fill the large book that has come down to us. What the book does not reveal is the truth of the reasonable tradition that often the student had other things than music in her mind, but that the teacher was inexorable, even to the administration of thimble-thumps on weary knuckles. At any rate, the virtue of both teacher and pupil had its reward in the gift from General Washington of a harpsichord that cost all of a thousand dollars.

Nelly Custis was ten years old when, one April day in 1789, Charles Thomson, the Secretary of Congress, brought to Mount Vernon official announcement of Washington's election as the first President of the United States. Washington lost no time in obeying the summons. Stopping in Alexandria to borrow from Captain Richard Conway ten thousand pounds for his expenses, he made his rapid way to New York, where he took the oath of office on April 30th. Mrs. Washington and 'the children' (as Washington constantly refers to Nelly and Washington Custis, in his diaries) followed on May 16th. Before setting out for New York, Washington made a visit to his mother at Fredericksburg. Both knew that the parting was final; for cancer was doing its rapid work with her. She died on August 25, 1789, in her eighty-second year.

The President's family took up their abode at No. 10 Cherry Street, New York City, and entered upon the formal life that, of necessity, is lived by the President of the United States. For company Nelly had her brother, eight years old; and on the daily drive 'the children' made half the party.

To-day the President of the United States walks the streets of Washington like any other citizen, and, out of respect for his privacy, is allowed to pass unnoticed by any whom he himself does not first recognize. When he drives, his automobile is unmarked save by the President's seal, about the size of a silver dollar, done in gold on the doors. His machine obeys the traffic rules punctiliously, but otherwise is undistinguished, save when on catching sight of it an indulgent traffic policeman hastens the turning of the 'go' sign.

Far otherwise was the equipage of the first President.

In Philadelphia six bay horses groomed under the direction of German John drew a cream-colored, English-built coach. The stables, one of the city sights, contained ten bays and two white chargers; and Solomon himself was not groomed like one of these saddle-horses. At night they were coated with a paste and swathed with body-cloths, and the straw of their beds was fresh and very clean; in the morning their coats were rubbed and curried and brushed until they shone like satin; their hoofs were blacked, their mouths were washed and their teeth picked; their leopard-skin housings were arranged; and then they were ready for the use of the finest and most fastidious of horsemen. The reputation of the Washington equipage had been established during Colonial days, in a rivalry at Williamsburg with Colonel Byrd, of Westover, when it was 'the bays against the grays.'

To a girl of ten all this pomp of state (where a drive through city streets was a continuous ovation, and over country roads was a series of bumps) doubtless became monotonous; but in the after years, amid the quiet of the Blue Ridge, Nelly was accustomed to tell to her grandchildren stories drawn from glorious memories of departed greatness.

For a time the New York rides were sadly interrupted by a serious illness of the President, caused by a malignant carbuncle on his thigh. 'Do not flatter me with vain hopes,' said the President to Dr. Samuel Bard. 'I am not afraid to die and can bear the worst. Whether to-night or twenty years hence makes no difference. I know I am in the hands of a good Providence.' Fortunately for the beginning nation, the illness left Washington in better health than it found him.

The Cherry Street house in New York proved all too small for the President and Mrs. Washington, the children, Mr. Lear, Colonel Humphreys, Mr. Lewis,[1] Mr. Nelson, and Major Jackson, especially as Colonel Humphreys was then composing his drama, 'The Widow of Malabar,' with whose lines he regaled his exasperated fellow secretaries when they courted Morpheus rather than Melpomene. So the family removed to the larger Macomb residence on the west side of Broadway, below Trinity Church. But their stay there was brief, for in December, 1790, Congress began a sojourn of ten years in Philadelphia.

Life in Philadelphia followed the precedents established in New York. On Tuesdays from three to four o'clock the President held a levee; he bowed to the persons presented to him, but did not shake hands with them. On Friday afternoons Mrs. Washington held drawing-rooms, at which she received the ladies. Each guest was met with a greeting and, after tea, coffee, and other refreshments, she made a second, silent obeisance to the hostess. 'Nothing could be more simple,' writes an English visitor, 'yet it was enough.' Indeed, it was too much for George Mason, of Gunston Hall, who feared that such display squinted toward monarchy, and was only half reassured by the consciousness that he could trust his neighbor, George Washington, although for himself he would have none of it. He declined even an appointment as United States Senator.

In Philadelphia the Presidential family occupied the Robert Morris house in Market Street, between Fifth and

[1] Robert Lewis, a son of Betty Washington Lewis.

Sixth Streets, and furnished it handsomely, but by no means extravagantly.

The hour before breakfast Washington Custis spent with his tutor, while Nelly attended her grandmother. On Thursdays the President gave official dinners. He talked with his guests in the drawing-room as they arrived, and five minutes after the hour named, the company proceeded to the dining-room, leaving late comers to be greeted with some such expression as: 'Gentlemen, we are too punctual for you. I have a cook who never asks whether the company has come, but whether the hour has come.'

In fact, the service of his table was perfection itself. He sat in the middle of one side of the table, Mrs. Washington being on his right at the end of the table, with the other ladies near her.[1] He invariably asked a blessing, or had one asked if a clergyman was present. He himself dined on one simple dish, drank beer from a silver pint-mug, with one glass of wine during dinner and one afterward. He withdrew shortly after the ladies had retired, turning over to his secretary the hospitality of the table, which 'supplied every sort of liquors liked by members of the Congress.'

Nelly Custis was eighteen years old when Washington appeared before the Congress at the inauguration of his successor, John Adams. The hall of the House of Representatives was packed with witnesses of the ceremony. Washington entered amid cheers, and was followed by Mr. Adams. After a moment of complete silence, the retiring President arose and, with great dignity, introduced Mr.

[1] The custom of the President having men on either side of him at dinner prevailed during Andrew Jackson's reign, as Senator Thomas Ewing's letters testify.

Adams to the audience, finishing by reading in a firm, clear voice a brief valedictory.[1] At the end, John Adams covered his face with his hands and wet his wrist-ruffles with tears; from the hushed assembly came nervous sobs; the great man himself was shaken, and large drops came from his eyes. Nelly, who could not trust herself to be near the foster-father whom she idolized, stood with Colonel Read. 'She was terribly agitated,' writes Mrs. Echard, a witness of the thrilling scene.

That night President and Mrs. Washington gave a dinner for Mr. and Mrs. Adams, at which the foreign ministers and their wives, Mr. Jefferson, Mr. Morris, and Bishop White were among the guests. When the cloth was removed, Washington filled his glass and said:

Ladies and gentlemen, this is the last time I shall drink your health as a public man. I do it with sincerity, wishing you all possible happiness.

It was not the words but the profound sincerity of the speaker that caused tears to flow down the cheeks of Mrs. Linn, the wife of the British Minister.[2]

When the Washingtons returned to Mount Vernon in the August of 1797, many changes had taken place in family affairs. The General was now the last of his generation. His mother, his half-brother Augustine, his sister Betty, and his brothers Samuel and John Augustine all had passed away.[3]

[1] The Farewell Address was delivered six months earlier.

[2] Custis: *Recollections.*

[3] Samuel Washington died at Harewood, near Charlestown, West Virginia, in 1781 leaving his affairs in confusion; John Augustine died at Bushfield in February, 1787; Augustine died at Wakefield in 1792. The will of Charles Washington was proved in Berkeley County, September 23, 1799; it is dated July 25, 1799. To his wife Mildred he left two slaves; and a life interest in three others, with reversion to his son Samuel. No real property is mentioned.

Betty, with her brother's advice, settled her mother's estate. Four years later she sold her home and went to live with her daughter, Mrs. Charles Carter, of Western View, Culpeper County; and there she died on March 31, 1797.[1]

Lord Fairfax had gone to a place where the loss of his quit-rents could no longer disturb him.[2] Belvoir had been burned never to be rebuilt, and its owner, George William Fairfax, had died in England at the end of a futile chase after the Fairfax properties. His widow was living in Bath, England, a saddened woman, indeed, but one who played the game unfalteringly to the end. To her in her old age Mrs. Washington sent a letter which her husband dictated, a letter of friendship born of years of neighborliness. Washington himself wrote of the Federal City then building on the Potomac, and assured her that the happiest days of his life were spent at Belvoir — a phrase which has been taken by the romantics to mean that she was his only love.

[1] For sixty years the Lewis estate was the home of Samuel Gordon, who named it 'Kenmore'; then it was a boys' school; next it was purchased and restored by W. Key Howard. The elaborate and beautiful stucco ceilings (the pride of the house) were restored with fidelity and taste by young Howard. In 1914, the place came on the market. On May 7, 1922, the one hundred and seventy-second anniversary of Betty Washington's marriage, the charter of the Kenmore Memorial Association was issued; and on June 6th the movement to raise thirty thousand dollars to save Kenmore was launched, with addresses by Vice-President Coolidge, Representative R. Walton Moore, and others. Through the efforts of the people of Fredericksburg, led by Mrs. H. H. Smith, the purchase price has been paid and a substantial sum has been raised toward restorations. The movement has commanded the interest and financial support of many men and women and organizations throughout the country. The buildings are to be used as a museum and as a center of genealogical research. *The Story of Kenmore* has been charmingly written by Mrs. Vivian Minor Fleming, the President of the Kenmore Association.

[2] Thomas, Lord Fairfax, died at Greenway Court in 1781, at the age of ninety-two years, and was buried in Winchester. In June, 1925, what are believed to be his bones were recovered and reburied. George William Fairfax died April 3, 1787.

MRS. FIELDING LEWIS (BETTY WASHINGTON)

COL. FIELDING LEWIS, OF FREDERICKSBURG

DRAWING-ROOM IN KENMORE, FREDERICKSBURG
Showing a portrait of Col. Fielding Lewis; also the ceiling designed
about 1775

Washington's forty years of happy married life, marked on both sides by tenderness and devotion, make such a theory absurd. That Sally Fairfax was fond of the boy whose character and manners she had done so much to mould was natural. So, too, it was quite natural that he should have a reminiscent affection for the gay, saucy, beautiful woman of the world, who took a discreet interest in him, and, within bounds, permitted him to make boyish love to her. People who lay stress on such things express their own natures, unhampered by the facts in the case.

At the same time, how could Sally Cary Fairfax keep from contrasting the life of George William Fairfax, her high-born husband, endowed with wealth and the brightest prospects, and whose end was a failure, with the career of George Washington, the son of a hard-working farmer, who had his own way to make in the world — and who triumphed gloriously? Such reflections are quite unavoidable, but they involve no questions of affection. It is sheer assumption to suppose that between the two there was any question of romantic love.[1]

Often General Washington's mind was so burdened with the affairs of state or the perplexities of his many private interests that he appeared abstracted and inattentive. At such times Mrs. Washington would reach up, seize a button of his coat, and give it a smart tug. Thus brought to earth, he would smile down at her and give immediate attention to her wishes, with which he always complied.

He rejoiced in the beauty of Nelly Custis. Indeed, he

[1] These conclusions are shared by two generations of Mistress Sally Cary's descendants, with whom I have discussed the matter at the present Belvoir.

never failed to take notice of the good looks of any lady. Nelly's powers as a mimic he appreciated as much as did any of the company; he laughed heartily at her saucy descriptions of persons and events; and he keenly relished a joke. It was a grief to him that his august presence put a wet blanket on the games of Nelly's companions, for he enjoyed watching their sports. On the occasion of her first ball he wrote her a long letter [1] in which shrewd sense is mingled with the weighty humor of that day. The subject was the inflammable nature of the human frame when subjected to the passion of love, and the necessity of loving with moderation — at least until the game is secured!

Nelly Custis at this time was described by a foreign traveler as 'one of those celestial beings so rarely produced by nature, sometimes dreamt of by poets and painters, whom one cannot see without a feeling of ecstasy. Her sweetness equals her beauty, and that is perfect.[2] She has many accomplishments. She plays the piano, she sings and designs better than the usual woman of America, or even of Europe.'

This tribute is one of many; every one speaks of her rare beauty and charm, her devotion to her parents, and her graciousness to strangers. The only wonder is that she reached the age of eighteen, mingling in the gayeties of Presidential life, without having a single serious love affair, in so far at least as the record shows.

[1] Custis: *Recollections*, p. 41.
[2] The extant portraits of Nelly Custis include a miniature by John Trumbull, 1792, owned by Yale University; a portrait by Gilbert Stuart, owned by Edward P. C. Lewis, of Hoboken, New Jersey; a pastel by James Sharpless, owned by Professor R. B. Widner, M.D., of Baltimore; a medallion by the Marchioness de Brahan, owned by Mrs. F. T. Morehead, of Allegheny City, Pennsylvania; a portrait and a miniature owned by Mr. Edward G. Butler, of Boyce, Virginia.

Fate, however, soon overtook the maiden. Two suitors appeared at Mount Vernon, and of the two she quickly chose Lawrence Lewis, the ninth of eleven children of Fielding and Elizabeth (Betty Washington) Lewis. It is said that Mrs. Washington would have preferred the son of Charles Carroll of Carrollton; but, naturally, the President would favor an alliance between the Washington and Custis families. It simplified the question of bequests; also, he was genuinely fond of both Lawrence and Nelly. In so far as Nelly herself was concerned, propinquity undoubtedly was a factor that counted in favor of Lawrence. He had been living at Mount Vernon as half secretary and half guest. After all contributory influences have been considered, it is quite certain that Nelly Custis would not have married Lawrence Lewis if she had not been in love with him.

Nothing, absolutely nothing, could have pleased General Washington more than the marriage of Nelly Custis to Lawrence Lewis, the son of his dearly beloved sister. The wedding took place at Mount Vernon very quietly, on the General's last birthday. When he came to write up his diary for February 22, 1799, he failed to record the event; so he had to refer to it in a footnote entered under the following day — a proceeding which has misled some historians. At the time of her marriage, Nelly lacked a month and a day of being twenty years old.

Mrs. Edward Carrington, writing to her sister, Mrs. Fisher, of Richmond, from Mount Vernon, less than a month before Washington's death, gives a picture of the household:

The General's reception of my husband [she writes] was that of a brother. He took us each by the hand and with a warmth of expression not to be described pressed mine and told me that I had conferred a favor never to be forgotten in bringing his old friend to see him; then bidding a servant call the ladies entertained us most facetiously till they appeared.

Mrs. W., venerable and kind, and resembling our Aunt A——; Mrs. Stewart [Stuart], her daughter-in-law, once Mrs. Custis,[1] with her two young daughters, Misses S——, all pleasant and agreeable; Mrs. H. Lewis, formerly Miss P—— of Richmond; and last though not least Mrs. L. Lewis. But how describe her?

Once I had heard my neighbor, Mrs. Tucker, give a romantic account of her when Miss Custis — how her lovely figure, made doubly interesting by a light, fanciful summer dress, with a garland of flowers she had entwined and an apronful she had selected — came in to throw the flowers at her grandmother's feet, — all I considered a fanciful effusion of my friend's romantic turn of mind.

But now when I see her the matron — for such her situation makes her appear — lovely as nature could form her, improved in every female accomplishment, and, what is still more interesting, amiable and obliging in every department that makes woman lovely and charming, particularly in her conduct to her aged grandmother and the General (whom she always calls Grandpa) I seem actually transported on beholding her.

---

[1] Eleanor Calvert Stuart (Mrs. John Parke Custis).

CHAPTER XIII

GEORGE WASHINGTON PARKE CUSTIS, THE CHILD OF MOUNT VERNON

'AT six months of age, my father became the Child of Mount Vernon, the idol of his grandmother and an object on which was lavished the caresses and attention of the many distinguished guests who thronged that hospitable mansion. His beautiful sister Nelly often observed: "Grandmamma always spoiled Washington." He was the pride of her heart; while the public duties of the Veteran prevented the exercise of his influence in forming the character of the boy, too softly nurtured under his roof, and gifted with talents which, under a sterner discipline, might have made him more available for his own and his country's good.'

So wrote Mrs. Robert E. Lee of her father, George Washington Parke Custis, of Arlington, in 1859, two years after his death. Here is, indeed, a case in which the sins of the children are visited on the parents — and quite unjustly. If Mr. Custis did not in his own person realize the fond wishes of his progenitors and his descendants, at least he rendered two services which will cause his name to shine in the history of his country. His recollections of Washington, in the form of newspaper articles, written as the spirit moved him during a period of thirty years, give to posterity the most authentic, consistent, and intimate account of the personal, family life of Washington. This statement is true notwithstanding the predominance of the personal equation, which of course must be corrected, much as one corrects the variations of the compass.

Again, he builded much better than he knew when all unconsciously he prepared in his estate of Arlington the most significant resting-place for the heroic dead of the Nation, a significance which will be realized more completely when the Memorial Bridge now building shall link Arlington with the Lincoln Memorial.

Therefore we may overlook the disappointment and chagrin of his relatives that as boy and man unconquerable indolence prevented George Washington Parke Custis from realizing the great expectations centered in him. Instead we may enjoy his career as the occasion for the exercise of Washington's solicitude, patience, forbearance, forgiveness, hope, and all those other exercises common to parents since the world began.

Also we may be thankful to him for preserving the atmosphere and flavor of Mount Vernon, even though at times he may seem to intrude the Roman fasces and to wrap his hero in the toga. We smile when he attempts to transform Mary Washington's short homespun garden-gown into the tunic of a Roman matron. Let it be his excuse that Roman history was the only study that interested him; and, besides, the Roman tradition predominated in this country down to the days of the Civil War. It was not until the very end of the nineteenth century that Greenough's colossal statue of Washington in all its Roman nudity was removed from the Capitol plaza to the shades of the National Museum.

In November, 1796, President Washington wrote from Philadelphia to young Custis, then a student at Princeton

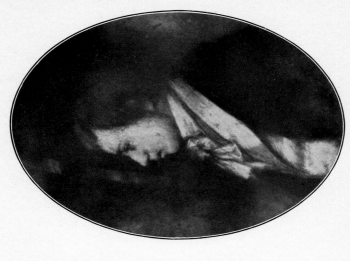

GEORGE WASHINGTON PARKE CUSTIS
By James Sharpless

GEORGE WASHINGTON PARKE CUSTIS
By R. E. Pine

GEORGE WASHINGTON
By Rembrandt Peale

College, enclosing a ten-dollar bill 'to purchase a gown &c., if proper.' At the time Washington was sixty-four years old and Custis was fifteen. Standing between the President, seriously burdened with the cares of state, and the boy who had grown up in luxury as the idol of a doting grandmother, was the boy's own mother, Eleanor Calvert, who had been the consort of John Parke Custis for seven years, and was now the wife of Dr. David Stuart and the mother of his annually increasing family. While the Stuarts were on terms of intimacy with the Mount Vernon family, they had only a consultative interest and no responsibility for the upbringing of either Washington Custis or his beautiful sister Nelly.

Washington had no children of his own to inherit his peculiar abilities and traits of character, but he strove to impress on his wife's children and grandchildren those ideas and ideals which the experiences of an arduous life had instilled in him. In these endeavors he had to contend with the erratic Parke and Custis blood.

On sending the money Washington cautioned Custis to consult his tutors as to the style of the gown, lest he be 'distinguished more by folly than by the dress.' He rejoiced at the assurance the boy gave that he was attending closely to his studies, adding, 'It is you yourself who is to derive immediate benefit from these. Your country may do it hereafter.' He adjures the youth to 'endeavor to conciliate the good will of *all* your fellow-students, rendering them every act of kindness in your power. Be particularly obliging and attentive to your chamber-mate. . . . But above all be obedient to your tutors and in a particular manner respect the president [Dr. S. S. Smith] of the seminary, who is both learned and good.' The letter closes with an injunction he himself had observed all his life: 'Never let an indigent person ask without receiving *something*, if you have the means; always recollecting in what light the widow's mite was viewed.'

In a second letter Washington urges his foster-son to be diligent in order, first, that he may become a useful member of society; 'and, secondly, that I may, if I live to enjoy the pleasure, reflect that I have been in some measure instrumental in effecting these purposes.' Here, indeed, is the yearning of a father.

The Washingtonian philosophy appears conspicuously in maxims such as these:

True friendship is a plant of slow growth; to be sincere there must be a congeniality of temper and pursuits.

I would guard you, too, against imbibing hasty and unfavorable impressions of any one. . . . Where there is no occasion for expressing an opinion it is best to be silent, for there is nothing more certain than that it is at all times more easy to make enemies than friends. . . . As Shakspere says, 'He that robs me of my good name enriches not himself, but renders me poor indeed,' or words to that effect.

To the President on his return to Mount Vernon, in March, 1797, Custis reports: 'The Roman history I have read, reviewed and am perfect in.' This would seem to be a true saying, for ever after in speech and writings he clothed all Washingtons in Roman garb. As for other studies:

The translating French has become quite familiar. . . . I have had a great many good authors and have particularly studied *Hume*; have obtained a tolerable idea of geography, and, sir, in justice to myself and my own endeavors, I think I have spent my time in a manner not to be complained of. I confess I have not made so much progress in arithmetic as I ought, owing to a variety of circumstances and the superficial manner in which I imbibed the first principles.

So much for Tobias Lear's teaching!

This letter gave Washington great satisfaction, but his complacency was rudely shattered a month later by a note from President Smith the contents of which may be inferred by the reply thereto:

Your favor of the 18th instant . . . filled my mind (as you naturally supposed it would) with extreme disquietude. From his [Custis's] infancy I have discovered an almost unconquerable disposition to indolence in everything that did not tend to his amusements; and have exhorted him in the most tender and parental manner often, to devote his time to more useful pursuits. His pride has been stimulated and his family expectations and wishes have been urged as inducements thereto. In short I could say nothing to him now by way of admonition, encouragement or advice that has not been repeated over and over again.

Most parents have had occasion to write such letters, wherein chagrin leads to extreme statement.

If contrition were amendment, then Washington's letter to Custis would have produced lasting results. The boy writes:

Dearest Sir, did you but know the effect your letter has produced, it would give you as consummate pleasure as my former one did pain. My very soul, tortured with the stings of conscience, at length called reason to its aid, and happily for me triumphed. That I shall ever recompense you for the trouble I have occasioned is beyond my hopes. However, I will now make a grand exertion and show you that your grandson shall once more deserve your favor.

To this effusion Washington made answer expressing willingness to forget 'and bury in oblivion all that has

passed.' Only Mrs. Washington and Nelly Custis knew of
the admonition. It was kept from Dr. Stuart and Custis's
mother and from his sisters, Mrs. Law and Mrs. Peter,
although all of them had been at Mount Vernon during
the trying days. At the same time, Washington warned
Custis against those who 'mistake ribaldry for wit, and
rioting, swearing, intoxication and gambling for manli-
ness.'

Then comes a delicious bit of renunciation. The boy
writes: 'The fourth of July will be celebrated with all
possible magnificence; the college will be illuminated and
cannon fired; a ball will be held at the tavern in the evening, which I shall not attend, as I do not consider it consistent with *propriety*.' To this Washington, touched to the
quick by apparent lack of patriotism on Custis's part,
made answer: 'If it has been usual for the students of
Nassau College to go to balls on the anniversary of the
Declaration of Independence, I see no reason why you
should have avoided it, as no innocent amusement or
reasonable expenditure will ever be withheld from you.'
So the boy scored. Not only did he get credit for asceti-
cism, but he also attended the festivities!

Custis having developed a propensity to write to Dr.
Stuart, Mr. Law, Tobias Lear, and a Mr. Z. Lewis, Washington cautions him against being drawn into correspondence at the expense of his college work. Particularly he objects to the Lewis letters. 'Mr. Lewis,' writes the discriminating Washington, 'was educated at Yale College,
and, as is natural, may be prejudiced in favor of the mode
pursued at that seminary, but no college has turned out
better scholars or more estimable characters than Nassau.'

Then he inquires about work in geography and mathematics, 'both necessary branches of useful knowledge. Nor ought you to let your knowledge of the Latin language and grammatical rules escape you. And the French language is now so universal and so necessary with foreigners, or in a foreign country, that I think you would be injudicious not to make yourself master of it.'

Custis did not return to Princeton. In March, 1798, Dr. Stuart took him to Annapolis and entered him at Saint John's College. In commending Custis to President McDowell, indolence of mind was Washington's charge against the boy, adding, 'I know of no vice to which this inertness can be attributed. From drinking and gaming he is perfectly free, and if he has a propensity to any other impropriety it is hidden from me. He is generous and regardful of truth.' Washington was correct as well as sincere. As Custis was at sixteen, so he remained to the end of his days.

The first letters from Annapolis renewed the hopes of the family. Custis settled to his studies with his usual good resolutions. He even turned his hand to match-making.

I find that young M. C.[1] has been at Mount Vernon, and report says to address my sister [Nelly]. It may be well to subjoin an opinion, which I believe is general in this place, viz., that he is a young man of the strictest probity and morals, discreet without closeness, temperate without excess, modest without vanity; possessed of those amiable qualities which are so commendable and with few of the vices of the age. In short I think it is a most desirable match, and wish it may take place with all my heart.

All of which sounds well, but will hardly bear analysis.

[1] A son of Charles Carroll of Carrollton.

However, Nelly Custis was not then in search of a paragon. Washington tells the story:

> Young Mr. C[arroll] came here about a fortnight ago to dinner and left us next morning after breakfast. If his object was such as you say has been reported, it was not declared here; and therefore the less is said upon the subject, particularly by your sister's friends, the more prudent it will be until the subject develops itself more.

Five weeks having elapsed without a letter from Annapolis, the family heard disquieting rumors in Alexandria that Custis was 'devoting much time and paying much attention to a certain young lady.' Washington's admonition was: 'Recollect the saying of the wise man, "There is a time for all things," and sure I am this is not a time for *a boy of your age* to enter into engagements which might end in sorrow and repentance.'

This letter was borne by Custis's mother who met him by arrangement at her former home and his birthplace, Mount Airy. There is something ironic in the situation of a mother advising her son against a course taken by herself and his father, and with happy results. However, she prevailed. Let the boy tell the story:

> The report, as mamma tells me, of my being *engaged* to the young lady in question is strictly erroneous. That I gave her reason to believe in my attachment to her I candidly allow, but that I would *enter into engagements* inconsistent with my duty or situation, I hope your good opinion of me will make you disbelieve. That I stated to her my prospects, duty, and dependence upon the absolute will of my friends, I solemnly affirm. That I solicited her affection and hoped, with the approbation of my family to bring about a union at some future day, I likewise allow. The conditions were not accepted and my youth being alleged by me as an obstacle to the consummation of my wishes

at the present time (which was farthest from my thoughts) I withdrew, and that on fair and honorable terms, to the satisfaction of my friends. . . . To my mother I disclosed the whole affair, who is now perfectly satisfied.

What mother is not satisfied when she gets a son out of an undesirable love affair, no matter on what terms?

Custis did not return to Annapolis in the September of 1798. He was ready to go because the family wished it; but his reluctance was so great that Washington knew the uselessness of a further stay there. In his hopelessness, the perplexed 'father of his country' sends to Dr. Stuart this confession of futility in his dealings with his foster-son:

What is best to be done with him I know not. My opinion has always been, that the university in Massachusetts would have been the most eligible seminary to have sent him to; first, because it is on a larger scale than any other; and, secondly, because I believe that the habits of the youth there, whether from the discipline of the school, or the greater attention of the people generally to morals, and a more regular course of life, are less prone to dissipation and excess than they are at the colleges south of it.

It may be asked, if this was my opinion, why I did not send him there? The answer is as short as to me it was weighty: being the only male of his line, and knowing (although it would have been submitted to) that it would have proved a heart-rending stroke to have him at that distance, I was disposed to try a nearer seminary, of good repute, which from some cause, or combination of causes, has not, after the experiment of a year been found to answer the end that was contemplated. Whether to send him there now or indeed to any other public school is indeed problematical, and to misspend his time at this place would be disagreeable to himself and me.

If I were to propose to him to go to the university at Cambridge, in Massachusetts, he might as has been usual with him on like occasions say he would go wherever I chose to send him, but if he should go contrary to his inclination and without a disposition to apply himself properly, an expense without any benefit would result from the measure. Knowing how much I have been disappointed, and my mind disturbed by his conduct, he would not, I am sure, make a candid disclosure of his sentiments to me on this or any other plan I might propose for the completion of his education, for which reason I would pray you (or perhaps Mrs. Stuart could succeed better than any one) would draw from him a frank and explicit disclosure of what his own wishes and views are; for if they are absolutely fixed an attempt to counteract them by absolute control would be as idle as the endeavor to stop a rivulet that is constantly running. Its progress while mound after mound is erected may be arrested, but this must have an end, and everything will be swept away by the torrent.

The more I think of his entering William and Mary, unless he could be placed in the bishop's family, the more I am convinced of its inutility on many accounts, which had better be the subject of oral communication than by letter. . . . I believe that Washington means well but has not resolution to act well.

How very few parents are as painstaking, forgiving, sagacious, and intelligent as Washington was. All these qualities were by no means lost on the boy. To be sure, he never took a place of leadership, but he was a useful citizen. And of how few boys brought up in luxury can as much be said?

What schools could not do for young Custis, Washington hoped the camp might accomplish. There he himself received his education. President Washington had able advisers; but his personality was dominating and his reputation for high-minded justice pervaded the Nation. When he came to deal with the foreign relations of the new Government with England and France, then at war with one another, all his patience and all his prestige were required to keep this country out of European quarrels. Even so he was forced to ask the recall of Genêt, the first

French Minister, a hot-headed young man who attempted
to trade upon the Revolutionary services rendered by
France to the Colonies. Also, he was compelled to recall,
in disgrace, Monroe, our Minister to France.

No sooner had Washington quitted the Presidency
than the troubles with the France of the French Revolution culminated in suspension of commercial intercourse
and preparations for war. At this juncture, President
Adams and Congress again turned to Washington, and he
was commissioned to command the new army.

Washington naturally selected Alexander Hamilton and
Charles Cotesworth Pinckney as major-generals, and the
latter took upon his staff young Custis, who had already
been commissioned a cornet of horse. Lawrence Lewis also
got a commission, which gave him the title of major, a
decoration he wore through life.

Happily, Napoleon, for reasons of his own, was ami-
cably disposed, and the peril of war was averted. So here
again Washington's hopes for Custis were thwarted.

CHAPTER XIV

LAST DAYS AT MOUNT VERNON

On Thursday, December 12, 1799, General Washington, as was his custom, rode out to his farms about ten in the morning and returned at three in the afternoon. Soon after he went out, the weather became very bad, rain, hail, and snow falling alternately, driven by a cold wind.

On coming in, he franked some letters, but said the weather was too bad to send a servant to the post-office. He told his anxious secretary, Tobias Lear, that his great-coat had kept him dry; but Lear saw with concern that his neck was wet and snow hung on his hair. He went to the dinner table without changing his clothes and in the evening he appeared as well as usual. The next day a heavy fall of snow kept him indoors, save for a brief sally into the grounds to mark some trees for cutting, to improve the view.

In the evening he sat in the parlor with Mrs. Washington and Mr. Lear. He was very cheerful, and read aloud from the papers items that interested or amused him. Being quite hoarse, he asked Mr. Lear to read to him while Mrs. Washington went up to Mrs. Lawrence Lewis's room. A fortnight before, Frances Lewis had been born, and the mother was still in a very weak state.

The General refused to take medicine, saying: 'You know I never take anything for a cold. Let it go as it came.' Between three and four in the morning of the 14th the General awoke Mrs. Washington. He said he felt very ill and had an ague. He spoke and breathed with difficulty; but forbade his wife to call a servant, lest she should take cold. At daylight, Caroline appeared to make the fire, and Mr. Lear was summoned.[1] Dr. Craik, at Alexandria, was sent for; then Rawlins, one of the overseers, was called to bleed the General. When Mrs. Washington remonstrated at the loss of so much blood, the General firmly called 'more.' Dr. Craik arrived at nine and applied the usual remedies. At eleven, Dr. Brown came from Port Tobacco, and at three Dr. Dick appeared. For the fourth time the General was bled — a remedy now superseded, but then the most efficacious method known. Even with modern science, it is doubtful if Washington's life could have been saved.[2]

About four o'clock the General asked Mrs. Washington to bring two wills from his desk. He selected one and asked her to burn it. She did so. He told her to put the remaining one in her closet. When this was done, he gave other directions, for he felt that his end was near. To his old friend and companion, Dr. Craik, he said: 'Doctor, I die hard; but I am not afraid to go.' He asked when Lawrence Lewis and George Washington Parke Custis would return from New Kent, whither they had gone for a visit.

About ten o'clock Saturday night, the 14th of December, the General died without a sigh or a struggle. Mrs. Washington, from her place at the foot of the bed, asked: 'Is he gone?' Mr. Lear lifted his hand in acquiescence.

[1] Tobias Lear left two accounts of the last days of General Washington.
[2] 'Washington's Death,' *Transactions* of the College of Physicians and Surgeons of Philadelphia, vol. 25; 1903. Also 'Washington's Death and Doctors,' by Dr. I. Solis Cohen, *Lippincott's Magazine;* 1889.

"'Tis well,' she said; 'all is over now. I have no more trials to pass through. Soon I shall follow him.'

Congress, on hearing of the death of General Washington immediately sent to his widow the request that she allow his body to be placed in a crypt in the Capitol, then building; and she, 'taught by the greatest example I had so long before me, never to oppose my private wishes to the public will,' consented to the request, 'and in doing this, I need not — I cannot — say what a sacrifice of individual feeling I make to a sense of public duty.' Clearly, firmly, and in writing that bears the marks of high breeding, she penned the words that, as she thought, separated her in death from the husband whose life she had shared to the fullest extent in camp and public office and home.[1] Fortunately the separation was never made in fact. It is not possible, in view of the modern examples in Europe and this country, to conceive the crypt of the Capitol converted into a shrine comparable in any particular to Mount Vernon.

The two years and five months that Mrs. Washington lived as a widow marked a period of adjustments for the household at Mount Vernon. The Lawrence Lewis family began to build Woodlawn, and George Washington Parke Custis meditated his reproduction at Arlington of the temple of Pæstum. Meantime, the daily routine was to be observed. Letters of condolence came by every post, and the task of answering the more intimate ones fell to Mrs. Lewis. Writing to Mrs. Charles Cotesworth Pinckney,[2]

[1] House of Representatives MSS. in the Library of Congress.

[2] The letters to Mrs. Pinckney are from the Alice Rutledge Felder collection of manuscripts now in the Library of Congress. These letters are now published for the first time.

Mount Vernon Jany 12th 1809

Accept Dear Madam the thanks of my Belov'd Grand-
Mama for your kind and sympathising letter.
The loss we have sustain'd is irreparable, the shock
was so sudden and unexpected, that I very much
fear'd my Revered Parent could not support it; but
that pious resignation to the dispensations of
Providence, however afflicting, which has through
life distinguish'd her, the most devout submission to his
Divine Will, has enabled her to support this severe
trial with uncommon fortitude. her health has
suffer'd but she is now pretty well, & I trust in Heaven
that she will be preserv'd many years to bless her children
and friends.
At the awful moment which depriv'd me of a Friend
and Belov'd Father, I was prevented paying the last
sad duties by confinement; my child was a fortnight
old and I in a very weak state. my confinement still

LETTER OF MRS. LAWRENCE LEWIS (NELLY CUSTIS) TO MRS.
CHARLES COTESWORTH PINCKNEY TELLING OF THE DEATH OF
GENERAL WASHINGTON

continues, although the weeks have elapsed since
her birth. I am extremely reduced and have had
constant illhealth — Accept Dear Madam my best
thanks for the affectionate manner in which
I am mention'd in your letter. My little Darling
grows very fast and is remarkably healthy.
Could her innocent smiles and caresses soften the
sorrows of my Belov'd and Rever'd Parent, it would
make me most happy; in time I hope she will afford
some amusement.

Grandmama, the Gentlemen of the family, & my-
-self, unite in best wishes for General Pinckney,
yourself and the young Ladies — Our compliments
to Mr & Mrs Thornton

      I am Dear Madam with perfect
   esteem,
      Yours affectionately
        Eleanor P. Lewis

NELLY CUSTIS TO MRS. PINCKNEY

less than a month after General Washington's death, she says:

The shock was so sudden and unexpected that I very much fear'd my Revered Parent could not support it; but that pious resignation to the dispensations of Providence, however afflicting, which has through life distinguished her, the most devout submission to his Divine Will, has enabled her to support this severe trial with uncommon fortitude. Her health has suffer'd but she is now pretty well, & I trust in Heaven that she will be preserved many years to bless her children and friends.

At the awful moment which depriv'd me of a Friend and Belov'd Father, I was prevented paying the last sad duties by confinement, my Child was a fortnight old and I in a very weak state.

On November 9, 1800, Mrs. Lewis writes to Mrs. Pinckney, acknowledging for herself and her sisters (Mrs. Law and Mrs. Peter) a gift of plumes [1] sent by General Pinckney. 'We are very vain of them, I assure you,' she says, 'and whenever I wish to look particularly smart, I become a *Major General.*'

She and her child had spent five weeks at Hope Park with her mother, Mrs. Stuart, 'but ague and fever still pursued us.' Mrs. Washington 'was very sick for a short time with a bilious attack, she is now recovered & looks better than when you were here.'

Six months later, Mrs. Lewis again writes to Mrs. Pinckney. Both the writer and her grandmother had been suffering from violent coughs, and her brother 'was for a long time ill with a bilious fever and something of a Pleurisy.' She 'had serious apprehensions of a decline in which my friends and Physician concurred, but the timely and constant use of milk punch and a conserve of roses, with

[1] Badges of the Federalists.

air and exercise, have removed those fears and I now begin to fatten a little.'

Writing on May 9, 1801, to Mrs. Pinckney, Nelly gives this description of the domestic life at Mount Vernon, together with some characteristic reflections on the political conditions following the defeat of General Pinckney by Thomas Jefferson in the Presidential election of that year.

I am sure it will please my dear Mrs. Pinckney to know that my little Frances is the darling of her good Grandmama and seems to afford her comfort and amusement. My Beloved Parent is delighted when my child is fond of her, calls her Grandmama and gives her sweet kisses. My only fear is that my daughter will be spoilt, she is indulged in every thing stays with Grandmama the most part of every day and is never denied anything she takes a fancy to.

I cannot describe to you how perfectly delightful my sensations are when I see my venerable Parent, to whom my utmost Gratitude and devoted attachment are due, fondling my darling cherub who is more necessary to my happiness than I can express.

I feel more grateful if possible for the renewed love of my Grandmama to my child, than for all the benefits and affection she has bestowed upon me; can I possibly fail my respected Friend in any of the duties and affections of a Mother when I have such an example constantly before me? when I remember the care, the anxiety, the unremitted attention and affection of my revered Parent to me.

My Frances runs about every where, sings, dances and is much delighted with a doll I bought for her in Alexandria, she is extremely fond of her Father and myself — he is as much attach'd to her as I am, as soon as he returns from his Farm he plays on the violin for her to dance and attends a great deal to her.

My Husband is much gratified by your kind remembrance of him, and I assure you allways thinks and speaks of you and General Pinckney with the sincerest esteem and affection. These his sentiments and mine are unalterable and will be renewed in our children.

The regard of Gen'l Pinckney and yourself is allways remember'd and mention'd with pride and pleasure, & I assure you with sincerity, that you have not more & zealous admirers in the world than are to be met with at this time at Mount Vernon.

Sincerely have we deplored the infatuation of our Countrymen and the triumph of democracy, we are compleatly degraded in my opinion, my only consolation is, that it is probably for the *best;* Americans have hitherto been so happy they did not properly appreciate the blessings they enjoyed, not experiencing calamity they were unmindful of felicity, and ungratefully repined without having a grievance to complain of. now the scene is changed, adversity will teach them repentance and submission, they will regret the blessings they have lost by their own folly — their eyes will be opened reformation be effected, and we may then hope for the *Millenium* so long predicted — what think you of my prophecy?

For Genl Pinckney's *own* comfort I should never wish him to be a President, happiness I am sure is not an attendant on that situation. I am persuaded he is far happier in his present employments, but for his Country I think the loss is irreparable for the present four years, — after that term expires, I trust America will retrieve her character by electing him unanimously and for life.

The much valued plume [1] was worn to an assembly the 7th of March, I was very much indisposed but as it was the only assembly during my stay in the City I went for the pleasure of wearing my badge of Federalism. My Sisters wore theirs during the Winter, it was a very dull party, and I was very glad to return early to my Frances with a resolution of not attending another dance for three years at least.

Col. Burr, his Daughter and her husband were there. Mrs. Alston is a very sweet little woman very engaging and pretty — but her husband is the most intolerable mortal I ever beheld. I can not enough congratulate my Dear Eliza on escaping an union with him, I think he is more calculated to break a Wife's heart than any person I ever have seen. He has rice and cotton they say in abundance, and good sense, the latter he is too partial to,

---

[1] The bravery of the Custis family in flaunting their party principles was greater than their tact.

to make his associates the better for it — it is securely lock'd up in the inmost recesses of his brain — the former, although agreeable apendages, will not compensate for the want of domestic comfort — affectionate attentions, all those virtues so necessary to the happiness of the conjugal state.

I remain'd seven weeks in the City with my sisters, was sick all the time and never felt more pleased than when I arrived safe at home with my child, and to my beloved Parent who was equally pleased with our return — our little dwelling will be finished this week, & the remainder of the walls run up this summer, so that by the next season I hope to be well and comfortably fixed — then shall I expect my good friends will have some curiosity to see me a house-keeper, and if possible, allow me the delight of entertaining them as amongst my most wellcome Guests. . . .

Writing again to her beloved Mrs. Pinckney, in the January of 1802, from Mount Vernon, the lively Nelly paints this picture of domestic bliss:

I have the happiness to inform you that my revered Parent [Mrs. Washington], with your other Friends here, are quite well. I am myself in better health than I have been for two years past, my children are fat & rosy. My precious Frances is her Grandmama's Darling & my little smiling Martha is one of the most quiet children I ever saw.[1] I love them equally, I do not feel the least difference in my affection for them.

My Dear Mother has just recovered from her confinement with her twentieth Child, it is a very fine Girl, large and healthy. Mama has suffered extremely, and is still weak.

I passed a fortnight with her & my two eldest single sisters have been with us since Christmas. My sister Law also dined with us on Christmas & staid a few days after. Sister Peter could not come, she has just recovered from her confinement with another charming Boy, who is to be called Daniel Parke after our revered Parent's first husband. She has put her little John in Boy's cloaths & has had a suit of uniform made for him, which I am told he looks very sweet in.

---

[1] Martha and a boy died in infancy.

I have not as yet paid my annual visit to Washington, indeed there are too great a number of Democrats there for any person to be comfortable who has a natural antipathy to those animals. You have no doubt heard of the *mammoth* cheese, which the Kind Ladies of Cheshire [1] [Massachusetts] thought proper to present our ruler with — it has arrived without accident at the President's House, who has appropriated a room to it, which he dignifies with the appellation of Mammoth room & invites the members of Congress to visit it. A number of the Federalists were here yesterday who had seen it. They say the crust is painted red and think the new representatives room looks like an *oven* intended for the *apple pye* which was supposed would be offered with the cheese.

Mr. Lowndes, a member from Carolina, with his agreeable wife staid a day and night here last week — they are very pleasing indeed. Mr. States Rutledge, a very handsome young man, paid us a visit, he only staid a few hours, we regretted he could not stay longer. In the summer, Mr. Osborne with his Daughter, Mrs. Lowndes, her husband and several others called here to see the place. Mrs. Lowndes is a beauty & very pleasing woman I think.

We have had the most charming mild weather I ever knew at this season. Yesterday my Husband, sisters and self went on a visit by water, we passed a charming day and returned without experiencing any inconvenience from our trip. It is a very remarkable thing with us to go on a water party in January.

On Thursday I dined, in company with my sisters & Mr. Lewis, at Woodlawn, our new House, it was so novel to me to preside in a House, that I spent a very happy day and my little Frances, who was with me, was delighted with everything. It is nearly ready for us, and I hope next summer we shall be favored with the company of yourself and Genl. Pinckney there.

Her two older sisters, Mrs. Law and Mrs. Peter, were settled in homes in the Federal City. For a time Nelly had been quite concerned lest the impulsive Eliza (Mrs. Law)

[1] Under the ministrations of a political Baptist preacher, Cheshire became a Jeffersonian oasis in the desert of New England Federalism; and to this day rejoices over the fact.

should be carried off her feet by Mr. Alston to whom Nelly took a vigorous dislike, because of his apparent neglect of those courtesies due ladies. She writes to Mrs. Pinckney:

I think Our Dear Eliza has had a very fortunate escape from a wedded life with a Mr A—— for the man who is so little minded as to think less of a worthy man, and endeavour to injure him, from the rejection of the daughter, deserves nothing but contempt, and can never make a good husband. His designs I trust will be defeated and that Gen'l Pinckney will be our next President.

Congress are to meet next monday in Washington & the inhabitants will be very gay I hear — We have had races in Alexandria, ball, plays &c — I was one morning there but could not leave my daughter for the evening parties, she is more amusing to me than eny entertainment.

Mr. Alston seems to have belied her judgment by proving a devoted husband to Theodosia Burr. He wrote to his wife a heart-broken letter as he watched her ship sail out of Charleston Harbor. She was at the bottom of the sea before the letter reached New York. How Nelly regarded Mr. Law, whom Eliza did marry, has not been revealed.

During the time of her widowhood, Mrs. Washington maintained the Mount Vernon house on the same hospitable scale established by her husband; and her friends and grandchildren and great-grandchildren kept her occupied. On Saturday evening, May 22, 1802, she succumbed to a prolonged attack of bilious fever, and died surrounded by relatives, to whom she gave the consolations of the faith that had maintained her steadfast through seventy-one years of an eventful life.

CHAPTER XV

MR. AND MRS. LAWRENCE LEWIS, OF WOODLAWN

SOME time before his death, Washington wrote to Lawrence Lewis that, unless he and Nelly did something to displease him (a remote contingency, but one to be guarded against, nevertheless), they might count on receiving from him two thousand acres, together with the mill and distillery, which were on the property. Washington himself picked out the site for the house, on a hill commanding a fine view of the Potomac, a location he conceived to be the very finest he knew of anywhere in the country. The plans for the house were drawn by William Thornton, the architect of the United States Capitol, and later of Colonel John Tayloe's house, The Octagon; of Tudor Place, the seat of Thomas Peter; and of the House on the Square, built by Colonel John Tayloe.[1]

Mrs. Washington inherited all the household furniture and supplies at Mount Vernon, most of which she divided among her four grandchildren; but a portion was sold to all the heirs at a private sale. For number these mementoes are equaled only by the original cargo of the Mayflower.

[1] The Octagon is now the home of the American Institute of Architects, and is to be restored and made a memorial of Charles Follen McKim; Tudor Place is still, and probably will long remain, the home of the Peter family; the House on the Square, after sheltering Senator Don Cameron of Pennsylvania and Senator Mark Hanna of Ohio, has become a portion of the Cosmos Club, with the prospect that ultimately it will be taken for Government uses, according to the Plan of 1901.

Very many of them have found their way back to Mount
Vernon, but each year some relics of the Washingtons appear in auction sales and bring fabulous prices. Much of
the furniture went to equip Woodlawn, the new home of
the Lewises; other portions were given to Mrs. Peter and
Mrs. Law; and a very considerable portion, acquired by
gift or purchase, found its way to Arlington.

Frances, the first child of the Lewises, was born at
Mount Vernon; and so, also, were Martha and a son, both
of whom died in infancy. Then came, in succession,
Angela, Lorenzo, and Agnes. The latter died at the age
of eighteen, while at school in Philadelphia. During the
three years succeeding Mrs. Washington's death, Nelly
was often on the brink of the grave, and suffering from a
nervous affliction which prevented sleeping.

We live at Woodlawn [she writes to Mrs. Pinckney], in a small
part of our intended House; it is rather inconvenient, but we are
allways pleased with our house, and our poor little Frances is a
constant comfort. Had my Martha & my little son lived we
should have been as fortunate Parents as any in the world, but
they are much more fortunate in being spared the trials which
attend every one in this life.
The last summer I passed in Frederick County, I went to
Harper's Ferry to the house where General Pinckney and yourself resided. I wished to have gone to Shepherds Town to see
your residence there. . . . Next season we propose passing entirely in the upper country. I shall then certainly visit Shepherds Town. . . . I am charmed with that Country and should
like very much to reside there entirely, or to leave Virginia for the
Eastern States. I live now in sight of Mount Vernon, and it is a
continued source of uneasiness to reflect on times past which can
never be recalled.

Establishing themselves at Woodlawn, the Lawrence

WOODLAWN

Designed by Dr. William Thornton, architect of the Capitol; built by Major
and Mrs. Lawrence Lewis on that portion of the Mount Vernon estate bequeathed to them by General Washington. Now the home of Senator and
Mrs. Underwood

KENMORE, THE HOME OF COLONEL AND MRS. FIELDING LEWIS

Sketch for the restoration, designed by Edward W. Donn, Jr., architect

HOUDON'S BUST OF WASHINGTON

Lewises pursued the even tenor of ways that ever straightened with the years. He and Bushrod Washington became the active executors of the Washington estate, and in 1835 carried out the provision of the will which directed that a new tomb be built on the spot marked by Washington. Fortunately, the Congress never carried out the plan to have the body of Washington (and possibly of Mrs. Washington also) placed in a crypt constructed for the purpose beneath the dome of the Capitol. To-day that chamber is occupied only by the catafalque used from time to time as the temporary resting-place of the body of a President when lying in state. Thus seeming indifference has resulted in making Mount Vernon itself the shrine of the Nation.

In building the new tomb, Lawrence Lewis proceeded with a meticulous care and a meagerness of imagination that are evidenced by the receipted bills.[1] His fellow executor, George Washington Parke Custis, with justifiable indignation, wrote:

The ancient family vault having fallen into a state of decay, the Chief surveyed and marked out a spot for a family burial place during the last days at Mount Vernon. The situation is particularly unfavorable and ill chosen, being a most unpleasant location for either the living or the dead. The executors, conceiving themselves bound by the provisions of the will to erect a vault on the spot marked out, proceeded to do so to the best advantage; but all their endeavors, together with the labors of skillful mechanics, have resulted in the tomb of Washington being universally condemned as unfit for and unworthy of the purpose for which it was intended, while it serves as a matter of reproach

[1] Library of Congress MSS. The contract for six hundred dollars was made with William Yeaton, of Alexandria, who objected to a portion of the design as 'out of all order.' The vestibule, where the bodies of General and Mrs. Washington now are, was built later.

to the crowds of pilgrims who resort thither to pay homage to the fame and memory of the Father of his Country.[1]

The care and thought given so abundantly to General and Mrs. Washington during their lives, Nelly afterward bestowed upon her children. The eldest, Frances, married Edward George Washington Butler, who entered the United States Army as a cadet in 1816, resigned after fifteen years of service, and settled in Louisiana. In 1847, he reëntered the army as a colonel of dragoons and served during the year of the Mexican War. He was of the famous Butler family, being the son of Edward, the youngest of five brothers, all of whom had distinguished Revolutionary War service. Edward and two of these brothers were in the terrible St. Clair defeat and massacre.[2] After removing the wounded General St. Clair from the field, he returned to find his brother Richard desperately wounded by the exultant savages. 'Leave me to my fate,' said Richard, 'and save my brother.'

On hearing the news of this disaster, Washington indulged in one of those few outbursts of justifiable profanity that have endeared him to mankind. But, when the tempest subsided, the still, small voice whispered that St. Clair should have justice; and so it was.

There is a letter written, evidently from Woodlawn, in May, 1827, in which Mrs. Lewis tells her daughter, Mrs. Butler, in Cincinnati, the gossip of the family and advises her in the matter of bringing up her children, as grandmothers might do in those far-off days. The Lewises were planning to go to Philadelphia on the 25th for the wedding

[1] Custis: *Recollections*, p. 439.
[2] November 4, 1791. *The Northwest under Three Flags*, p. 360.

of Lorenzo and Miss Coxe, a daughter of Dr. John Red-
mond Coxe. Miss Coxe was arranging to furnish her own
rooms at Woodlawn, as was the practice of Philadelphia
brides in those days.[1]

There is news in the letter of Boston friends — of Mr.
Nat Emery, who was in financial difficulties; of W. Otis,
a great beau, although the lively Nelly forgets whom he
was then addressing; of Ellen Coolidge, who has made
herself much beloved and respected. Also Nelly was
looking forward to having money and an escort to go to
Cincinnati in June, although Mr. Lewis thought her '*too
old* [forty-six years] to visit so much.'

Five years later in 1832, she writes again to Mrs. Butler,
then in Iberville, Louisiana, of the Clay Convention, attended by '300 young and midle-aged men'; also of the
families at Tudor Place and at Arlington, of the doings of a
host of friends, and especially of Chapman's portraits.
That artist was about 'to shut himself up in Alexandria
and paint the return of Jephtha, with the whole host of
Israel,' and from that art center he was sending his portraits to Boston, Philadelphia, and Baltimore.

The next letter in the group is from Lawrence Lewis to
Major Butler. He has sent his negroes south to be hired
out; he cannot go to Louisiana because of a severe attack
of gout of the stomach; he sends his love to his wife, who
evidently has been visiting the Butlers. Again from
Audley, Lawrence writes in January, 1837: he intends
that Mrs. Conrad in New Orleans shall have the principal
sum paid for the negroes, but he must have part of the

---

[1] In 1833, Thomas Sully painted a portrait of Mrs. Lorenzo Lewis for her
mother, Mrs. Coxe, at a price of sixty dollars.

interest, else he could not live. His income has been reduced to nothing; Lorenzo, who was bound to give him part of the crop at Audley has not made expenses for many years. Woodlawn is worse than nothing, as it eats up the little interest of $420 he receives from debts due him in Clark County. This with the small sum he has in the bank enables him to get along pretty well without being in debt.

Nelly had already divided her negroes among her three children, with her husband's approbation. If we are to take Lawrence literally, he puts the blame on his wife for the financial backsliding of the family.

Angela [he writes] is better acquainted with my affairs than either of my children, as every day some transaction occurred to convince her things were going on badly & could not last long under a course so imprudent as my wife was running. She often, I know, mentioned the subject to her mother, & always under the mildest persuasion, but alas the habit had become a disease without a cure. Angela no doubt has mentioned these things to Conrad, & he therefore declines at this time to accept anything from me.

I shall however take the true course, the one I think best to secure my Childrens interest. My Son, God bless him, is everything to me heart can wish in my present condition of health. It was necessary I should inform him of my intention toward his Sister's & if they did not know the proposal he made it would indear him more than ever to them. He has a generous heart & cares I fear two little for himself.

A little while will bring all things right, his family is increasing & appearances at present indicate an increase of two more which I sincerely hope may not be the case. We have at this time truly a sick house. Lorenzo is unwell with a bad cold, as also is Esther and the three boys.

A letter written by Lawrence Lewis indicates that his

LAWRENCE LEWIS

MRS. LAWRENCE LEWIS

AUDLEY, CLARKE COUNTY, VIRGINIA
The last home of Nelly Custis

wife was in Pass Christian when her daughter, Martha
Eleanor Angela Conrad, died there on September 21, 1839,
in her twenty-seventh year.[1] Only two months later, on
November 20th, Major Lawrence Lewis died at Arlington,
the home of his brother-in-law, George Washington Parke
Custis. A record simply of his death is to be found in the
'Washington Intelligencer,' no circumstances being given.
Being a member of the Washington family, his body was
admitted to a place in the vault, which is now permanently
sealed. Therefore, no tombstone bears record of him.

His latter days were not happy. Tradition in the
Washington family says that Lawrence Lewis thought
that Bushrod Washington should have left Mount Vernon to him instead of to his own nephew; and therefore
the intercourse between Mount Vernon and Woodlawn
became so official that messengers sent from one to the
other were cautioned not to dismount.

Mr. W. H. Snowden, of Andalusia, tells that in 1845,
seven years before Nelly's death, Woodlawn had long been
a scene of desolation.

Only here and there a patch of ground was under cultivation
— not a handful of grass-seed was sown, not a ton of hay cut.
The fields were overgrown with sedge, brambles, sassafras and
cedars, and all traces of fencing had disappeared. Not a white
man was living on an acre of it. Only a few superannuated
slaves remained in some rickety cabins and these were subsisting
on products from a farm in another county. A tax assessment
was thirty dollars — one and one half cents an acre, although

[1] The monument at Mount Vernon bears this inscription: 'Sacred to the
memory of Mrs. M. E. A. Conrad, wife of Charles M. Conrad, of New Orleans,
daughter of Lawrence and Eleanor P. Lewis, and grandniece of Gen. George
Washington. Born April 1, 1813, at Woodlawn, Fairfax County, and died at
Pass Christian, September 21, 1839, in the 27th year of her age. Erected to the
memory of a beloved wife by her husband.'

the buildings had cost near one hundred thousand dollars forty-three years before. It was at this period that a New Jersey colony purchased the property at $12.50 an acre, and subsequently the whole tract was subdivided into small farms and occupied by improving proprietors.[1]

Lorenzo, the only son of the Lewises, born at Woodlawn in 1803, settled on family lands in Clark County. The estate, known as 'Audley,' is on the outskirts of the town of Berryville.[2] Beautiful for situation, amid the rich lands of the Shenandoah Valley, in a neighborhood occupied by descendants of the best families of Virginia, Audley offered a refuge to the tired but still indefatigable widow. So it came about that her heart's desire was realized. In the beauties of nature she found solace. No longer did the sight of Mount Vernon and the surroundings of Woodlawn awaken sad memories. For a time she had her son and her grandchildren for consolation. Seven years before her death, Lorenzo died, leaving six sons, one of whom, Edward Parke Custis (born at Audley, February 7, 1837) served as a colonel in the Confederate Army, was a prisoner of war for fifteen months, was Minister to Portugal under President Cleveland, and died at his home in Hoboken, New Jersey, September 3, 1892.

Nelly Custis died at Audley, July 15, 1852, at the age of seventy-four years, the last thirteen of which she had passed as widow. Even in these days of motors, it is a long journey from Berryville through the mountains to Mount Vernon. The hearse that brought back the body of Nelly

---

[1] *Some Historic Landmarks of Virginia and Maryland.*
[2] Audley is now a prosperous stock farm, owned by Mr. B. B. Jones.

was followed by one carriage in which rode two surviving
grandsons. Late at night Mount Vernon was reached and
her body was placed in the room whence, fifty-three years
before, she had gone forth a bride. Many old friends came
from Alexandria and the neighboring country to bury the
dead, whose life seemed to stretch back into a remote past
almost prehistoric. The body of her husband had long
been reposing in the vault of the Washingtons. Nelly
Custis, the child of Washington's heart, is buried with her
daughter, Eleanor Angela Conrad, outside the tomb. It
is just as well so.

CHAPTER XVI

GEORGE WASHINGTON PARKE CUSTIS
OF ARLINGTON

GOVERNOR SIR WILLIAM BERKELEY, in 1669, granted to Robert Howser six thousand acres of land, for bringing settlers to Virginia. In 1735, John and Gerard Alexander asserted title under the grant made sixty-six years previously, and their title was sustained. On Christmas Day, 1778, Robert and Gerard Alexander sold two tracts on the Potomac to John Parke Custis. The one of these tracts, embracing eleven hundred acres, now known as Arlington, brought eleven thousand pounds Virginia currency. The other tract, which included Abingdon, where Custis made his home, was purchased for twelve pounds per acre, the principal payable at the expiration of twenty-four years with compound interest. This latter bargain came near being the ruin of the Custis estate, because of the fluctuations of currency values occasioned by the Revolution. Dr. David Stuart, who married John Parke Custis's widow, extricated the estate. As the guardian of Washington Custis, Dr. Stuart was permitted to effect a compromise, the Virginia Legislature stipulating by law that no agreement should be legal until approved by General George Washington. In 1796, what are now the Arlington lands were allotted by the Court to the legal representatives of John Parke Custis. Mr. Custis died intestate; and, by the law of primogeniture, the estate descended to his only son, G. W. P. Custis, who

ARLINGTON TO-DAY: FORT MYER IN THE DISTANCE

GEORGE WASHINGTON PARKE CUSTIS

named it 'Arlington,' after the Custis ancestral home in
Northampton County, on the Eastern Shore of Virginia.
There he elected to build his home.[1]

After Mrs. Washington's death, and while his house was
being completed, Custis occupied a small house near the
river. In 1803, he moved into the mansion, where he lived
for more than half a century. In its architecture Mr.
Custis indulged his classical propensities by making the
principal feature a Doric portico, fashioned, as he believed,
after the temple at Pæstum. Happily he thus brought the
structure into harmony with the style adopted by Washington and Jefferson for the Capital City then building.
At that time the Arlington estate was included in the
District of Columbia.[2]

One summer evening in 1902, a small party of men were
enjoying a ride on the Potomac. In the party was Charles
McKim, the architect, who was then restoring the White
House. Pointing to Arlington he said: 'See how that bit
of classic architecture carries over all this wide area.
Those columns are whitewashed — yet what is whitewash
but a form of marble!' So it was that, in planning the
connection between parks of the Potomac, Mr. McKim
made the future Lincoln Memorial and the mansion at
Arlington the termini of the Memorial Bridge, symbol of
the union of North and South as well as the pathway between Lincoln and the soldier dead. Verily in selecting as

[1] *Historic Arlington*, by Karl Decker and Angus McSween; 1892.
[2] In 1846, that portion of the District of Columbia ceded by Virginia to the
United States, comprising about three square miles, was retroceded to the State.
This action was taken with the sanction of Congress and in pursuance of a vote
of the citizens of Alexandria County. There were 763 votes for retrocession to
222 against. Washington Custis voted with the majority. See *The Alexandria
Gazette* for September, 1846.

the model for his dwelling the temple at Pæstum, Mr. Custis builded far wiser than he knew.

The structure having been completed, Mr. Custis made of it a home by installing therein his bride of sixteen years, Mary Lee Fitzhugh, whose father was the owner of Chatham at Falmouth, but who had fled from the temptations of a hospitality too abundant for his means, and had found refuge at the more secluded Ravensworth, near Alexandria.[1]

Arlington House (as Mr. Custis called the mansion) became the repository of a large and most interesting collection of relics of the Washingtons, that were either given to him by his doting grandmother, or that fell to his lot in the final division of the household goods, or that were purchased from less affluent possessors. First and foremost of these treasures was the capacious bed on which the General and Mrs. Washington talked and slept, and on which he died. That bed is now in the room they occupied at Mount Vernon.

The tent that sheltered the General during the Revolution in after years often was pitched on the Arlington lawn for the awed admiration of Washingtonians and old residents of Georgetown, who were ferried across the Potomac to attend annual sheep-shearing festivals held near the famous spring at the foot of the hill near the present Ord and Weitzel Gate.[2] A barbecue was the reward and an oration by Mr. Custis was the penalty of attendance

[1] Ravensworth, now owned by Dr. Bolling Lee, a grandson of General Robert E. Lee, contains much of the Custis and Lee furniture and silverware, and many family portraits.

[2] On June 4, 1812, Mr. Custis sent two pieces of the tent of Washington to the museum of Masonic Lodge, No. 22, at Alexandria, one for that museum and one for the Grand Lodge of Boston. Custis letter; Library of Congress MSS.

— at least, that is the way a not irreverent great-grandson
used to put it. The breeding of merino sheep was Mr.
Custis's hobby, and one of his proud possessions was a
letter from President Madison commending him for his
patriotic services.

As the only son of the family, Washington Custis
inherited the lands owned by his father in Fairfax County,
and by his grandmother in New Kent County. To these
General Washington added twelve hundred acres of the
Mount Vernon estate and his square of land in the City of
Washington; so that Mr. Custis was a very wealthy man
according to the standards of his day. Yet he was usually
hard-pressed for ready cash, as Washington himself often
was. On one occasion he asked the bank to defer payment
of a note of sixty-five dollars; and in 1831, he applied to
the Bank of the United States at Washington for a loan of
twelve thousand dollars in order to finance a trip to France.

It is probably known to you [he writes] that I have been for
many years engaged on a work of no little interest to the American People in particular & to the good & wise of the World in
general: *The Private Memoirs of the Life & Character of Washington.* G'nl La Fayette has kindly promised me all his Revolutionary papers and all his personal Recollections of the venerated
Chief. But the condition of my obtaining these treasures is a
visit to LaGrange. No tongue but that of LaFayette can now
tell the *private memoirs* of gone by days from 1777 to the end of
the War of the Revolution. You will I am sure be aware, my
Dr. Sir, of the importance of my voyage across the Atlantic to
rescue these precious mementoes from accident if not oblivion.
Large possessions in the South do not by any means allways
comprise funded resources, and to accomplish, I may say, the
pious and National object I have in view, I must raise pecuniary
resources by a pledge of valuable real property.[1]

---

[1] Library of Congress MSS.

Mr. Custis's own letters are the best commentary on his character and mode of life. The indolence of youth was never outgrown, nor yet was his confidence in his own abilities and attainments. When, in 1836, General John P. Van Ness [1] and John Boyle were arranging a ball to celebrate Washington's birthday, Mr. Custis offered as a decoration his 'Equestrian Painting of Washington resting on a White Charger & contemplating the cannonade at Trenton at sunset, previous to the ever memorable Battle of Princeton the ensuing day.'

He adds quite naïvely, 'It is the work of a purely self taught artist and the first human figure or horse he ever attempted, and it is the work of the Last male survivor of Washington's Domestic Family.' The picture was seven feet by five.

In a postscript Mr. Custis explains that he was occupied in getting up a little National Interlude, 'The Launch of the Columbia; or Our Blue Jackets Forever,' the scene of which was laid in Washington City, in 'witness of our humble & most grateful acknowledgment of the very great kindness and favour' with which the citizens of Washington had been pleased to receive his 'National Dream of Pocahontas; or The First Settlers of Virginia.' Of Mr. Custis's paintings the only fragment remaining is a decoration of coursing hounds in the hall of Arlington House; his

[1] John Peter Van Ness, Member of Congress from New York in 1800, forfeited his seat by becoming a major of the District of Columbia militia in 1803. He married Marcia, a daughter of David Burns, one of the thirteen original proprietors with whom Washington negotiated for the lands comprised in the Federal City and the one with whom he had most trouble. Marcia was the wealthiest woman in this region, and she became so esteemed for works of philanthropy that a public funeral was accorded to her in 1832. General Van Ness was mayor of Washington. His mansion, on the site of the present Pan-American Building, was a center of lavish hospitality.

dramas and poems have not found a place in anthologies.
And yet the 'Pocahontas' was played in Charleston and
Columbia, South Carolina; Mr. Custis's 'Railroad' ran
seven nights in Baltimore, and upwards of twenty nights
in all.

The former play was criticized as being melodrama, but,
as Mr. Custis truly observes to Carter Lee, 'melodrama
is all the go now, and even in Historical Plays you must
sprinkle show & pageant & things to please the senses as
well as the judgment. . . . The Play is in London in the
hands of Washington Irvin[g] & J. Howard Payne, who will
under their able auspices bring it out on the London Stage.
If successful there, why, I may be considered here as something of a Dramatist.' [1]

But if his fame as artist and dramatist was destined not
to survive, his 'Recollections' will keep his memory green
forever. In a letter to Mr. Donoho, of the 'Intelligencer,'
written in April, 1851, he truly remarks that his handwriting, unlike good wine, does not improve with age.
The impending Civil War weighed upon him. 'Surely,' he
writes, 'in these perplexing times,

> When civil dudgeon runs so high,
> And men fall out they know not why,

a reminiscence of the glorious and happy past and of *the
brave old days of '76* should come "freshly o're all our
senses."'

The most interesting event that ever took place at
Arlington House, during the Custis incumbency, was the
marriage, on June 30, 1831, of Mary Custis, the only

[1] Library of Congress MSS.

daughter of the House of Custis, to Lieutenant Robert Edward Lee, of the United States Army, Corps of Engineers, which was solemnized in the room on the westerly side of the mansion. From Ravensworth, Lieutenant Lee wrote to his superior officer, Captain Talcott, at Fortress Monroe: [1]

So, Captain, you would not come up to Arlington on that memorable Thursday. . . . However, you would have seen nothing strange, for there was neither fainting nor fighting, nor anything uncommon which could be twisted into an adventure. The Parson had a few words to say, though he dwelt upon them as if he had been reading my Death warrant, and there was a tremulousness in the hand I held that made me anxious for him to end. I am told I looked 'pale & interesting,' which might have been the fact. But I felt as 'bold as a sheep' & was surprised at my want of Romance in so great a degree as not to feel more excitement than at the Black Board at West Point.

The party kept together till the following Tuesday, when most of them departed, particularly the Gentlemen. Some of the Ladies remained the rest of the week, and we were then left alone. I would tell you how the time passed, but fear I am too much prejudiced to say anything more, but that it went *very* rapidly & still continues to do so.

Lieutenant Lee was a member of a family that had been prominent in Virginia affairs ever since Richard Lee came to America as secretary of the Colony and member of the King's Council before 'the usurpation of Oliver Cromwell,' to use a phrase common among Virginians of Cavalier stock. The seat of the family was Stratford on the Potomac, in Westmoreland County, about seven miles below the ancestral estate of the Washingtons. The second Richard Lee, who died in 1690, was a Hebrew and Greek

[1] Letter of July 13, 1831; Library of Congress MSS.

scholar as well as a King's Councillor. His fifth son Henry had a third son Henry, who had a first son Henry, born January 29, 1756.

The latter Henry graduated at Princeton in 1774, and two years later Governor Patrick Henry appointed him a captain of the cavalry raised for the Continental service. 'Light Horse Harry' Lee served during the Revolution with high distinction under Washington's direct control. In 1782, he married a daughter of Philip Ludwell Lee, of Stratford, the ancestral home, and there he lived with his father-in-law when he was not serving in Congress or as Governor of Virginia. In the funeral oration on Washington, written by him but delivered by John Marshall, occurs the famous phrase 'first in war, first in peace and first in the hearts of his countrymen.'

Henry Lee was fifty-one years old when his third son, Robert, was born at Stratford, January 19, 1807. With Robert Morris he had been carried away by the mania for land speculations, and had become so seriously involved that he found refuge in the West Indies. Moreover, he had been wounded in a political riot in Baltimore, and his injuries shortened his life. In 1811, on his way home to join his family, he was overtaken by death on the South Carolina estate of his companion in arms, General Greene; and there his body remained until 1913, when it was removed to Lexington, Virginia, where the Lees have found honored sepulture. Meantime the family had removed to Alexandria for the sake of better schools. Carter Lee, the first child, was then at Harvard; the second, Sidney Smith Lee was in the Navy. The youngest boy, Robert, was the steady, reliable, devoted son of an invalid mother. At the age of eighteen he entered West Point, graduating second in a class of forty-six. He was stationed at Fortress Monroe at the time of his marriage to the playmate of his youth, Mary Ann Randolph Custis, the only child of George Washington Parke Custis.

During the quarter of a century between the marriage of Mary Custis Lee and the death of her father, seven children were born. The first was George Washington Custis Lee, who graduated first in his class at West Point, was aide to President Jefferson Davis during the Civil War, and afterward a professor in the Virginia Military Academy. He succeeded his father as President of Washington and Lee University.

Next came Mary Custis Lee; third, William Henry Fitzhugh Lee, a graduate of Harvard, a major-general in the Confederate Army, and a Member of Congress; fourth, Agnes; fifth, Captain Robert Edward Lee, Jr., C.S.A.; then Mildred Lee and Anne Carter Lee.

Only two of all these years (1833–34) were spent in Washington. In 1852–55, Colonel Lee was Superintendent at West Point, a reward probably for his distinguished service in the Mexican War in 1847.

Mrs. Custis died in 1853, at the age of sixty-five years; and four years later, on October 10, 1857, her husband followed her. Both are buried at Arlington, in the midst of the graves of the defenders of the Union. The modest monuments, erected by their daughter, have been made inconspicuous by Time's mantle; and no garish granite erection disturbs the quiet of their particular location. The serried ranks of small, moss-covered headstones of the private soldiers keep them company, and overhead are the trees they loved.

LIEUT. ROBERT E. LEE, U.S.A.

MARY CUSTIS LEE

THE GRAVES OF MR. AND MRS. GEORGE WASHINGTON PARKE CUSTIS IN THE ARLINGTON NATIONAL CEMETERY

With the death of George Washington Parke Custis, the last human link with the Father of his Country ('Pater Patriæ,' as Mr. Custis was fond of calling him) was broken. And so he was mourned throughout the land, because of the sentiment that accorded to him in death, if not in life, the affectionate regard due to the Child of Mount Vernon.

Colonel Lee obtained leave to repair to Arlington to settle the Custis estate; and, during his brief stay, he brought order out of chaotic conditions, and developed, if not a taste for farming, at least an aptitude for it. Again, he was at Arlington when the John Brown raid occurred at Harper's Ferry. He was sent with a force to quell the disturbance. This he did; and, having turned his prisoners over to the civil authorities, he returned to Texas, where he remained until 1861, when that State seceded from the Union, and he was ordered to Washington. In the estimation of General Winfield Scott, Lee was the ablest officer in the Army.

Every effort was made to keep Colonel Lee from going with his State. His own judgment and opinions were hostile to secession and to slavery; but, after a long struggle, he found that he simply could not bring himself to go counter to his native State. He felt, as his father had felt before him, that his first allegiance was to the Commonwealth of Virginia.[1]

Mr. Custis bequeathed the Arlington House estate of three hundred acres, together with the mill on Four Mile

[1] It so happened that the period for the manumission of the Arlington estate slaves, as provided for in the will of Mr. Custis, ended in 1863, in the midst of the Civil War. The slaves within the Confederate lines General Lee called together, and gave them freedom, with promise of safe-conduct for those who desired to go North. No one doubts the entire good faith of this transaction.

Run, to Mrs. Lee, and at her death to the eldest grandson, George Washington Custis Lee. The Custis family plate might be divided; but all of the Mount Vernon plate, and every article he possessed that related to Washington and came from Mount Vernon, was to descend entire and unchanged to his latest posterity. It has been assumed, both in and out of Congress, that Arlington contained Lee family possessions; but, as a matter of fact, the Lee belongings were at Ravensworth. Arlington was a Custis seat, and was furnished largely from Mount Vernon.

On April 22, 1861, Colonel and Mrs. Lee left Arlington for Richmond, where he immediately entered the military service, first of Virginia and afterward of the Confederacy. With them the family took only their most valued possessions. The family letters of Washington were buried; and, when exhumed, they were found to be in such bad condition that Mrs. Lee burned them.[1]

By Mr. Custis's will, the estate called 'White House,' containing four thousand acres of land, went to the second grandson, W. H. F. Lee. To the third grandson, Robert E. Lee, Jr., he left the King William County estate, called 'Romancock,' containing another four thousand acres. Both were living on their estates when the Civil War came. About the end of the war White House, where George Washington and Martha Custis were married, was burned, and it has not been rebuilt.

To each of his granddaughters Mr. Custis gave ten thousand dollars; and, as a result, their father, as executor, was pressed for ready money to pay the expenses of the estate, although the payment was to come from the sale of

[1] Mrs. R. E. Lee's letter; Library of Congress MSS.

lands in Stafford, Richmond, and Westmoreland Counties and of Smith's Island, a remainder of the original Custis properties on the Eastern Shore.

In the early hours of May 24, 1861, three detachments of Federal troops invaded the sacred soil of Virginia. Colonel Ellsworth at the head of his Zouaves, went by boat to Alexandria. There the young officer was killed by the inn-keeper as he was descending the stairs of the Marshall House, with the Confederate flag that he had hauled down. His command reported to Colonel Orlando B. Wilcox, of the First Michigan Infantry, who had marched by land. A force under Colonel Heintzelman occupied Arlington.[1]

After Bull Run, McDowell's army entrenched itself on Arlington Heights; the mansion was occupied by officers; soldiers were encamped on the open spaces; hospitals were established and two strong forts were built for the defense of the Capital. Of the two, Fort Whipple, on the grounds of the present Fort Myer, has disappeared, but Fort McPherson still presents its grass-grown ramparts to the visitor.

After the battles of the Wilderness, Quartermaster General M. C. Meigs ordered burial at Arlington for all soldiers dying in the military hospitals in and about Washington. The official records of such burials begin with May 13, 1864. Afterward the bodies of the soldier dead buried between the Potomac and the Rappahannock were removed to Arlington, bringing the total of Civil War burials to sixteen thousand.

General Lee died in 1870. Four years before his death,

[1] Library of Congress MSS.

on January 27, 1866, he wrote to Senator Reverdy Johnson:

I have been awaiting the action of President Johnson upon my application to be embraced in his proclamation of 29 May, and for my restoration to civil rights, before attempting to close the estate of Mr. G. W. P. Custis, of which I am sole administrator. His servants were all liberated agreeably to the terms of his will, but I have been unable to place his grandchildren in possession of the property bequeathed them. A portion of his landed property has been sold by the Government, in the belief, I presume, that it belonged to me, whereas I owned no part of it, nor had any charge than as administrator. His will, in his own handwriting, is on file in the Court of Alexandria Co. Arlington, and the tract on 'four mile run' given him by Genl. Washington, he left to his only child, Mrs. Lee, during her life; and at her death, to his eldest grandson. Both of these tracts have been sold by the Government. It has also sold Smith's Island (off Cape Charles), which Mr. Custis directed to be sold to aid in paying certain legacies to his granddaughters.

If in your opinion there is anything that can be done to enable me to bestow the property as bequeathed by the testator, and to close my administration of his estate, I would be greatly obliged to you to inform me.

Again, on July 7, 1866, General Lee wrote to Senator Reverdy Johnson:

I had hoped when passion had subsided and reason resumed her sway, that the people of the country would prefer, from former associations, seeing Arlington in possession of Mr. Custis' descendants than appropriated to its present use. But that day seems to me now as distant as at the beginning, and I may never see it.[1]

Arlington was held by confiscation until January 11, 1864, when the Government bid it in for unpaid taxes, at a cost of $26,800. Mrs. Robert E. Lee died in 1873, and four years later her son successfully upset the Govern-

[1] Reverdy Johnson MSS. in the Library of Congress.

ment title under the tax sale, only to be barred by the Supreme Court.[1] Then by the Act of March 31, 1883, Congress appropriated $150,000 to purchase the property from Mr. Lee, and the transaction was completed.

From the close of the Civil War to this day, Arlington House has remained a deserted mansion, visited by thousands of pilgrims who have enjoyed the view off over the Potomac to the City of Washington. The room in which the marriage of Lieutenant Lee and Miss Custis took place is occupied by the Superintendent; the great parlors are filled only with emptiness, save for a useless and inappropriate marble case containing a list of Spanish War dead. In the spacious hall two large ungainly tablets of bronze, placed during the second Cleveland administration, tell in official language the history of Arlington.

Congress has decreed that Arlington House shall be restored as a Custis and Lee mansion, but has made no appropriations for the purpose. It is quite proper to recreate there a typical home, representing the first half-century of the Republic, the best period of American architecture, and plans have been made to carry out this idea in an adequate manner. As a Lee shrine Arlington can never detract from the Washington and Lee University,[2] where General and Mrs. Lee spent the peaceful

---

[1] United States *v.* Lee, Supreme Court Reports, vol. 106, p. 196, October, 1882. The Court held that if the United States was satisfied that its title to the Arlington estate was invalid, it might purchase the property by fair negotiation, or condemn it by a judicial proceeding, in which a just compensation shall be ascertained and paid according to the Constitution.

[2] In 1796, Washington gave to Liberty Hall Academy, near Lexington, Virginia, the shares of stock in the James River Canal voted to him by the legislature of Virginia in 1785, and thereafter held in trust by him, awaiting some public use to which he might devote the gift. The name of the institution was then changed to Washington Academy, and later it became Washington and Lee University.

years of their later life, and where they have found honored graves among their kindred.

The restoration of Arlington House has been facilitated by the erection of the elaborate Arlington Memorial Amphitheater, with ample provision for offices. Through its white marble arches one looks out upon serried lines of stately cedars, under the bluest of skies. In front of the building, on the terrace overlooking the Potomac, reposes the Unknown Soldier of the World War, while near by sleep tens of thousands of his companions in arms. Every man and every woman who has worn the uniform of the United States may here find a last resting-place; and so quickly are large areas coming into occupation that plans have been made to extend the cemetery to the Potomac, by taking back the present experimental gardens of the Department of Agriculture. In no long time the silent population of Arlington may come to equal the numbers of the Capital itself. The possibilities run into millions; and the desirability of this place of burial is daily becoming more manifest.

CHAPTER XVII

THE VICISSITUDES OF MOUNT VERNON

WHEN George Washington entered military service in the French and Indian War, he intimated to his brother, John Augustine, that, if he should fall therein, the Mount Vernon estate should become the property of that brother. That ancient intimation colored all of Washington's thoughts as to the final disposition of his property; and so far from feeling constrained by an implied promise, events strengthened him in adhering to it.

Not only were these two brothers held together by the strongest ties of friendship, but also John Augustine's eldest son, Bushrod, was the one on whom Washington could depend confidently to carry on the high traditions of public service he himself had established. He knew Bushrod well. He had commended him to James Wilson, of Philadelphia, as a student in law, and in a remarkable letter had furnished to the young man a compass by which to steer his course through life. He had made Bushrod a companion in western travel; he had watched the young lawyer's slow legal progress in Westmoreland County and Alexandria to a successful practice in Richmond; and had been gratified when President John Adams appointed him a Justice of the Supreme Court, although he himself had scrupulously avoided any suggestion of such action. Bushrod was thirty-six years old when he succeeded his preceptor, James Wilson, on the bench, where he served for thirty-one years.

To Bushrod, therefore, was bequeathed the Mount Vernon mansion house, together with four thousand acres, including the original twenty-five hundred acres that had been granted to John the immigrant. With these went the books and papers, public and private. Justice Washington's court duties kept him much away from home, and he had an invalid wife, to whom he was devotedly attached and who always accompanied him on his travels.

Anne (Blackburn) Washington, the daughter of Colonel Thomas Blackburn, an officer on General Washington's staff, early received so great a shock by reason of the tragic death of her sister that she never took an active part in social affairs. An occasional dinner to members of the Supreme Court was the limit of her entertaining.

All these circumstances combined to break up the customs of hospitality long established at Mount Vernon; and, furthermore, the new owner was no farmer and he had endless trouble with his slaves.[1]

George Washington by will gave freedom to his slaves after Mrs. Washington's death, this postponement of emancipation being ordered in consequence of their intermarriage with the dower slaves of Mrs. Washington's first marriage, who were not at his disposal. A very few years after the General's death, Judge Washington came into court one morning to announce that he was compelled to proceed to Mount Vernon. He and Chief Justice Marshall had been summoned by Mrs. Washington, in consequence of an attempt to set fire to the mansion. The slaves were implicated in the transaction. For twenty years, Justice Washington testifies, he struggled to pay the expenses of

[1] Bushrod Washington was born in Westmoreland County in 1762. He graduated at William and Mary College, was appointed to the Supreme Court, December 20, 1798, and died in Philadelphia, November 26, 1829. His wife died two days later.

his farm and to afford, for those who cultivated it, a comfortable support from the produce of their labor; but his annual loss was from five hundred to one thousand dollars, which amounts were paid from his other resources.

The insubordination of my negroes [he continued], and their total disregard of all authority, rendered them more than useless to me. . . . But if it should be asked . . . why this temper was more observable at Mount Vernon than upon other plantations in the neighborhood, I answer that that place has at times been visited by some unworthy persons who have condescended to hold conversations with my negroes and to impress upon their minds the belief that, as the nephew of General Washington, or as the President of the Colonization Society, or for other reasons, I could not hold them in bondage, and particularly that they would be free *at my death.* . . . I called the negroes together in March last, and, after stating to them what I had heard, and that they had been deceived by those who had neither their or my good in view, I assured them most solemnly that I had no intention to give freedom to any of them, and that nothing but a voluntary act of mine could make them so. That the disappointment caused by this declaration should lead to the consequences which followed . . . was to be expected.[1]

The only alternative he saw was the sale of his negroes. Emancipation without deportation he could not think of. He was already contributing to the support of the most promising of his servants, whom he had liberated and sent to Liberia; for he believed thoroughly in the work of the Colonization Society, whose first president he was.[2]

---

[1] Letter of Bushrod Washington to *Niles' Register*, 1821, quoted by Lawrence Washington, *Westmoreland County, Virginia*, compiled by T. R. B. Wright; 1912. (See also *Niles' Register*, September 29, 1821, vol. 21, p. 71.)

[2] George Washington's slaves were given freedom in accordance with his will, and some were regularly supported from the estate for more than a quarter of a century. The originals of the accounts of Bushrod Washington and Lawrence Lewis, executors, are at the United States Naval Academy; photostats are in the Library of Congress.

Horace Binney, who knew Justice Washington both in court and in private life, describes him as kind and good-humored in general society, but not above the common level of educated men. His reading, except in the law, and in novels (of which he became a most voluminous *viva voce* reader, for the amusement of his valetudinary wife), did not appear extensive. His taste, particularly in music, of which he was passionately fond and of which he thought himself a judge, was rather unrefined. Like his great uncle, he was fond of the society of ladies; he liked to have things flow smoothly rather than to have a keen relish, and he 'had a more decided inclination to the disengaged talk of a club supper-table, and the circulation of a temperate glass, than to anything else on the round earth.' He used half-Scotch snuff.

On the bench he was another man.

Without the least apparent effort, he made everybody see at first sight that he was equal to all the duties of the place, ceremonial as well as intellectual. His mind was full, his elocution free, clear and accurate, his command of all about him indisputable. His learning and acuteness were not only equal to the profoundest argument, but often carried the Counsel to depths which they had not penetrated; and he was as cool, self-possessed and efficient at a moment of high excitement at the Bar, or in the people, as if the nerves of fear had been taken out of his brain by the roots.

He came to the bench from a practice chiefly in chancery and was thoroughly grounded in the common law, but was unfamiliar with commercial law, or with jury trials.

Nevertheless, it was in these two departments or provinces, commercial law and Nisi Prius practice and administration [says Horace Binney], that he was eminent from the outset and in a

JUSTICE BUSHROD WASHINGTON, TO WHOM MOUNT VERNON
WAS BEQUEATHED

THE LAST PRIVATE OWNERS OF MOUNT VERNON

Mrs. John Augustine Washington; her daughter, Mrs. Alexander (*left*); her
son, Richard Blackburn Washington; her nephew, Noblet Herbert; her son,
John Augustine Washington (*right*)
Painted by Chapman on the porch at Mount Vernon

short time became as accomplished a Nisi Prius Judge as ever lived. I have never seen a judge who in this speciality equalled him. I cannot imagine a better. Judging of Lord Mansfield's great powers at Nisi Prius by the accounts which have been transmitted to us, I do not believe that even he surpassed Judge Washington.

As the clock struck ten, he was always found on the bench, ready to begin the day's work. During his latter years he adjourned court exactly at three. On one occasion Mr. Binney was in the middle of a sentence when the clock struck. The Judge said, with a smile, as he arose from his chair, 'Mr. Binney, I will hear the rest of that sentence to-morrow morning.' As the two walked away from court, the Judge explained:

The sound of that clock is as distinctly heard by Mrs. Washington at our lodgings as it is heard by us in the court-room; and if I am not in her parlor within five minutes afterwards, she imagines some evil has happened to me, and her nerves are disordered for the rest of the day. . . . I give the whole of the evening to reading aloud to her such books as will amuse and interest her, until drowsiness comes on. I look at neither book nor paper in the cause until the next morning, and then, by early hours, I endeavor to redeem the time.

When his death occurred, in Philadelphia, it broke her down; and, although she attempted to get home when his remains were attended to Mount Vernon, she died upon the road.[1]

When Bushrod Washington came to make his will, some five months before his death, he divided his four thousand acres among his kindred. To John Augustine Washington, the son of his brother Corbin, he devised the mansion house of Mount Vernon and the lands between Gum

[1] *Bushrod Washington;* an address by Horace Binney; Philadelphia, 1858.

Spring and the ferry. To the sons of Mrs. Mary Lee Herbert (his deceased sister), Bushrod W. Herbert and Noblet Herbert, he gave a second portion. A third portion he gave in trust for Bushrod Washington, Jr.; and the remainder he bestowed upon George Corbin and Bushrod Corbin Washington.

John Augustine Washington, son of Justice Bushrod Washington's brother Corbin, was thirty-seven years old when he inherited Mount Vernon. He was born at Walnut Grove, Westmoreland County, in 1792; and, after the death of his father, Corbin Washington, he and his brothers, Richard Henry Lee Washington and Bushrod Corbin Washington, made their home at Mount Vernon with their uncle and guardian.

At the age of twenty-two years, John Augustine Washington married Jane, the daughter of Richard Scott Blackburn, U.S.A., and the family home was at Blakely, Jefferson County. Of their four children the first two died in youth, leaving John Augustine the younger and Richard Blackburn.

After an occupancy of less than three years, John Augustine died on June 16, 1832, leaving Mount Vernon to his wife, who might give it to one of the boys, or sell it to Virginia or the Nation. For twenty-five years she was the mistress of Mount Vernon. When she died at Blakely on September 6, 1855, in her seventieth year, her body was the last to be placed in the tomb of the Washingtons.

The features of Washington were seen for the last time October 7, 1837, when the remains of George and Martha

Washington were placed in two solid marble coffins, given
by John Struthers, a Philadelphia stone-cutter, whose
generosity Lawrence Lewis rewarded by allowing him to
place thereon the record of his gift. The vault had been en-
larged by building a chamber large enough to permit the
coffins to be placed in dry air, the dampness of the inner
tomb having thrice destroyed the wooden cases enclosing
the lead coffins. On making the change, the lid of the lead
coffin containing the remains of the General was found to
be broken. 'At the request of Major Lewis, the fractured
part of the lid was turned over the lower part, exposing to
view a head and breast of large dimensions, which appeared, by the dim light of the candles, to have suffered
but little from the effects of time. The eye-sockets were
large and deep, and the breadth across the temples, together with the forehead, appeared of unusual size.' [1] The
leaden lid was replaced, and the body, raised by six men,
was carried and laid in the marble coffin, the cover of
which was set in cement. The body of Mrs. Washington
was similarly treated; only Mrs. Washington's sarcophagus
is plain, while that of the General has an emblem carved
upon the lid. Major Lewis and his son Lorenzo, Mrs. Jane
Washington and her son John Augustine, and George
Washington Parke Custis, were present.

John Augustine Washington was ten years old when the
family took up their residence at Mount Vernon, and he
was thirty-two when his mother placed him in possession of
the estate. He married Eleanor Love, the daughter of
Wilson Cary Selden; and between 1844 and 1858 five

[1] Account of James Strickland, quoted in Lossing's *Mount Vernon and its Associations*, p. 341.

daughters and two sons were born to them, all at Mount Vernon. Of the five daughters, three were living in 1925.[1]

In 1846, Vice-President Dallas, the President of the Senate, the Speaker of the House, Senators, Representatives, the Secretaries of State, of War, of the Navy, of the Treasury, the mayors of Washington and Georgetown, and private citizens, submitted to Congress a memorial, asking the Government to purchase Mount Vernon. The memorial was accompanied by a statement to the effect that for nearly half a century the descendants of Washington had guarded and watched over his remains, and had gratuitously entertained all who visited the tomb of the Father of his Country. The average number of visitors was ten thousand annually, in spite of bad roads and lack of near-by places of entertainment. 'At first sight,' says the memorial, 'the sum of one hundred thousand dollars, the price asked by the owner, Mrs. Jane C. Washington, for one hundred and fifty acres of poor land, having nothing of visible importance upon them saving a group of ancient and dilapidated buildings, with an old and untenanted tomb rapidly crumbling into dust, and a plainly

[1] The children of John Augustine and Eleanor Love Washington were: Louisa Fontaine, born 1844, married Colonel R. P. Chew, and lives in Charles Town, West Virginia; Jane Charlotte, born 1846, married Nathaniel H. Willis, Rock Hall, Jefferson County, West Virginia, and died in 1924; Eliza Selden, married Major Robert W. Hunter, of Winchester, Virginia, and died in Charles Town, West Virginia, in 1909; Anna Maria, born 1851, married the Right Reverend Beverley Dandridge Tucker, Bishop of Southern Virginia, and lives in Norfolk, Virginia (they are the parents of thirteen children); Lawrence, born 1854, married Fannie, daughter of Thomas Lackland, and died in Washington in 1920, leaving twelve children; Eleanor Selden, born 1856, married Julian Howard, of Richmond County, Virginia, and lives in Washington; and George, married Emily Serena Davenport, and died in Charles Town, West Virginia, in 1905, leaving one son.

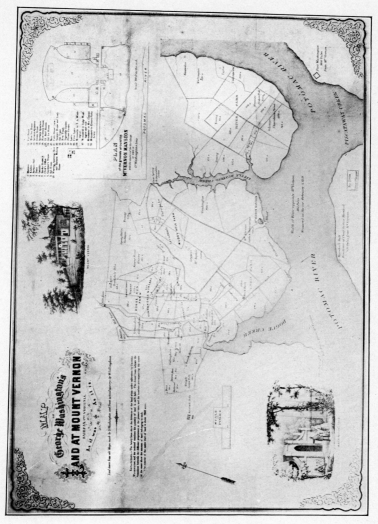

MAP OF THE MOUNT VERNON ESTATE, 1850

BIRD'S-EYE VIEW OF MOUNT VERNON IN 1852

MOUNT VERNON MANSION AT THE TIME OF THE SALE TO THE
LADIES' ASSOCIATION

constructed new tomb, may appear an *exorbitant* price';
but the memorialists pointed to the fact that, unless the
Government made the purchase, the estate might fall into
the hands perhaps of 'the agent of some Turk or other
foreigner, who would then have the power to exact *tribute*,
or levy a *tax* in the shape of admission *fees* on all persons
visiting those consecrated grounds.'

The contingency, however, moved Congress not at all,
probably for the excellent reason that the signers did not
bestir themselves to carry out their own vehemently expressed desires.[1]

The tolling of the ship's bell as the steamer was passing
Mount Vernon one night in 1853 started sympathetic
throbs in the heart of one of the passengers, Mrs. Cunningham, of South Carolina. The sad conditions prevailing at
the estate were matters of common knowledge; but how
to bring about a change was not so apparent. Both the
United States and the State of Virginia had refused to be
interested. In the National Capital work on the Washington Monument had stopped;[2] the half-finished monument
to Mary Washington at Fredericksburg was interesting
only to relic-hunters; the shadow of civil war hung over the
country. To Mrs. Cunningham only one resource was left:
'Let the women of America own and preserve Mount
Vernon,' she wrote to her daughter, Miss Ann Pamela
Cunningham.

[1] Sen. Misc. Doc. 82, 30th Cong., 1st Sess.
[2] The Washington Monument was begun in 1848, by an association that depended on gifts and subscriptions. Work was pursued intermittently for a few
years, and then stopped entirely; and for twenty years a melancholy stump of a
monument stood as a memorial of national inertia. In 1876, Congress, fired by a
patriotic Fourth-of-July outburst by Senator John Sherman, voted to complete
the monument, a task accomplished in 1884.

Into the troubled waters plunged Miss Cunningham, a helpless invalid in body but a determined spirit. She organized The Mount Vernon Ladies' Association, and began work quite anonymously, under the pseudonym of 'The Southern Matron.' For seven years she buffeted the storms. The purchase was begun as a Southern enterprise, but the North insisted on sharing. There were encouragements and rebuffs. Contribution boxes in Independence Hall were fast being filled when, in 1858, the substantial citizens refused to support women who were mixing in public affairs.

One happy day in 1856, the orator, Edward Everett, succumbed to the eloquence of Miss Cunningham, who so won him over to her cause that thenceforth he devoted to the Mount Vernon fund the proceeds of his eulogy of Washington, thus raising $69,064 of the $200,000 needed for the purchase. The greatest obstacle, time only excepted, with which Miss Cunningham had to deal was the owner of Mount Vernon, John A. Washington, who objected to the charter granted by Virginia. So long a journey by rail being too fatiguing, 'The Southern Matron' went from her home by canal-boat as far as Baltimore, from whence the railroad ride would be short. Arriving at Mount Vernon on a hot June day, she was carried in a chair up to the mansion. She put forth all those powers of persuasion that had won Edward Everett; but in vain. Fortunately she missed the mail-boat, which she had hoped to take at Mount Vernon in returning. That night and the next morning she renewed the attack. He would not yield. He believed that the Ladies' Association and Virginia had conspired to put an indignity upon him. 'His feelings were wounded, goaded,' writes Miss Cunningham, 'and lo! in explaining *my* feelings I had shown him *his* error.' She made him see that he must let the Association pay the money, and must not feel that his State or himself were lowered by the act. 'I held out my hand,' she continues, 'he put his in mine; then with quivering lips, moist eyes, and a heart too full to speak, our compact was closed in silence. . . . None but God can know the mental labor and physical sufferings Mount Vernon has cost me.'

Meantime public interest had died out. On July 4, 1857, Miss Cunningham, from her air-bed, blew a blast in Charleston that awoke echoes through the land. Then came the memorable financial panic of that year. Edward Everett again came to the rescue. At Richmond the charter was defeated: if Virginia paid Mr. Washington, what assurance had the State that the price would ever be refunded? But Mr. Washington's heart had been reached. The noble, gallant struggle had won him over; he would wait. Reaction came at Richmond, also, and on March 19, 1858, the act was passed. The purchase was completed on February 22, 1859. In the appeal for funds for restoration 'The Southern Matron' disappeared, and Miss Cunningham signed the paper with her baptismal name. From 1859 to 1861 she perfected the organization of the board of control, consisting of the Regent, and Vice-Regents representing all the States of the Union.[1]

Then the Civil War came, and for four years Mount Vernon had a care-taker. Both Confederates and Federals

[1] *Historical Sketch of Ann Pamela Cunningham, ' The Southern Matron.'* 1911.

respected the tomb of Washington. Meanwhile Miss Cunningham was managing, still from a sick-bed, a South Carolina plantation. Her mother was a partisan, her brothers were in the Southern army, her heart was in Mount Vernon. How she won from the Government seven thousand dollars, to pay for the seized Mount Vernon steamer, on which the support of the estate depended; how she found an ally in Senator Charles Sumner; how she failed in one Congress and succeeded in the next — this story belongs among the tragedies and triumphs of persevering womanhood with which the National Capital is replete.

Meantime John Augustine Washington with his family retired to a new home near Warrenton; he entered the Confederate army, and was on General Lee's staff when, on September 13, 1861, he was killed at Cheat Mountain. So ends the tale of the tenth owner of the Mount Vernon estate, representing six generations of the family, and covering a period of exactly two centuries of ownership since the coming of John the immigrant in 1658.[1]

[1] The succession of Mount Vernon in the Washington family is: John (1658, about, to 1667); Lawrence (1667–1697); Mildred and Augustine (1697–1743); Lawrence (1743–1752); George (1752–1799); Bushrod (1799, subject to life-interest of Martha, to 1829); John Augustine (1829–1832); Jane C. (who was at liberty to sell to the United States or to give to one of her children, and who held from the death of her husband in 1832 until her deed of gift to her son, September 18, 1849); John Augustine (1849–1860). Jane Washington died in 1855, and her remains were the last to be placed in the vault.

The Regents of The Mount Vernon Ladies' Association of the Union incorporated under the laws of Virginia, hold the legal title to the property. In case of the dissolution of the Association, the property goes to the State of Virginia. Congress has no authority in the premises and can have none, excepting with the consent of Virginia. Therefore, the movements (that start when some organization objects to paying the twenty-five cents admission fee, or when some one has the theory that the grounds should be opened on Sunday) to have the Govern-

From time to time spasmodic attempts are made to dis-
possess the women of America from the ownership and
management of Mount Vernon and to make it Government property; but the ownership is so well entrenched
both in law and in public approval that all such attempts
must prove abortive. Year by year the devoted and con-
servative Regents are bringing the mansion and grounds
into conditions that prevailed during their best days. No
one who cherishes the memory of Washington can desire a
change from a form of management nation-wide in scope,
well advised in all restorations, and ever actuated by the
purest motives of patriotism and reverence.

ment purchase Mount Vernon and reduce it to the level of the Arlington Mansion
and Wakefield (both owned by the Government) must prove abortive.

Miss Cunningham was the Regent from 1853 to 1873, when she resigned. She
was succeeded by Mme. Lily L. Macalester Berghmans, of Pennsylvania, who in
1876 became Mrs. Lily L. Macalester Laughton, and continued as Regent until
her death in 1891. The third Regent was Mrs. Justine Van Rensselaer Townsend, of New York (1891–1909); and the fourth, Miss Harriet Clayton Comegys,
of Delaware (1909–   ) who is the present Regent.

Miss Cunningham died May 1, 1875, at Laurens, South Carolina, and was
buried at Columbia, South Carolina. Since her retirement there have been two
superintendents: Colonel J. M. Hollingsworth (1872–1885); and, since the latter
date, Harrison H. Dodge, who happens to be a descendant of Admiral Vernon's
brother, and who, in his presence and personality, embodies the spirit of gracious
hospitality characteristic of the halcyon days of Mount Vernon.

CHAPTER XVIII

AN AUTOBIOGRAPHIC WILL

DURING the long July days of the last year of his life George Washington made up his final accounts with this world. As a boy he had learned the two cardinal principles of a valid will — no contingencies, no remainders. His trained mind saw clearly and his trained hand recorded distinctly. He was in no haste.

One can see him as he sits at his writing-table in the library at Mount Vernon, well-tied bundles of papers at hand, methodically putting down each parcel of land (whether in Virginia, Maryland, Kentucky, New York, Pennsylvania, or the Ohio Country) and recording his equities therein, preparatory to final disposition. From time to time he looks up from his long task to gaze out of the wide windows, across the grassy slopes, to the broad Potomac flowing leisurely to the sea.

His memoranda ready, he begins to write:

In the name of God, Amen.

There has been discussion as to Washington's religious beliefs, and as to whether he partook of the communion. Born within the pale of the visible church, he was dedicated to God in baptism. Like every great mind called upon continuously to bear grave responsibilities, he believed in God the maker and ruler of the universe. Throughout his entire career he lived an active Christian life, according to the standards laid down by Christ him-

THE NATIONAL SHRINE: THE TOMB OF WASHINGTON AT MOUNT VERNON

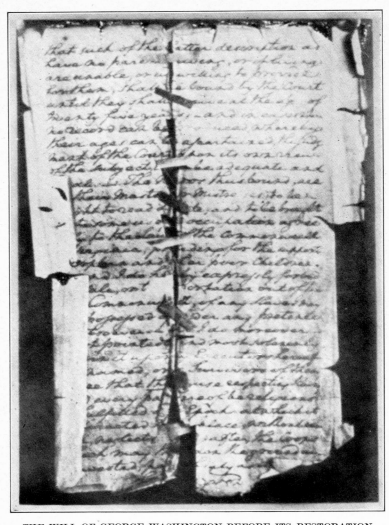

THE WILL OF GEORGE WASHINGTON BEFORE ITS RESTORATION
IN 1910

self. Probably he was as charitably disposed toward the
theology of his day as he certainly was toward the lax conduct of its exponents.

He found Robert Morris in prison and he came unto
him. He gave Lund Washington to understand that no
needy person, though a stranger, should be turned from the
doors of Mount Vernon. He inculcated in his foster-son
the virtue of giving. He clothed and provided for the
widow who claimed to be a relative, although he had never
seen her. Every page of his will records forgiveness of both
debts and trespasses.

I, George Washington of Mount Vernon, a citizen of the
United States, and lately President of the same.

This phrase is to be interpreted in connection with the
reasons he gives for making a gift to establish a national
university at the seat of government.

It has always been a source of serious regret with me [he
writes] to see the youth of these United States sent to foreign
countries for the purpose of Education, often before their minds
were formed, or they had imbibed any adequate ideas of the happiness of their own. . . . It has been my ardent wish to see a plan
devised on a liberal scale, which would have a tendency to spread
systematic ideas through all parts of this rising Empire, thereby
to do away local attachments and State prejudices, as far as the
nature of things would or indeed ought to admit, from our National Councils.

He therefore created a fund to establish a university,
'wherein the youth of the land might acquire knowledge in
the principles of politics and good government, and (as a
matter of infinite importance in my judgment) by associat-
ing with each other, and forming friendships in juvenile
years, be enabled to free themselves in a proper degree

from those local prejudices and habitual jealousies which have just been mentioned; and which, when carried to excess, are never-failing sources of disquietude to the Public Mind and pregnant of mischievous consequences to this country.'

Washington feared, and strove to overcome, the spirit of disunion that had already begun to manifest itself in Jefferson's and Madison's Virginia and Kentucky Resolutions. He called Patrick Henry back into public life to stem the rising tide of sectional opposition to a strong central government. Also, he exerted himself to remove any causes which might prevent the growth of the spirit of nationalism among the youth. Fortunately, help came from a source undreamed of by him — from John Marshall, his friend and biographer, who, from his place on the Supreme Bench, and with the aid of his fellow judges, built up through judicial decisions a body of national law which has persisted in spite of every turn of the political tides.

Washington could not 'receive pecuniary compensation for any services rendered his Country in its arduous struggle with Great Britain for its Rights,' but he did permit the Legislature of Virginia to bestow upon him James River and Potomac River canal shares, to be held for *public uses.*

To his mind no public use could transcend that of education in America for American youths. The canal shares had a par value of upwards of $200,000; and he believed firmly that they would come to have a much larger intrinsic value. This sum, he believed, would form a beginning for a national university. Congress never has had the con-

structive wisdom to found a national university; and up
to the present time there has not been enough interest in
the problem, or sufficient cohesion in educational forces to
weld together and coördinate into one organization the
abundant materials for higher education which abound in
the national capital. Some day, in the very nature of
things, an organizing and directing force will appear, and
then George Washington's elaborate dream will be realized
according to the fashion of that future time. Unfortunately, the canal shares did not prove of the value he anti-
cipated.[1]

To his 'dearly beloved wife' he gave the profit and benefit of his estate for her life. The little house, at the corner
of Pitt and Cameron Streets in Alexandria, which they
together had built and in which they had spent many
happy hours quite by themselves, went to her absolutely.
She, too, had the household furniture to dispose of as she
pleased; and it became her pleasure to bestow it upon her
grandchildren. Much of it naturally went to Mr. and Mrs.
Lawrence Lewis at Woodlawn, a disposition that kept the
balance between Washingtons and Custises. After Mrs.
Lewis's death her heirs sold the articles to the Government,
and they are now in the National Museum. The furniture
that was acquired by Washington Custis, either by inheritance or by his purchases among the heirs, went far
toward the furnishing of Arlington, and much of it is now
back at Mount Vernon. Mrs. Eliza Custis's and Mrs.
Thomas Peter's shares are still owned by their heirs. In

[1] The George Washington University is consciously striving to grow into the
stature of a national university. After years of vicissitudes, good progress is
now being made under the presidency of Dr. William Mather Lewis.

the main these latter possessions consist of Mrs. Washington's personal belongings or Custis family relics, all of which naturally went to her grandchildren.

Before Washington could get down to the matter of actual gifts, he of necessity had to clear his decks for action by throwing overboard certain indebtedness. His brother Samuel inherited business qualities from his mother rather than from his father. Samuel had taken over certain lands, but had made no payments; and had conveyed the property to his son Thornton. Both died without obtaining title from George, who by his will directs his executors to make good the title in Thornton's heirs. Meantime George had paid for the support and education of Samuel's sons, George Steptoe and Lawrence Augustine, at a cost of $5000. All these advances he wiped out. So, too, he treated an item of £425 and thirty-three negroes, against the estate of his wife's deceased brother, Bartholomew Dandridge, provision being made for the gradual emancipation of the slaves. Other like entanglements he straightened.

Already Washington had contracted to sell his lands in various States, among them Great Meadows in Pennsylvania, 'where the first action with the French in the year 1754 was fought.' There must have been a touch of real sentiment in his purchase of his first battle-field, where he himself began a war that reached three quarters of the way around the world — even to India. Not content with such a modest reference to the historic battle-ground, he hides sentiment under a laudation of the fertility of the land and the eligibility of the site 'on Braddock's road from Fort Cumberland to Pittsburgh.' [1]

For political as well as economic reasons, Washington exerted every influence at his command — time, money, and persuasion — to open up the Western country by canals extending back from tidewater through the mountains. Had he lived until the days of railroads, he would have been equally enthusiastic over that improved method of transportation. He sought the end by every practicable means. It is only within the past year or two that the canal from Washington to Cumberland has sunk from a bearer of traffic to a purveyor of water-power on a small scale.

Washington and Governor George Clinton had united in a purchase of two thousand acres on the Mohawk River, in Montgomery County, New York, and had made money by the transaction. Then, too, he had a twenty-thousand dollars interest in the Great Dismal Swamp; and that proved a good venture. Also, he owned a tract at Difficult Run near the Great Falls of the Potomac, a location now fast becoming a portion of the suburbs of Washington.

His holdings extending forty miles along the Great Kanawha he had contracted to sell for $200,000, and he was not anxious to have the bargain carried out, for he thought the land would bring more rather than less; and he knew, for he personally had cruised it. There he and General Andrew Lewis had found 'a bituminous spring of so inflammable a nature as to burn as freely as spirits, and is as nearly difficult to extinguish.'

[1] This property was bought by Andrew Parks, of Fredericksburg, who married Harriot Washington.

These conditional sales amounted to upwards of $230,-000, leaving about $300,000 worth of property to be sold to provide for the bequests made in his will. Of this remainder a third was in lands on the Ohio, $15,000 in the North-Western Territory, and $10,000 in Kentucky. Then there was $44,000 worth of lands near Bath in Berkeley County, a peninsula covered with finest walnut trees, around which lands the Potomac River flowed. On the whole they were all sagacious selections; and most of the lands had been won by hard service in the French and Indian War, when he held a British commission.

Washington next used two pages of his clear, firm handwriting to give immortality to the names of half a score of those whom he held dear. Save for this act of kindly remembrance, most of those names would have crumbled with their tombstones in neglected Virginia graveyards. There were Lawrence and Robert Washington, 'acquaintances and friends of his juvenile years'; Sarah Green, Ann Walker, Sally B. Haynie, and a band of Washington widows. Then came his 'compatriot in arms and old and intimate friend Doct.r Craik,' the beloved physician. The Doctor preserved and believed firmly in the Indian Chief's prophecy, made at the time of Braddock's defeat. Then every enemy bullet missed the intrepid young warrior who 'was not of the red-coat tribe, but hath an Indian's wisdome' in fighting. 'The Great Spirit [said the prophet] protects that man, and guides him. He will become the chief of nations. He cannot die in battle.'

No wonder Washington's soldiers believed him invulnerable. Over and over again during the Revolution they had seen him expose himself in battle, as at Monmouth, where his uniform was spattered with dirt by a British cannon-ball. Did Washington also believe it? He had reason to.[1]

Five months after those loving words were written, Dr. Craik was summoned to attend the last hours of Washington, when the hero of many battles quickly succumbed to an uncared-for cold.

Next came Dr. David Stuart, on whom he had relied to start aright the beginnings of the City of Washington, and Eleanor Stuart, his high-born wife; 'the Reverend, now Bryan Lord Fairfax,' endeared by a lifetime of wrong-headedness; 'General de la Fayette,' whose name needed no explanatory words; and simple-hearted Tobias Lear, as devoted a secretary as ever great man had.

'AND NOW
'Having gone through these specific devises, with explanations for the more correct understanding and design of them,' he proceeded to the distribution of the more important parts of his estate.

First and dearest to his heart was Mount Vernon, lands granted to his great-grandfather by the Culpepers, who with difficulty had saved the Northern Neck of Virginia as a Utopian remnant from the great properties once owned by their besotted ancestor. These lands, little regarded by Washington's grandfather, had passed to his Aunt Mildred, and from her to her brother Augustine, who realized the possibilities of the situation and set about making it the future seat of the Washington family. With large

[1] Custis, *Recollections*, p. 223.

prevision, Augustine Washington arranged that, in case of
the failure of the line in his eldest son, Lawrence, the
estate should pass to George; and so in due time it did.

Into Mount Vernon George Washington's life was built.
Every structure on the estate was an expression of himself
— of his sense of order and proportion, thoroughness and
sincerity, simplicity and taste. Every tree and shrub, each
road and walk, the gardens of fruit and of flowers — all
were manifestations of his large and generous nature. The
reluctant soil, the uncertain water-courses, and the capri-
cious fisheries, seemed but the opportunity for the mani-
festation of his foresight, skill, and patience. From Mount
Vernon he departed always with reluctance, and to it he
ever returned with joy and satisfaction. 'And now' the
time had come for him to depart and to leave to his suc-
cessors the task and the enjoyment of carrying on the great
tradition.

It was to no unappreciative hands that he confided his
dearest possession. Between Bushrod Washington's father
and George Washington there had existed from boyhood
an affectionate regard, at once intimate and strong. Together they took counsel over the affairs of their mother
and their less successful brothers, being keen to maintain
the family honor. To this younger brother George always
felt that he could reveal himself in mental undress. The
love for the father became paternal affection toward the
son. Then, too, among all the wide connection, whether
Washingtons or Custises or Dandridges, Bushrod Washington was preëminently the one to maintain the prestige
of Mount Vernon. Mentally he was the superior of them
all, and his position on the Supreme Bench of the United

MOUNT VERNON AND ITS SURROUNDINGS

WASHINGTON AT TRENTON
By John Trumbull

States gave him national standing. He afterward fell short, but the causes of his failure were quite beyond his control.

During his lifetime George Washington had acquired not only the other moiety of the original grant of five thousand acres on the Potomac made to his great-grandfather and Spencer, but he had increased his holdings in the vicinity to about ninety-three hundred acres. Four thousand were included with the mansion in the gift to Bushrod. Two thousand went to George Fayette and Lawrence Augustine, then boys of ten and nine years, the grandsons of his brother Charles, and the sons of Colonel George Augustine Washington, who had married Mrs. Washington's niece, Frances, the daughter of Colonel and Mrs. Burwell Bassett, of Eltham. No tribute could possibly be finer than the one Washington pays to the parents of the boys, when he records that the gift is made 'in consideration of the consanguinity between them and my wife, being as nearly related to her as to myself, as on account of the affection I had for, and the obligation I was under to, their father when living, who from his youth had attached himself to my person and followed my fortunes through the vicissitudes of the late Revolution — afterwards devoting his time to the superintendence of my private concerns for many years, whilst my public employments rendered it impracticable for me to do it myself, thereby affording me essential services, and always performing them in a manner the most filial and respectful.' Of these two brothers, George Fayette was educated at William and Mary College; he lived for a time at Wellington on his estate, but removed to, and died at, Waverly, near Winchester, in 1867. The other, known as Charles Augustine, died at Cadiz, on a voyage in search of health, taken with his brother.

The gift of two thousand acres, together with the mill and distillery, to Lawrence Lewis and Eleanor Parke Lewis, has already been dealt with in preceding chapters. Washington adverts to it as 'the residue of my Mount Vernon Estate not already devised to my nephew Bushrod Washington,' from which one infers that the two thousand acres given to the children of Colonel George Augustine Washington, and the twelve hundred acres on Four Mile Run, bequeathed to George Washington Parke Custis, were held as separate properties.

Finally came the great assize in which the entire family connection — his own and his wife's, equally — were named in the distribution of the remainder of the estate. There were to be twenty-three parts: to the four children of his half-brother Augustine, four parts; to the five children of his sister Betty Lewis, five parts; to the sons and daughters of his brother Samuel, four parts; to Corbin Washington and the heirs of Jane Washington, son and daughter of his brother John Augustine, two parts; to the three children of his brother Charles, three parts; to the three children of his nephew George Augustine, the one part their father would have received had he lived; to Elizabeth Parke Law, Martha Parke Peter, and Eleanor Parke Lewis, three parts; and to Bushrod Washington, Lawrence Lewis, and Washington Custis, one part.

The administration of the estate fell upon Bushrod Washington and Lawrence Lewis. This task occupied

more or less of their time until 1823, when, at their instance, a friendly suit was brought in the United States
Court at Alexandria, by Lawrence Augustine Washington
and others against the executors, to settle the final accounts. The first sale of properties under the will had been
made in 1802; the principal sale took place in 1805; and the
net result was $126,801.03. This amount gave to each of
the twenty-three shares a principal sum of $5513.08. June
1, 1824, was fixed as the interest date; interest was charged
on advances to the legatees and interest credits were made
accordingly.[1]

These legacies were expended in various ways. A number of them went toward the education of children of the
recipients, as Washington himself would have approved.
He had a passion for education often found in persons who,
having been denied adequate training in youth, are forced
to supply the deficiency by continuous self-instruction
throughout life. It is true that in 1776 Harvard College
took the opportunity offered by the General's presence in
Cambridge to confer on him the second degree of Doctor

[1] The manuscript accounts of Bushrod Washington are at the United States
Naval Academy, Annapolis. Photostats are in the Library of Congress. The
final settlement of the estate seems to have devolved on John Augustine Washington. To him G. W. P. Custis writes from Arlington House, December 17, 1847:
'Enclosed you will find your commission & will proceed as to you may seem best
to a speedy, sure & satisfactory settlement of the affairs of General Washington's
Estate. There is but little left to do. . . . I am of the opinion that a decree of
your Court should be obtained to sell the undivided interest that General Washington's Estate holds in the land in Nansemond County near the Dismal Swamp.
. . . It appears the land is suffering much by delay. This done there only remains
to divide the dues of the debtor legatees among the creditor legatees; and, after
47 years, the affairs of the Estate of General Washington will be brought to a
final close. I am so poor a man of business that I do not feel myself competent to
advise in matters of which I have neither knowledge, nor have had any experience, but with the energy and method of your illustrious ancestor I feel assured
that you, my Dr. Sir, will "go ahead."' Library of Congress, Custis MSS.

of Laws granted by that institution, thereby anticipating
Yale, the University of Pennsylvania, Washington (Maryland), and Brown. Also, William and Mary College made
him its chancellor, an office he accepted with the expressed
hope that the learned faculty would provide a system of
education 'beneficial to the state and the republic of letters, as well as to the more extensive interests of humanity
and religion.' [1]

The institution most favored in the Washington family,
however, was the far-off Phillips Academy at Andover,
Massachusetts, which numbers among its former students
no fewer than nine nephews and grandnephews of General
Washington, and their descendants even to these days.
The General was partial to the brand of education supplied
at Andover, and he was particularly fond of Judge Samuel
Phillips, Jr., whom he came to know well in Boston, during
the earliest days of the Revolution. The acquaintance was
renewed in 1789, when President Washington was the
guest of Judge Phillips, and thus had an opportunity to
observe the progress the school had made in the fifteen
years since it had been started through the benefactions of
the Phillips family.

Howell Lewis, the first of the nine to climb Andover
Hill, came in 1785, at the age of thirteen. He was the
fourth child of Betty Washington Lewis. From 1812
until his death, in 1822, he lived on the Kanawha lands
which he had inherited.

Four years before Washington's death, Colonel and Mrs.
William Augustine Washington, of Westmoreland County,
appeared at Andover, bearing a letter from their Uncle

[1] *History of the College of William and Mary*, Richmond, 1874.

George [1] to General Lincoln. They entered their two sons:
Augustine (aged fifteen), who early died of consumption,
and Bushrod (aged ten), who entered Harvard, but did not
graduate. In later life he inherited from his uncle, Justice
Bushrod Washington, a portion of the Mount Vernon
estate, which he named Mount Zephyr. There he lived
with his wife, Henrietta Bryan Spotswood, and their eight
children, until his death in 1830.

The Washington boys had two cousins at Andover, sons
of their Aunt Mildred Washington, who married Thomas,
a son of Richard Henry Lee. Of the Lees, Cassius died
while a student at Princeton, and Francis Lightfoot
(Harvard B.A., 1802; M.A., 1806) lived until 1850.

Four Washingtons entered Phillips Academy in 1803.
The first was George Corbin, a younger son of Colonel
William Augustine, who afterward became a Member of
Congress from Maryland and the president of the Chesa-
peake and Ohio Canal Company. The three others were
sons of Corbin Washington, who had died in 1800 and left
the care of his children to his brother Bushrod. So the boys
were brought up at Mount Vernon and took its traditions
with them to their school. The first, Richard Henry Lee
Washington, died in 1819, unmarried. The second brother,
Bushrod Corbin, enjoyed a farmer's life in Jefferson
County.[2] The third, John Augustine, inherited Mount
Vernon from his uncle in 1829, lived to enjoy it only
about three years, and left the property to his widow, who

---

[1] He was the son of George's half-brother Augustine, and she was the daughter
of his brother John Augustine.

[2] *The Phillips Bulletin*, October, 1914: In spite of statements to the contrary,
the only persons named Washington who have received degrees from Harvard
are George, LL.D., 1776; Bushrod, LL.D., 1827; Booker T., LL.D., 1896; George
Augustine (B.A. Yale, 1903), LL.B., 1906.

deeded it to her son, John Augustine, who sold to the Mount Vernon Association. All four of these boys may well have been sent to school as beneficiaries of their uncle's will.

In the final distribution there was no caprice or favoritism — no rewards and no penalties: relationship to him or to his wife alone counted. He placed no restrictions on his executors, but he advised them to be slow in selling Western lands, which 'have been progressively rising and cannot long be checked in their increasing value.' And he 'particularly recommended to such of the legatees as could make it convenient to take each a share of his stock in the Potomac Company,' inasmuch as he was 'thoroughly convinced that no uses to which the money can be applied will be so productive as the Tolls arising from this navigation when in full operation (and this from the nature of things must be ere long) and more especially if that of the Shenandoah is added thereto.'

With characteristic distrust of his own abilities, Washington wrote that 'it will readily be perceived that no professional character has been consulted or has had any agency in the draught [of the will] and that, although it has occupied many of my leisure hours to digest and to through it into its present form, it may notwithstanding appear crude and incorrect. — But having endeavored to be plain and explicit in all the Devises — even at the expence of prolixity, perhaps of tautology, I hope and trust that no disputes will arise concerning them.' But if unhappily disputes should arise they were to be settled by arbitrators, 'unfettered by Law or legal constructions,' who shall declare their sense of the testator's intention; and such decision shall be as binding 'as if it had been given in the Supreme Court of the United States.'

Martha Washington; his nephews William Augustine, Bushrod, George Steptoe, and Samuel Washington; Lawrence Lewis and George Washington Parke Custis ('when he shall have arrived at the age of twenty years'), were named as executors. Each page of the will save one is signed by the testator, and the final signature was appended on 'the ninth day of July in the year one thousand seven hundred and ninety.' This most methodical of men actually omitted the last 'nine' in the date.

Twenty miles out of Washington three concrete roads converge at Fairfax Court-House, where the first blood of the Civil War was shed in battle. In the fireproof room of the County Clerk's office, the wills of George and Martha Washington are exhibited in a glass case.[1] In the records on the shelves are wills of Washingtons, Fairfaxes, Lewises, Masons and Fitzhughs, from 1742 to 1854 — seven score documents of high historical value. In Westmoreland County the Washington wills number twenty-two. Then there are Stafford, Clark, and still other counties to be searched.

[1] The will of Washington consists of forty-three pages, each written and signed by himself, except page twenty-three, where his signature was omitted. The will, having become badly mutilated, was, on recommendation of the late Gaillard Hunt, chief of the Division of Manuscripts in the Library of Congress, repaired and bound in book form in 1910, by the late William Berwick, a man of international fame as a restorer of manuscripts. In 1911 it was enclosed in a steel case and placed on exhibition in the County Clerk's office at Fairfax, Virginia.

It is commonly said that George Washington was altogether too perfect, too cold and calm and dispassionate, too just; that he lacked those foibles and weaknesses which endear lesser historic characters to the public in their own day and in historic times as well. No one who has studied the character of Washington as it developed slowly from youth to maturity could possibly make such a mistake. We have a great mass of correspondence written by his own hand; we have his diaries in which his daily life is mirrored; and we have the many records of visits made by personal friends and by strangers; by foreigners and by his fellow citizens; by soldiers, statesmen, artists, travelers, and curious people. In one and all of these records he is ever the incarnation of friendliness and courtesy, and of dignity without austerity. He preferred listening to talking; he avoided the hasty and censorious word about either the present or the absent. At the same time, those who were with him privately knew how hot the lava could be and under how thin a crust it boiled.

Others have given him his due rank among the world's great generals, or have extolled him for his deep wisdom as the first President of a new nation. The purpose of these pages is to show that he was the finest gentleman of America.

THE END

WASHINGTON CHRONOLOGY

WASHINGTON CHRONOLOGY

1602. Lawrence, son of Lawrence Washington of Sulgrave, Northamptonshire, England, born. He matriculated at Brasenose College, Oxford, 1621; B.A., 1623; fellow, 1624–33; M.A., 1625; proctor, 1631; rector of Purleigh, Essex, 1633; married Amphilis Rhoades, 1633.

1634. John Washington born in the rectory at Purleigh.

1643. The Reverend Lawrence Washington ejected from the living at Purleigh, on account of loyalty to the Crown.

1652–53. The Reverend Lawrence dies, leaving Amphilis, widow, and six children: John, Lawrence, William, Elizabeth, Margaret and Martha. Rev. Lawrence W. buried at Maldon, Essex, Jan. 21, 1652–53.

1654. Amphilis, widow of Lawrence, dies at Tring in January, and is buried there January 19. February 8, letters of administration granted John.

1658. John comes to Virginia; settles at Bridges Creek (now known as Wakefield), Westmoreland County; marries Ann, daughter of Nathaniel Pope.

1659. September. Lawrence, eldest son of John, born at Wakefield.

1668. Ann (Pope) Washington dies.

1669. John marries Ann Gerrard, widow of Walter Broadhurst and of Henry Brett. The date of her death is unknown.

1676. May. John marries, for a third wife, Frances, widow of Captain John Appleton.

1677. January. John dies, leaving a widow, Frances, and three children by his first wife, Ann Pope: Lawrence, John and Ann. His third wife was provided for by a marriage settlement, without alteration of his will, which was dated September 21, 1665.

1694. Augustine, second son of Lawrence, born at Wakefield; is taken to England by his mother; educated at Appleby, England.

1697. Lawrence, eldest son of John, dies. His widow, a daughter of Augustine Warner, goes to England to settle her husband's estate; she marries George Gale of White Haven, Cumberland, and is buried there January 30, 1700–01.

Lawrence's issue are John, Augustine, Mildred.

1710. December 7. Colonel Daniel Parke killed by a mob in Antigua.

1711. October 15. Daniel Parke Custis born.

1715. Augustine Washington returns from England and (April 20) marries Jane, daughter of Caleb Butler, lawyer.

1716. Butler, first child of Augustine and Jane (Butler) Washington, born at Wakefield; dies in infancy.

1718. Lawrence, second child of Augustine and Jane (Butler) W., born at Wakefield. Educated at Appleby.

1720. Augustine, third child of Augustine and Jane (Butler) W., born at Wakefield. Educated at Appleby.

1722. Jane, fourth child of Augustine and Jane (Butler) W., born at Wakefield; died 1735.

1725. July 7. Fielding Lewis born at Warner Hall, Gloucester County.

1726. Augustine Washington buys the Potomac property (Mount Vernon) from his sister Mildred.

1728. Jane, first wife of Augustine, dies and is buried at Wakefield.

1731. March 6. Augustine married for his second wife, Mary, fifth daughter of Colonel Joseph Ball, of Lancaster County; she was born in 1704.

1731. June 21. Martha, eldest child of Colonel John and Frances (Jones) Dandridge, born at White House, New Kent County.

1732. February 22. George, first child of Augustine and Mary (Ball) Washington, born at Wakefield. Baptized April 5.

1733. June 20. Elizabeth (Betty), second child of Augustine and Mary (Ball) W., born at Wakefield.

1734. November 16. Samuel, third child of Augustine and Mary (Ball) W., born at Wakefield.

1734-35. Augustine removes to Upper Potomac lands (Mount Vernon); granted to his grandfather for bringing immigrants to America; and bought by Augustine from his sister Mildred in 1726.

1735. Augustine Washington a vestryman of Truro Parish, indicating residence on his Upper Potomac property. Sits as Burgess for Prince William County till 1739.

1736. January 13. John Augustine, fourth child of Augustine and Mary (Ball) W., born.

1738. May 2. Charles, fifth child of Augustine and Mary (Ball) W., born.

1739. Mildred, sixth child of Augustine and Mary (Ball) W., born. Died 1740.

1739. Thomas Lord Fairfax visits his American estates.

1740. Augustine removes to Ferry Farm, opposite Fredericksburg, near his business with the Principo Iron Company; conveys to his son Lawrence the 2500 acres on the Upper Potomac, which Lawrence names Mount Vernon.

1740. Lawrence appointed one of four Virginia captains, under Admiral Vernon, in the Cartagena expedition against the Spaniards in the West Indies.

1742. Lawrence appointed adjutant general of Virginia. At his death, in 1752, the colony was divided into four districts, and George Washington was appointed adjutant of the Southern district. In 1753 George was transferred to the Northern Neck district.

1743. April 12. Augustine dies at Ferry Farm and is buried at Wakefield. George makes his home with his half-brother Augustine at Wakefield, where he has for teacher a Mr. Williams. He is much at Fredericksburg, where he attends the school of the Reverend James Marye. The facts in relation to his schooling are uncertain.

1743. Augustine, son of Augustine and Jane (Butler) W., returns from school at Appleby, England; and marries Anne, daughter and co-heiress of Colonel William Aylett. He inherits Wakefield.

Their children were: Elizabeth, wife of General Alexander Spotswood; Jane, wife of Colonel John Thornton; Anne, wife of Burdet Ashton; and William Augustine, who married his cousin, Jane Washington, daughter of John Augustine of Bushfield.

1743. July 19. Lawrence marries Ann, eldest daughter of Hon. William Fairfax of Belvoir. Their four children died in infancy.

1745. Benedict Calvert, son of the fifth Lord Baltimore, comes to America. In 1751 resides at Mount Airy, Maryland.

1746. Mary Washington refuses consent to Lawrence's proposal that George shall go to sea.

174. Deborah Gedney Clarke, wife of the Honorable William Fairfax, dies at Belvoir, aged 67.

1747. March. George Washington begins surveys for Lord Fairfax in the Shenandoah Valley.

1748. George goes to Mount Vernon to live with his half-brother, Lawrence.

March. George keeps a journal of his surveys for Lord Fairfax in the Shenandoah Valley.

Town of Alexandria surveyed by George Washington, for Lord Fairfax, Lawrence and Augustine Washington.

George William Fairfax marries Sarah, daughter of Colonel Wilson Cary of Ceelys. They live at Belvoir.

1749. Daniel Parke Custis (son of John Custis IV and Frances, daughter of Colonel Daniel Parke) marries Martha Dandridge. Her father gave them the White House farm in New Kent County. He was 38; she was 18.

1750. May 7. Elizabeth (Betty) Washington marries Colonel Fielding Lewis of Fredericksburg. He builds for her the house now known as Kenmore.

1751. Lawrence and George Washington in the Barbadoes.

1752. July 26. Lawrence Washington dies at Mount Vernon.

November 4. George Washington joins the Masonic Lodge at Fredericksburg.

Carlyle House at Alexandria built by Colonel John Carlyle, who emigrated to Virginia in 1740, and married Sarah, daughter of William Fairfax, of Belvoir.

1753. George Washington writes a journal of his expedition to the Ohio country to warn the French against encroachments on British territory. The journal was printed at Williamsburg, Virginia; in England; and in France.

John Parke Custis born at White House.

1754. May 28. George Washington attacks the French at Great Meadows, where first he 'heard the bullets whistle and found something charming in the sound.' Beginning of the Seven Years' War.

Eleanor Calvert (daughter of Benedict and Elizabeth Calvert) born at Mount Airy, Maryland.

1755. March. George Washington accepts the invitation of General Braddock to become a member of his military family.

July. Braddock's defeat.

Martha Parke Custis born at White House.

1756. George Washington visits Philadelphia, New York, New London, Newport, Providence, and Boston. Meeting with Miss Philipse.

April 14. John Augustine Washington, manager at Mount Vernon, brings thither his bride, Hannah Bushrod.

August. John Dandridge (father of Martha Custis) dies and is buried at Fredericksburg.

1757. William Fairfax dies at Belvoir. He was a son of Henry Fairfax of Yorkshire, England, and grandson of Thomas, fourth Lord Fairfax. Married, second, daughter of Major Thomas Walker; third, Deborah Gedney Clarke, of Salem, Massachusetts. Was agent of his cousin, Thomas, sixth Lord Fairfax, of Greenway Court. His eldest daughter, Ann, married, first, Lawrence Washington; second, George Lee.

Summer. Daniel Parke Custis dies at White House, aged 45 years.

Charles Washington marries Mildred, daughter of Colonel Francis Thornton, of Spotswood County.

1758. May. George Washington meets Mrs. Martha Dandridge Custis.

July 24. George Washington elected to House of Burgesses from Frederick County, while he is with troops.

Receives a vote of thanks from the General Assembly of Virginia.

1759. January 6. George Washington marries Martha, daughter of John Dandridge and widow of Daniel Parke Custis, at White House, New Kent County, the Reverend David Mossum, minister of Saint Peter's Church, officiating. By this marriage he was entitled to one third of her husband's estate, and, by decree of the court, to the care of the other two thirds, belonging to the Custis children.

1762. June 5. Bushrod Washington born at Bushfield, Westmoreland County; eldest son of Colonel John Augustine Washington and Hannah Bushrod.

Augustine Washington, half-brother of George, dies at Wakefield, leaving widow, Jane; son, William Augustine; and daughters, Betsy, Nancy, Jane.

1763. George William Fairfax and George Washington made church wardens of Truro Parish.

1765. George Washington elected to the House of Burgesses from Fairfax County.

Lund Washington comes to Mount Vernon as manager; remains until 1785.

1766. New Pohick Church provided for. Mr. Lee Massey recommended to the Bishop of London and Governor of the Colony for minister, in place of Charles Green, deceased.

John Parke Custis placed with the Reverend Jonathan Boucher, who had a private school at Saint Mary's, Maryland.

1772. May 21. First portrait of Colonel George Washington painted by Charles Willson Peale at Mount Vernon. First original sketch owned by the Historical Society of Pennsylvania since 1892.

1773. June 19. Martha Parke Custis dies at Mount Vernon, aged 17.

Mr. and Mrs. George William Fairfax go to England, never to return to Belvoir.

1774. February 3. John Parke Custis and Eleanor Calvert married at Mount Airy, Maryland, the home of her father, Benedict Calvert, son of the fifth Lord Baltimore. He was 19 and she 16. George Washington and Lund Washington present, staying three days.

1775. May. George Washington attends second Continental Congress in Philadelphia. Writes to George William Fairfax in England that the Americans will fight for their liberties and property.

June 15. Elected General to command all Continental forces. Writes Mrs. Washington of his acceptance; and goes to Boston.

December 30. Mrs. Washington, accompanied by Mr. and Mrs. J. P. Custis, at Cambridge.

1776. April. Mrs. Washington and Mrs. J. P. Custis at headquarters in New York. Mrs. Washington inoculated for smallpox.

August 21. Eliza Parke Custis born at Abingdon.

1777. December 31. Martha Parke Custis born at Abingdon.

1778. John Parke Custis buys Arlington estate from Gerard Alexander.

1779. March 21. Eleanor Parke Custis born at Abingdon.

1781. April 30. George Washington Parke Custis born at Mount Airy, Maryland.

October 19. Cornwallis surrenders at Yorktown.

Fielding Lewis dies at Fredericksburg.

November 5. John Parke Custis dies at Eltham; Washington adopts the two younger children.

Thomas Lord Fairfax dies at Greenway Court, aged 92.

Samuel Washington dies at Harewood.

November 11. Washington, Rochambeau, and officers attend a ball at Fredericksburg.

1782. December 19. George Washington resigns his commission as Commander-in-Chief, at Annapolis, and spends Christmas at Mount Vernon.

1783. Eleanor (Calvert) Custis, widow of John Parke Custis, marries Dr. David Stuart.

1784. George Washington sells Bank of England stock belonging to his wife, for £1650.

> In September he visits Charles Washington at Berkeley Springs.
> Chevalier de la Luzerne and Lafayette at Mount Vernon.

1785. Mrs. Dandridge and Bartholomew Dandridge (stepmother and brother of Mrs. Washington) die.

> George Augustine Washington and Fanny Bassett marry.
> October 2. Houdon, 'the first statuary of the world,' arrives at Mount Vernon from Paris to make studies for the statue of Washington provided for by Act of the Virginia legislature, June 22, 1784. He was selected by Franklin and Jefferson. Stays fifteen days, leaving a copy of the bust he made to work from after his return to Paris, where the statue was completed.

1787. February. John Augustine Washington dies at Bushfield: — 'the intimate companion of my youth, and the friend of my ripened years.'

> March. Washington visits his mother in Fredericksburg; and goes to the Constitutional Convention.
> April 3. George William Fairfax dies at Bath, England, aged 63.
> Gideon Snow comes to Mount Vernon as tutor.

1788. Benedict Calvert dies at Mount Airy, Maryland.

1789. April. Charles Thomson brings to Mount Vernon notification that George Washington has been elected President. Washington pays a last visit to his mother; borrows £10,000 in Alexandria; and goes to New York.

> May 16. Mrs. Washington starts for New York, with Nelly and Washington Custis.
> August 25. Mary Washington dies at Fredericksburg, aged 82.

1793. Corner-stone of the United States Capitol laid, with Masonic ceremonies, by President Washington.

1794. Kenmore sold to Samuel Gordon, who gives it its present name.

> Betty Lewis goes to live with her daughter, Mrs. Charles Carter, Culpeper County.

1795. January 6. Thomas Peter and Martha Parke Custis married at Hope Park.

1796. March 20. Thomas Law and Eliza Parke Custis married at Hope Park.

> George Washington Lafayette at Mount Vernon.

1797. March 3. Presidential term expires. George Washington returns to Mount Vernon.

March 31. Elizabeth (Betty) Washington Lewis dies at Western View, Culpeper County.

1798. July 3. Washington commissioned Lieutenant-General of the Provisional Army.

1799. February 22. Eleanor Parke Custis marries Lawrence Lewis at Mount Vernon.

December 1. Frances Lewis born at Mount Vernon.

December 14. George Washington dies.

1800. British House of Lords confirms right of the Reverend Bryan Fairfax, son of William Fairfax, to title as eighth Baron Fairfax. From him the present Lord Fairfax, eleventh baron, descends.

1802. Arlington built on the 1160 acres left to G. W. P. Custis by his father.

Bryan Lord Fairfax dies at Monteagle, near Alexandria.

1803. May 22. Martha Washington dies at Mount Vernon.

Justice Bushrod Washington comes to Mount Vernon to live.

1803. Lorenzo Lewis born at Woodlawn.

1804. Thomas Law and Eliza Parke Custis Law separate; she takes the name of Mrs. Custis.

1805. G. W. P. Custis marries Mary Lee Fitzhugh, daughter of Colonel William and Anne (Randolph) Fitzhugh of Chatham and Ravensworth.

1807. January 19. Robert Edward Lee born at Stratford, Westmoreland County, the son of 'Light Horse Harry' Lee.

1810. Colonel William Augustine Washington, son of Augustine of Wakefield, dies at Georgetown, Virginia. His first wife, Jane Washington, died in 1791; he married, second, Martha, daughter of Richard Henry Lee; and, third, Sally, sister of Colonel John Tayloe of Mount Airy, Virginia. He was an executor and legatee of George Washington.

1811. Eleanor Calvert, widow of John Parke Custis and wife of Dr. David Stuart, dies at Hope Park.

1813. April 1. Martha Eleanor Angela Lewis born at Woodlawn.

1815. January 28. Britannia Wellington Peter born at Tudor Place, Georgetown; married (1842) Commodore Beverly Kennon, U.S.N.; he was killed (1844) by explosion of a gun on the U.S.S. Princeton; she died in 1911, aged 96 years.

1820. Colonel John Augustine Washington born at Blakely, Jefferson County. Son of John Augustine and Jane Charlotte (Blackburn) Washington.

1822. Howell Lewis dies. He inherited 1300 acres on the Kanawha, and lived there from 1812 until his death. He was the fifth child of Betty Washington Lewis.

1825. Lafayette at Arlington and Tudor Place.

1826. Lawrence Lewis buys Audley, Clark County, from son of Warner Washington. The estate remained in the Lewis family until 1900, when it was bought by Mr. Cummings, who sold (1921) to B. B. and Montfort Jones.

1827. Lorenzo Lewis marries Miss Coxe of Philadelphia.

1829. November 26. Justice Bushrod Washington dies, leaving Mount Vernon to his nephew, John Augustine, son of his brother Corbin.

November 28. Ann Blackburn, wife of Bushrod Washington, dies.

1831. June 30. Mary Ann Randolph Custis marries Lieutenant Robert E. Lee at Arlington.

1832. June 16. John Augustine Washington, son of Corbin, dies at Mount Vernon, aged 43. His widow inherits Mount Vernon.

Eliza Parke Custis (Mrs. Law) dies in Richmond.

1837. October 7. Remains of General and Mrs. Washington placed in the new vault.

1839. September 21. Martha Eleanor Angela Conrad, wife of Charles M. Conrad and daughter of Lawrence and Eleanor P. Lewis, dies and is buried at Mount Vernon.

November 20. Major Lawrence Lewis dies at Arlington.

1842. John Augustine Washington marries Eleanor Love, daughter of Wilson Cary Selden.

1845. Woodlawn purchased by the New Jersey Colony for $12.50 per acre.

1846. Alexandria County, D.C., ceded back to Virginia.

1847. Lorenzo Lewis dies at Audley, Clark County.

1848. Corner-stone of the Washington Monument laid.

1852. July 15. Mrs. Lawrence Lewis (Nelly Custis) dies at Audley and is buried at Mount Vernon.

1853. Ann Pamela Cunningham starts the Mount Vernon Ladies' Association, to purchase Mount Vernon.

April 23. Mrs. G. W. P. Custis dies at Arlington.

1855. Jane Blackburn, widow of John Augustine Washington, dies at Blakely. She had given Mount Vernon to her son, John Augustine Washington, who arranges to sell the estate to the Mount Vernon Ladies' Association.

1857. October 10. G. W. P. Custis dies and is buried at Arlington.

1859. February 22. Purchase of Mount Vernon by the Mount Vernon Ladies' Association completed, and the work of restoration begins.

1860. February 22. Formal possession of Mount Vernon taken by the Association.

1861. April 22. Robert E. Lee and family leave Arlington for Richmond.

September 13. Colonel John Augustine Washington, the last of the Washington family to own Mount Vernon, was killed at Cheat Mountain, while an aide on General R. E. Lee's staff.

1870. October 12. General Robert E. Lee dies at Lexington, Virginia.

1873. Mrs. Robert E. Lee dies.

1883. Congress appropriates $150,000 to pay George Washington Custis Lee for all rights to Arlington.

1885. The Washington Monument completed at a cost of $1,500,000.

Mrs. Lorenzo Lewis dies at Audley.

1890. H. L. D. Lewis, administrator of the estate of Mrs. Lorenzo Lewis, sells the Washington relics at Audley, which were bought by the National Museum.

1891. Washington relics owned by Lawrence, Bushrod C., and Thomas B. Washington, and J. R. C. Lewis, sold at private sale in Philadelphia.

1893. Mary Washington Monument at Fredericksburg dedicated.

1904. J. R. C. Lewis, of Berryville, the last child of Lorenzo Lewis, dies.

1905. Restoration of the Washington church at Purleigh, Essex, England, started. There are two other 'Washington churches' in England — one at Sulgrave, and one at Great Brinckton, Northamptonshire, where Lawrence Washington lived after his expulsion from Purleigh in 1643.

1924. Wakefield National Memorial Association purchases seventy acres of Wakefield.

1925. Kenmore, the home of Mr. and Mrs. Fielding Lewis at Fredericksburg, dedicated to the public.

INDEX

pany's property confiscated, 22; 25, 41, 49, 74; on the Potomac, 97.

Rhoades, Amphilis, mother of John and Lawrence Washington, 18.

Richmond, Virginia, 4.

Richmond Pike, 5.

Robinson, Beverly, 47, 49, 53.

Robinson, John, Speaker of the House of Burgesses, 56, 72.

Rochambeau, Comte de, at Gunston Hall, 10; at Fredericksburg, 13.

Rogers, Edmund, 112.

Rogers, Eleanor, 112.

Rogers, Eliza, 112.

Rogers, Lloyd Nicholas, 112; bequeaths Druid Hill Park to Baltimore, 112.

Rogers, Mrs. Lloyd Nicholas (Eliza Law), 10; marries Lloyd Nicholas Rogers, of Druid Hill, Baltimore, Maryland, 112; children of, 112; death of, 112.

Rome, fountains of, 1.

Romney, George, paints portraits of Bishop Law, 105.

Roosevelt, Theodore, President, 75; restoration of the White House, 125.

'Rules of Civility,' origin of, 29, 30.

Sabine Hall, Virginia, seat of the Welfords, 19.

Saint Clair's defeat, 172.

Saint John's Cemetery, 114.

Saint John's College, Annapolis, Maryland, 155.

Sangster family, 38 n.

Savage's painting of the Washington family, 123.

Scarborough, Edmund, 58.

Selden, Eleanor Love. See John Augustine Washington, III.

Selden, Wilson Cary, 199.

Seven Years' War begins, 41.

Sharpe, Horatio, Governor of Maryland, 42 n.

Sharpe, Miss Elizabeth, restores Woodlawn, 5.

Sharpless, James, artist, 146 n.

Shenandoah Valley, 2, 7, 34.

Sherman, Senator John, moves to complete Washington Monument, 201 n.

Shirley, William, Governor of Massachusetts, 42 n.; Washington appeals to, on question of rank, 47; 49.

Shirley, Captain William, 43.

Shooters Hill, Alexandria, Virginia, site of Masonic Temple, 4.

Sinclair, Sir John, 33 n.

Smallpox, 92.

Smith, Mrs. H. H., raises money to pay for Kenmore, 144 n.

Smith's Island, 189; confiscated, 190.

Snow, Gideon, tutor at Mount Vernon, 136, 137.

Snowden, W. H., 175.

Snuff, 76.

Soldiers' Home, District of Columbia, 7.

'Southern Matron' (Miss Cunningham), 202.

Spectator, The, 34.

Spotswood, Alexander, Governor of Virginia, 75.

Stafford Court House, Virginia, 11.

Stewart, Dr. George, 93.

Stratford, home of the Lee family, 19; burned by convicts, 24.

Strickland, James, on reburial of George and Martha Washington, 199 n.

Struthers, John, gives marble coffins for remains of George and Martha Washington, 199.

Stuart, Dr. David, marries widow of J. P. Custis, 102; ancestry of, 102; one of first Commissioners of City of Washington, 103; 121, 151; extricates J. P. Custis's estate, 178; 213.

Stuart, Mrs. David (Eleanor, daughter of Benedict Calvert, wife of John Parke Custis and, second, of Dr. Stuart), 3, 102, 103, 148, 151.

Stuart, Gilbert, his Washington portraits, 146 n.

Sulgrave, English home of the Washington family, 17, 18 n.

Sully, Thomas, artist, 173 n.

Sumner, Senator Charles, 204.
Sun Tavern, Fredericksburg, Virginia, 13.
Sussex, England, 58.

Talcott, Captain, 184.
Tayloe family, 19, 126.
Tazewell Hall, Williamsburg, Virginia, 74.
Thomson, Charles, Secretary of Congress, announces Washington's election to the Presidency, 138.
Thornton, Dr. William, architect, designs Woodlawn, 5, 69; architect of the Capitol and other buildings, 124, 125 n.; Mrs. Thornton's diaries, 125 n.
Tobacco, 19, 77.
Toeplet, William, 9 n.
Townsend, Miss Amy, raises funds to restore Pohick Church, 8.
Trumbull, John, 146 n.
Tucker family, 74.
Tudor Place, Mrs. Washington's possessions at, 56; 125, 126; society and politics, 128; during Civil War, 128.
Tyler, Dr. Lyon G., 62 n., 74.

Underwood, Senator Oscar, purchases Woodlawn, 6.
United States Capitol, 1, 2, 118; crypt for Washington's body, 162.
United States Constitution, 9.
United States Corps of Engineers, headquarters of, 6.
Unknown Soldier of the World War, 192.

Valley Forge, Mrs. Washington at, 98.
Van Braam, Jacob, causes trouble by mistranslation, 42.
Van Ness, General John P., sketch of, 182 n.
Venango, 39.
Venice, flagstaffs of, 1.
Vernon, Admiral Edward, 28.
Versailles, model for the City of Washington, 118.

Virginia, Northern Neck of, 7; Constitution and Bill of Rights, 9; production of iron in, 21; Virginia Magazine, 34 n.; claim to Western lands, 39; bravery of Virginia soldiers at Braddock's defeat, 44; inns, 52; hospitality, 52; Eastern Shore of, 58; 'Papers relating to the Church in,' 61 n.; Journals of the House of Burgesses, 72 n.; Virginia Magazine of History and Biography, 136 n.; education of girls, 137.
Visiting in Colonial days, 91.
Viviani, M. René, at Gunston Hall, 10.

Wakefield (birthplace of George Washington), 4, 15, 18, 19, 24; site of house marked, 25; President and Mrs. Coolidge visit, 26; present conditions, 26.
Walker, Ann, 212.
Walker, Sarah, second wife of William Fairfax, 32.
Walker's 'Sufferings of the English Clergy,' 18 n.
Walpole, Horace, laughs at George Washington, 41.
Walpole Grant, 78.
War College, District of Columbia, 7.
Warburton Manor (Fort Washington), 90.
Warden, Dr. David Bailie, first American Consul in Paris; his friendship with Mrs. Eliza Custis, 109; her letters to, 110, 113, 114.
Warner, Colonel Augustine, of Warner Hall, Gloucester County, Virginia, 20.
Warner, Mildred, marries Lawrence Washington, 20.
Warner Hall, Gloucester County, Virginia, seat of the Lewis family, 13, 20.
Washington, Ann, daughter of John the immigrant, 19.
Washington, Augustine, father of George, vestryman at Pohick Church, 7; will of, 11; changes of residence,

INDEX

247

12, 24; inherits Wakefield, 21; purchases Mount Vernon property from his sister, 21; his interests in Principo Company, 21; marriages, 22; death and will, 28; disposes of Mount Vernon property, 37; 136.

Washington, Augustine, half-brother of George, educated in England, inherits Wakefield, marries Anne Aylett, 28; 35, 83; death, 143.

Washington, Betty, sister of George (Mrs. Fielding Lewis), 14; 126; death, 144.

Washington, Booker T., Harvard degree, 219 n.

Washington, Justice Bushrod, son of John Augustine I, 193; sketch of, 194 n.; trouble with his slaves, 195; President of the Colonization Society, 195; character of, 196; devotion to his wife, 197; bequeaths Mount Vernon to his nephew, John Augustine II, 197; bequest to, 216; administrator accounts, 217 n.; Harvard degree, 219 n.

Washington, Bushrod, Jr., 198.

Washington, Bushrod Corbin, 198, 219.

Washington, Charles, brother of George, will of, 143 n.

Washington, Charles Augustine, grandson of Charles, 216.

Washington, Elizabeth, daughter of John the immigrant, 19.

Washington, George, birthplace, 1, 15, 19; lays corner-stone of the United States Capitol, 1; plans Federal City, 1; plans town of Alexandria, 3; his house in Alexandria, 4, 88 n.; seat of, in Christ Church, 4; member of Alexandria Masonic Lodge, 4; lands owned by, 5, 20; bequest of Woodlawn to Maj. and Mrs. Lawrence Lewis, 5; fox hunting, 6; related to Fairfax family, 6, 31; pew in Pohick Church, 9; at Gunston Hall, 10; at Chatham, 11; at Ferry Farm, 12; joins Masonic Lodge at Fredericksburg, 13, 39; visits to his mother, 13;

ancestry, 16; birth, 23; birthplace marked by G. W. P. Custis, 25; public neglect of birthplace, 25, 26; on death of his father becomes a member of his brother Augustine's family, 28; education, 29; 'Rules of Civility,' 29; his mother refuses to allow him to go to sea, 30; goes to Mount Vernon to live, 31; friendship with William Fairfax, 31; meets Mrs. George William Fairfax, 32; employed to survey Lord Fairfax's lands, 33; his reading, 35; first experiences on the frontier, 35, 36; inherits Mount Vernon, 37; smallpox, 37; attentions to Betsy Fauntleroy, 38; encourages Masonry in Continental Army, 39; begins his military career, 39; expedition to the French in the Ohio Country, 39; his report published in Virginia, England and France, 40; attacks the French, 40; 'hears the bullets whistle,' 41; begins Seven Years' War, 41; joins General Braddock's military family, 43; campaign friendships, 43; personal bravery at Braddock's Defeat, 45; contradicts report of his own death, 46; Sally Fairfax summons him to Belvoir, 46; his profanity as historical judgments, 46; correspondence with Sally Fairfax and Sarah Carlyle, 46, 47; dispute over relative rank, 47; rides to Boston, 47; the Mary Philipse episode, 47, 48; amusements of the journey, 48; on the Forbes expedition to Fort Duquesne, 49; his death again reported, 50; goes a-wooing, 50; meets Mrs. Custis, 52; a secret engagement, 53; adjustments of Mary Philipse and Sally Fairfax affairs, 53; idle tales of his love, 54; Mount Vernon put in order, to receive the bride, 55; marriage, 56; relationships and responsibilities, 57; elected to the House of Burgesses for Frederick County, 71; his legislative career, 71, 72, 73; receives the thanks of the House, 72; administers the

INDEX

boyhood in Purleigh rectory, 18; executor of his mother's estate, 18; marries Ann Pope, 18; colonel in Indian war, 19; member of House of Burgesses, 19; houses built by, 19; marries, second, widow of Walter Broadhouse and of Henry Brett, and, third, Mrs. Frances Appleton, 19; with Nicholas Spencer obtains grant of lands which become Mount Vernon, 20; death, 20; his property, 20.

Washington, John, son of John the immigrant, 19.

Washington, John, son of Lawrence the immigrant, 21, 23.

Washington, John Augustine I, brother of George, 41; famous letter to, 45; manager of Mount Vernon, 76; marries Hannah Bushrod, 76; member Mississippi Company, 78; consulted as to mother's affairs, 133, 134; death, 143.

Washington, John Augustine II, inherits Mount Vernon, 197; sketch of, 198; marries Jane Blackburn, 198; death, 198; leaves Mount Vernon to his wife, 198.

Washington, John Augustine III, receives Mount Vernon from his mother, 199; marries Eleanor Love Selden, 199; his family, 200 n.; on General Lee's staff, 204; killed in battle, 204.

Washington, Lawrence of Sulgrave, 17.

Washington, Rev. Lawrence, M.A., ancestor of the Virginia Washingtons, 17; his Oxford career, 17; rector of Purleigh, Essex, 17; deprived of his living by Parliament, 17; death, 17.

Washington, Lawrence, comes to Virginia, 17, 18; settles in Rappahannock County, 20.

Washington, Lawrence, son of John the immigrant, inherits Bridges Creek property, 20; marries Mildred Warner, 20; death, 21.

Washington, Lawrence, of Mount Vernon, half-brother of George, marries daughter of William Fairfax, 6; 7, 22 n.; educated in England, member House of Burgesses, in Cartagena expedition, 28; 30, 31, 35; death, 36, 37.

Washington, Mrs. Lawrence (Anne Fairfax), marries George Lee, 37; death, 38.

Washington, Lawrence of Chotank, 212.

Washington, Lund, manager of Mount Vernon, 92, 101; 131, 132 n., 207.

Washington, Martha, sister of John the immigrant, 18.

Washington, Martha, wife of George, 24, 52, 53; marriage, 56, 70; ancestry, 57; former marriage to Daniel Parke Custis, 58, 69; children, 70; house in Williamsburg, 73; gowns, 75; domestic duties, 78; attack of measles, 79; expectation of children, 86; indignant letter of, 98; leave-taking letter, 128; drawing-rooms, 141; 145; widowhood, 162; death, 168.

Washington, Mary Ball, mother of George, removes from Ferry Farm to Fredericksburg, 13; ancestry and married life, 22; no portrait of her, 22; 28, 43, 80; proposition for pension, 134; her maintenance, 135; her troubled life, 136; affection of friends, 136; her belated monument at Fredericksburg, 136; death, 139.

Washington, Mildred, daughter of Lawrence the immigrant, 21.

Washington, Mildred, wife of Charles, 143 n.

Washington, Richard Henry Lee, 198, 219.

Washington, Robert, 212.

Washington, Samuel, brother of George, 80; financial troubles and death, 133; 143, 210.

Washington, Samuel, son of Charles, 143 n.

Washington, Thornton, 210.

250 INDEX

Washington, Sir William of Packington, 17.

Washington, Colonel William Augustine, 218.

Washington, City, planned by Washington and L'Enfant, 1; squalid entrances to, 2; 18; burned by the British, 111; plans for, 117, 120; land speculations, 121; Washington's lands in, 122, 123; his vision of, 123.

Washington Intelligencer, 175.

Washington Monument, 1, 3; completion of, 201 n.

Washington and Lee University, 64, 186; beginnings of, 191 n.

Washington's Life Guard, 14.

Washington Parish, Westmoreland County, 20.

Washington relics, 129, 180, 209.

Washington tomb, 171.

Waters, Henry F., discovers the English ancestry of the Washingtons, 17.

Welford family, 19.

Welles, Albert, his 'Pedigree and History of the Washington Family,' 17.

Wellington House, 137 n.

Westmoreland County, extent of, 18; the Athens of America, 23; distinguished men of, 24; Washington wills in, 221.

Westover, lost by gaming, 69 n.

Wharton, A. H., 'Martha Washington,' 58 n.

White, Bishop, 143.

White House, The (the President's House), 1, 2, 3, 118, 179.

White House (home of Mrs. Daniel Parke Custis), 11, 53, 57; burned, 188.

Whiting, Mrs. Beverly, 23.

Widner, Professor R. B., 146 n.

Wilderness, Battles of the, 14.

William and Mary College, 59, 73, 74, 194 n., 215, 218.

Williamsburg, 42, 56; plan of, 73, 82, 118; social life, 89, 90.

Willing, Mary, marries William Byrd III of Westover, 69 n.

Willing, Mr. and Mrs. Mark, owners of Bushfield, 76 n.

Wilson, Justice James, 193.

Winchester, 34 n.; sanitary legislation, 73.

Wirt, William, his 'Life of Patrick Henry,' 72 n.

Wise, Colonel Jennings Cropper, his history of the Eastern Shore of Virginia, 66 n.

Woman's Party, occupies Old Capitol Prison building, 111.

Woodlawn, estate of, given to Lawrence Lewis and Nelly Custis, 5; present ownership of, 5; occupied, 167; deserted, 175.

World War, 7, 51.

Wren, Sir Christopher, reputed designer of Williamsburg buildings, 74; 123.

Wythe, George, 71, 74.

Yale University, 146 n., 154, 218.

Yeaton, William, 171 n.

Yorktown, 13, 99.